STUDIES IN MEDIEVAL ENGLISH ROMANCES

Some New Approaches

STUDIES IN MEDIEVAL ENGLISH ROMANCES

Some New Approaches

Edited by Derek Brewer

D. S. BREWER

© Contributors 1988

All Rights Reserved. Except as permitted under current legislation
no part of this work may be photocopied, stored in a retrieval system
published, performed in public, adapted, broadcast,
transmitted, recorded or reproduced in any form or by any means,
without the prior permission of the copyright owner

First published 1988 by D. S. Brewer, Cambridge
Reprinted in hardback and paperback 1991

D. S. Brewer is an imprint of Boydell & Brewer Ltd
PO Box 9, Woodbridge, Suffolk IP12 3DF
and of Boydell & Brewer Inc.
PO Box 41026, Rochester, NY 14604, USA

ISBN 0 85991 247 7 hardback
ISBN 0 85991 324 4 paperback

British Library Cataloguing in Publication Data
Studies in medieval English romances: some new
    approaches.
    1. English literature. 1066-1400. Romances. Critical
    studies
    I. Brewer, Derek, 1923-
    820.9′001
    ISBN 0-85991-247-7
    ISBN 0-85991-324-4 pbk

Library of Congress Cataloging-in-Publication Data
Studies in medieval English romances.
    Bibliography: p.
    1. Romances. English – History and criticism.
2. English literature – Middle English, 1100-1500 –
History and criticism. I. Brewer, Derek, 1923-
PR321.S78 1988 820′.9′001 88-7339
ISBN 0-85991-247-7 (hbk. : alk. paper)

The paper used in this publication meets the minimum requirements
of American National Standard for Information Sciences —
Permanence of Paper for Printed Library Materials, ANSI Z39.48-1984

Printed in Great Britain by
St Edmundsbury Press Ltd, Bury St Edmunds, Suffolk

CONTENTS

ARTICLES REPRINTED FROM OTHER JOURNALS

Excerpt in 'Escape from the Mimetic Fallacy' from Derek Brewer, 'The Interpretation of Dream, Folktale and Romance with special Reference to *Sir Gawain and the Green Knight*', *Neuphilologische Mitteilungen*, 77 (1976), 569 – 81

Derek Pearsall, 'The Development of Middle English Romance', *Mediaeval Studies*, XXVII (1965), 91 – 116

Claude Luttrell, 'The Folk-Tale Element in *Sir Gawain and the Green Knight*, *Studies in Philology*, LXXVII (Spring 1981), number 2, 105 – 127

Thanks are due to the Editors of these journals for permission to reprint the articles.

INTRODUCTION

The following Studies in Medieval English Romances arose out of a lecture course given some years ago in the University of Cambridge. Not all the lectures given could be published, and some of the essays printed here were not given as lectures. They exist as a series of studies in an ever expanding topic, concentrating on the main great works. There have been delays in the production of the volume for which the editor apologises to the various authors, but which have not limited the value of their essays.

Derek Brewer

Escape from the Mimetic Fallacy

DEREK BREWER

An explosion of interest in medieval English Romances has taken place in the 1980s. This is part of a general expansion of English studies which has shown a new readiness to consider previously unfamiliar approaches to literature, a new sense of the complexities of literary texts, and of their openness to interpretation. In all kinds of ways the 'fluidity' of a text, the importance of the reader's response, of the conditioning imposed by the original culture, of the historical biases built into language and into the general consciousness, have been realised with enthusiasm by literary critics and theorists.

It is no longer possible to dismiss medieval romances with patronising weariness or derision or dismissive association with the repeated patterns of folktale. Indeed folktale in many respects offers us the key to understanding romance, and the study of folktake itself is undergoing a revolution and an expansion comparable with and linked with the study of romance.

The new understanding of romance, as of folktale, comes from recognising what may be called 'the mimetic fallacy'. The mimetic fallacy is based on the belief that actions, people and things can and should be closely imitated in words. With this belief are linked two others. One is, that the actions and people so imitated should be such as could be met with in ordinary life. The second belief is that people cause actions, which affect people, and so forth — that is, that life is a series of identifiable materialistic causes and effects, which of course stories should in consequence imitate. Strictly speaking neither the belief in ordinary reality, nor that it is a sequence of cause and effect, need logically be associated with the mimetic fallacy, but it is easy to see that all three notions fall close together. It is a matter of historical fact in the history of literature that they did emerge together as a result of complex multiple

1

factors in the course of the sixteenth century in Europe and began to predominate in the European mind from the second half of the seventeenth century. The grand marker in terms of literary history is the appearance of that great satire on romance, *Don Quixote*, (1605). Nothing less was in issue, ultimately, than a profound and only partly conscious change in the European sense of ultimate 'reality'. Formerly, as still in traditional worldviews, ultimate 'reality' was believed to lie *behind* the surfaces, the appearances, of things. Increasingly from the late seventeenth century the world of appearances, or, more subtly, the phenomenal world, the material world, has been taken to be the ultimate and indeed the only real world.

So brief an account is necessarily crude and oversimplified. Moreover, the twentieth century has seen so much more deeply into material 'reality' that it may almost be said to have come out on the other side. Hence indeed the new interest in romance, which is essentially a non-mimetic mode of writing. We note that twentieth-century art since Cubism, music since Stravinsky, literature since James Joyce's *Ulysses*, (to take outstanding examples) have all become non-mimetic.

This rough sketch of a particular materialist 'commonsense' world view as prevailing from the mid-seventeenth to (say) the mid-twentieth century may make more credible the prevailing literary theory, which was predominately mimetic. It was introduced into England with Sir Philip Sidney's *The Defence of Poesie*, written 1579 – 80, published in 1595, drawing on the resources of Continental Humanism. It combined with great skill the conflicting demands of mimesis and literary idealism. Although so great a critic and literary theorist as Coleridge was restive under its constraints the fundamentally mimetic bias of literary criticism remains strong even (paradoxically) in the criticism of T. S. Eliot. It is best thought of as Neoclassical, since it derives from the Humanist revival of Aristotelian criticism. Most poetry fits uneasily into a Neoclassical frame, and this restiveness is the source, for example, of Blake's railing against Newton. But the supreme achievement of the Neoclassical literary worldview, in the field of literature, is the novel. In English the novel may be said to gather its strength in the late seventeenth century from various strands and to achieve its typical style with Defoe's *Robinson Crusoe* (1719). At the same time romance loses its last popularity and becomes the material of chapbooks. Even the so-called Revival of Romance, that is, Romanticism, in all its vast European ramifications, can be shown to be largely based on, even when apparently reacting against, the literary theories and worldview of Neoclassicism.

Now things are different. We can accept with gratitude the huge achievements of the Neoclassical period but we see them in a different perspective. Their mimetic worldview is no longer self-evidently the true

2

reality (what *is* 'reality' remains more mysterious than ever). In literary terms we can see that the fundamental premises of the novel, an extended verbal fiction, are quite different from those of the romance, though that is also an extended verbal fiction.

We can see a stranger truth. It is now clear that even the most realistic or naturalistic novel may, for all the Neoclassical assumptions of writer and first readers, incorporate below its surface structures which are in fact more like the romance or even the folktale than at first appears. So realistic a novel, for example, as Henry James' *Princess Casamassima*, (first published 1886) has at its heart a romance fantasy, akin to fairy-tale, about the lost child of a noble parent. Jane Austen, Charlotte Bronte, Dickens, offer more examples.[1] But in these instances the romance or folktale theme lies beneath the realistic surface.

The persistence of the non-realistic fantasy theme within the Neoclassical novel itself suggests the fallacy of mimesis. A moment's further thought is enough to make clear that words can never *imitate* the non-verbal word, except in the few and rare cases of genuine onomatopoeia. (These are rarer even than may be thought. In English the noise made by cows is described as 'moo'; in Japanese the same sound is rendered by the equivalent of 'maw').

A fuller argument against, (and a warmer tribute to) the mimetic fallacy would occupy more pages than are available in this short account. Interesting as they could be, they are no longer strictly necessary. Many books and essays now testify to the self-sufficient, self-enclosed, or self-reflexive elements in literary structures and in language itself which at best parallel but certainly never imitate non-verbal experience. Many books are now devoted to the conduct of stories and a whole new subject, often called 'narratology', has developed. The symbolic nature of language and of narrative is now well established. The power of linguistic, stylistic and narrative conventions and traditions is recognised.[2] Such symbols and conventions can now be related both to the inner psyche and to the outer worlds of nature and society, themselves symbolically rendered, and penetrated by cultural concepts of all kinds which we are now beginning to recognise through the symbolic structures of romance.

Having escaped from the mimetic fallacy, we may turn in several directions, some of which are indicated in the following essays. The first principle must be to follow the text and be led by it. An obvious test case

[1]   Henry James, *The Princess Casamassima*, edited with an Introduction by Derek Brewer, Penguin Books, Harmondsworth, 1986. For others see Derek Brewer *Symbolic Stories*, D. S. Brewer, Cambridge, 1980; repr. Longman, London, 1988.
[2]   See for example Carol Fewster *Traditionality and Genre in Middle English Romance*, D. S. Brewer, Cambridge, 1987.

here is Chaucer: he is well aware of the mimetic fallacy. At its simplest he
sees its impracticality.

> But now, paraunter, som man wayten wolde
> That every word, or soonde, or look or cheere
> Of Troilus that I rehercen sholde,
> In al this while unto his lady deere —
> I trowe it were a long thyng for to here;
> Or of what wight that stant in swich disjoynte,
> His wordes alle, or every look, to poynte.
>
> For sothe, I have naught herd it don er this
> In story non, ne no man here, I wene;
> And though I wolde, I koude nought, ywys;
> For ther was som epistel hem bitwene,
> That wolde, as seyth myn autour, wel contene
> Neigh half this book of which hym liste nought write,
> How sholde I thanne a lyne of it endite?

Troilus and Criseyde III, 491 – 504

Yet Chaucer is much more 'realistic' than most of his contemporaries,
as many instances even in *Troilus and Criseyde* demonstrate. Whether that
poem can even rightly be called a 'romance' has been debated, and since
William Godwin's *Life of Chaucer* (1803 – 4) *Troilus and Criseyde* has often
been called a novel. That it is not, for there are too many gaps in the
apparently realistic structure, too little relationship between character
and action, and, at the end, too rapid a transition to the 'eighthe spere'
(V, 1809). This last brings in, though paradoxically, such elements of the
romance mode as its supra-worldly concept of true reality, and the happy
ending, as have been suppressed during the conduct of the story and
which effectively destroy mimesis, as the discomfort of many critics
unconsciously committed to the mimetic fallacy demonstrates. Nevertheless, Chaucer's careful narration of a sequence of connected events in this
poem does bring him closer to the normal assumptions of the novel than
any of his English contemporaries.

With the other romances we are in almost a different world, and with
them most often what may still seem the problem of romance. Apart from
the accepted fantasies of science-fiction (which Professor Shippey
effectively lays beside the Breton lays) we still find it hard to account for
the acknowledged draw of self-evidently implausible, not to say improbable, sequences of events, where characters are stereotypes and where we
often know as it were innately, or at least from pre-literary experience,
what the outcome of the narrative will be.

One major factor that soon becomes apparent in romances is the importance of pattern as opposed to either the arbitrariness or the determinism of a chain of cause and effect. In many romances what happens, though it may be surprising or improbable, not to say impossible, (as also in so-called fairy-tales) 'feels right'. Why is this?

Recourse must be made here to two associated factors, the symbolical power of certain stories, and the key to that symbolism in the generalised psychology of the individual.

We have at hand phenomena closely related to the implausible yet compulsive stories of *Sir Gawain and the Green Knight* and most other romances. These are myth, folktale (including fairytale) and dreams. All have been studied vigorously and illuminatingly in the last half-century precisely in the terms that apply to romance, that is in terms of the significant yet non-naturalistic story. The general meaning is seen to lie in the inner shape of the story itself, which controls the less 'deep' (though not necessarily less valuable) qualities of characterisation, description, authorial comment, etc. In such stories there is no point in saying, for example, that Little Red Ridinghood must have been a very stupid little girl not to recognise a wolf dressed up as her grandmother, and also wolves can not dress up and speak. Her character is not revealed by what she does and has little importance. Anybody who cannot see both the similarity between a wolf and a granny, and the relationship between a wolf and a wolfwhistle, (even though some wolves cannot whistle either) is unlikely to sympathise with my enterprise here. The same will hold true of the foolishness of dreams.

The analysis of dreams, folktale and myth offers us some concepts for analysing romance, ultimately for explaining some of our interest. The interpretation of such symbolism, especially of dreams, varies among different schools of thought and there are some sharp controversies. Any interpretation of any romance which adheres narrowly to any one such school might be suspect, but enough is generally agreed for our purposes. 'The images of a dream are pictures of conceptions.'[3] Freud regarded dreams as mere wish-fulfilments, but most people would now agree with Jung and later writers such as Calvin S. Hall that at least some dreams are more than this; they may be an autonomous but purposive function of the whole personality when released from the need for action. Everyone agrees that the images of dreams, being symbolic, can be interpreted, at least in part. Apart from a relatively brief period in English culture, (that

---

[3]   Calvin S. Hall, 'A Cognitive Theory of Dreams', *Journal of General Psychology*, 49 (1953), 273 – 82, reprinted in *Dreams and Dreaming*, ed. S. G. M. Lee and A. R. Mayes, Penguin Books, London, 1973; quotation from p. 363. Hall continues that a dream is a work of art. The collection of articles is a very useful general survey.

is, the Neoclassical and empirical scientific period from mid-seventeenth to the late nineteenth century, and even then with notable exceptions), men have always felt that dreams *can* be, and have often felt that they *must* be interpreted.[4] We may say much the same for literary works.

Some well-established concepts in the interpretation of dreams correspond to, and may supplement, concepts used in literary criticism. It may be useful briefly to recall the few general terms that I need for my purposes here.[5] The most important as it is the most general, is that of symbolism. In the interpretation of dreams the ostensible subject-matter is *manifest*, the inner significance *latent*. This obviously corresponds with many types of literary interpretation and all that is necessary here is to note, for the purpose of avoiding it, the trap which medieval exegetes sometimes fell into, of assuming that the manifest content is a shell to be cracked and thrown away once one has discovered the latent fruit. In literary questions the latent may well govern the manifest content, but it is the manifest which realises the latent and gives it some uniquely interesting force. The latent is often relatively simple, and, by definition, general; similar to other expressions of the same deep human need, and thus repetitious. If this investigation has value it is in establishing relationships between an individual manifestation and general latency of meaning in a romance.

Methods of interpretation are mainly concerned with establishing the relationship between the manifest and the latent. An important element is the recognition of repetition under different guises. Repetition is also extremely important in myth. It has been well argued that the stories of the Old Testament, taken as mythology, constantly recur to the same general topic.[6] Our basic personal concerns are relatively few. Repetition is not much in favour as a literary device nowadays, for historical reasons, but traditional literature is full of it, on a small scale, in verbal devices, or at large. Romances are full of it.

After repetition we may note *condensation*, the multiple (and possibly contradictory or ambiguous) significations of a single image. This concept offers no difficulty to students of literature, though the practice does. There is an art in selecting the correct significations which must be guided by the context provided by the individual poem. Mechanical application

---

[4]   Brief historical accounts, up to and including Freud and Jung, are given in *Dreams and Dreaming*, 1⸰ – 80, and in E. Fromm, *The Forgotten Language*, Victor Gollancz, London, 1952, 99 – 129.

[5]   The most thoroughgoing psychoanalytical theory of literature known to me is N. Holland *The Dynamics of Literary Response*, which has a useful glossary. See also Earnest Jones, 'Freud's Theory of Dreams' *American Journal of Psychology*, 21 (1910), 283 – 308, reprinted *Dreams and Dreaming*, 39 – 67.

[6]   E. R. Leach, *Genesis as Myth*, Cape, London, 1969.

of significations from handbooks or from quite different works, will not do. We may also notice *substitution* of one manifest image for another, either by likeness or association. Likeness is familiar as metaphor; association in literature, as in language, is metonymy.[7] *Projection* is the attribution of one's own feelings to other people. *Splitting* is the division of various desires, inhibitions and fears, and representing them in different characters. A 'split' hero occurs in *The Knight's Tale* and the various tales, of world-wide distribution, of *The Two Brothers* type exemplified in the late romance *Eger and Grime*.[8]

It has sometimes been remarked that literature is a dream dreamed for us.[9] This is particularly obvious in the case of folktale and fairytale, but also in major works of traditional literature from an early period. Thus in an early study, dated in some respects, but containing some very fruitful remarks, Otto Rank remarks, in identifying a general pattern in certain hero-myths, that 'The true hero of the romance is, therefore, the ego, which finds itself in the hero . . .'[10] Rank associates such a process with retrograde childish fancies in a manner we need not follow, but amply proves the father-son conflict, with various resolutions, in many different mythical stories, associating it with 'The family romance of paranoiacs'. The degree to which the reader of the story associates himself with the hero, and then may regard the story as if it is the hero's own dream will clearly vary according to the individual work of art, but the vigorous presentaion of such identification has led to some most illuminating interpretations by Dr A. Wilson.[11] From the work of Rank, Fromm, Holland, Wilson and others, it has been clearly established that myth, folktale and romance may be effectively interpreted in terms similar to those used in the interpretation of dreams. The protagonist is central, and all must be interpreted in relation to his interests. Other characters are often 'splits', substitutes and projections of various kinds, who have no effective relationship between each other independent of their relationship to the protagonist. (This is most important. It is of no use to enquire, e.g. in the case of *Sir Gawain and the Green Knight*, into the actual marital relationship between Sir Bertilak/Green Knight and his wife. The poem is not interested.) Thus in folktales brothers represent various aspects of the

---

7   Derek Brewer, 'Metonymy in Chaucer', *Poetica*, Tokyo, 1 (1973), 1–20.
8   *Eger and Grime*, edited with introduction by J. R. Caldwell, Cambridge, Mass 1933.
9   Holland, op. cit., p. 73.
10 Otto Rank, *The Myth of the Birth of the Hero*, translated by F. Robbins and S. A. Jelliffe, Robert Brunner, New York, 1957. (The original, which I have not seen, published about 1912).
11 A. D. Wilson, *Traditional Romance and Tale*, D. S. Brewer, Cambridge, 1976. Cf. also, apart from Rank, Fromm, *The Forgotten Language* (n. 2 p. 571), especially his final chapter. See also, apart from valuable remarks by Holland, op. cit., M. Loeffler-Delachaux, *Le Symbolisme des Contes de Fées*, Paris, 1949.

protagonist; witches, stepmothers and other villains are substitutes for the protagonist's view of mother and father; helpful animals much the same. Such characters may also represent how the protagonist feels toward himself.

The centre of many folktales, and of almost all romances, as in dreams, is the nuclear family. Often it may be said that there are only three main characters, protagonist, father, mother. Situations are often repetitions with variation and ultimately progress, of the conflict between the protagonist and his parents.

Perhaps the most crucial and often painful passage in our lives is that by which we emerge from dependent childhood to independent maturity (in so far as we ever do), divesting ourselves of the authority of the parents. This involves testing in and by loneliness, and often, by extension, establishing a stable loving relationship with a member of the opposite sex. One of the tests is often fear of death, associated with loneliness, or, maybe, with victory of the parents and failure to achieve independence. This transition, which is a universal human necessity, is almost always the subject of medieval romance (there are exceptions), and in all societies there are various rituals to mark it. One of the most obvious in Western society is the wedding. Such transitions are now well-recognised since the work of van Gennep as *rites de passages*.[12] Ritual has much in common with dream, and of course myth. It is symbolic, independent of naturalistic cause-and-effect, exemplary, full of projections, splits and substitutes.

The feelings engaged in the struggle for emergence as a full human being, with all the conflicts involved, are so strong as to call for deep disguises. Such feelings, as latent forces, easily manipulate the manifest content. We are not troubled by naturalistically improbable sequences when such important issues are being worked out beneath.

It is important here, when noticing the specific similarity of romance to that middle *rite de passage* of our lives, to recognise that a *rite de passage* is by definition successful. Otherwise it would deny its nature. By the same token, it is the nature of romance to have a happy ending. It expresses, most naturally, the successful achievement of maturity and the beloved. The characteristic pattern of romances, from those of antiquity up to the seventeenth century, shows a hero or heroine escaping from the authority of parents, being tested (often by the very conflict with parents, but also by the endurance of hostility in the solitude which is the consequence of escaping from the parents) and then establishing a stable relationship with a member of the opposite sex of the same age as the protagonist. The

[12] Van Gennep is discussed and further references given, by J. A. Senn 'Arnold van Gennep', *Folklore* 85 (1974) 229 – 43.

protagonist may be male or female. Sex is important because chastity represents, or used to represent, personal integrity as opposed to the regressive or dissipating forces of promiscuity. Death may well be invoked because there is a natural association between sex and death, traditionally much more powerful than the association between sex and life, (because the life involved is that of an at present non-existent third party without rights). Such a third party has little emotional or imaginative appeal to the adolescent obsessed with his or her own struggle to emerge from the now constricting chrysalis.

It is apparent in these phenomena of dream folktale and romance that the chain of material cause and effect is either of no importance at all, or is merely a superficial rationalisation of something 'far more deeply interfused'. In other words, there are patterns of expectation and effect deep in our minds, and it is the expression of these patterns which is of such moment to us. They are truly in our minds, and we may hold several versions of the same pattern, i.e. that of conflict between child and parent, simultaneously in our minds. One of the great values of stories is to articulate a version of the pattern. We may respond equally to a tragic or a happy outcome of the underlying pattern as represented in a story, which will be fundamentally non-mimetic.

Literary history shows us that these patterns, especially of what I have called elsewhere 'the family drama'[13] are extraordinarily wide-spread and longlasting. Many though perhaps not all cultures have them.

The association with folktale, and particularly with the so-called 'fairy tale', better called 'wonder-tale', may enlighten us as to the non-mimetic nature of the story, its reliance on pattern rather than cause-and-effect, its continuing appeal, and also the way it can change. Succeeding periods or writers make the story their own. In no case is this more striking than with Shakespeare. His reliance on medieval romance has often been noted, but the further lessons of the relation to folktale and its narrative quality deserved further exploration as suggested here by Mrs Burton. From this point of view Shakespeare deserves to be recognised as the last and greatest of English writers of romance, and by the same token, the last great English medieval author.

The essays in the present volume take various aspects of the medieval English romances, and an approach to one may by extension often be found fruitful when applied by the reader to other romances, not only those studied here. The present set of studies make no claim to be definitive. They are exploratory. They illustrate the great variety of

---

[13]   In *Symbolic Stories*, see note 1 on p. 3.

English medieval romances. Those romances studied here are unquestionably fine works of art, but there are many others also to be read and
studied in a variety of ways. The admirable survey by W. J. R. Barron,
English Medieval Romance (Longman, London, 1987) follows a series of
valuable studies by other scholars, and gives full bibliographical details.
There is no need to duplicate that work here. The reader is invited to
explore for himself or herself the many interesting relationships, internal
and external, to be found in the English medieval romances.

The Development
of Middle English Romance

DEREK PEARSALL

The purpose of this article is to offer a tentative outline of the growth and development of Middle English romance from 1240 to 1400. The initial date for the discussion is not difficult to arrive at, for it is simply the date, on palaeographical evidence, of the Cambridge MS fragment Gg.4.27, containing *King Horn* and *Floris and Blauncheflur*, the earliest extant Middle English romances.[1] The final date is arbitrary, and some of the romances to be discussed may possibly be from the early years of the fifteenth century. However, a distinction may be drawn between fourteenth and fifteenth century romance which is not arbitrary and which justifies the choice of 1400 as a terminal date.

The corpus of Middle English romance, from the period of its great flourishing between 1280 and 1380, gives the strongest impression of homogeneity, a homogeneity which makes quite possible a general analysis of the 'type' such as Dorothy Everett gave in her fine essay.[2] This homogeneity is most evident in the observance of a wide range of formal and literary conventions, what we might call the 'grammar' of romance. The same plot-patterns, the same situations, the same phrases, recur insistently from romance to romance, providing much of their popular strength. The reason for this close stereotyping, however, is to be found in the social context of Middle English romance, which is overwhelmingly popular and non-courtly. True courtly romance had no real vogue in

---

[1] The MS is described briefly in *King Horn*, ed. Hall (Oxford, 1901), p. x. See also K. Brunner, "Middle English Metrical Romances and their Audience", in *Studies in Medieval Literature in Honour of Professor A. C. Baugh*, ed. MacEdward Leach (Philadelphia, 1961), 219–226, especially 220–222.

[2] "A Characterization of the English Medieval Romances", in *Essays on Middle English Literature*, ed. Patricia Kean (Oxford, 1955), 1–22.

English, since the audience which could appreciate it, at the time when it was fashionable, was French-speaking. The only exceptions are the alliterative romances and the late adaptations of the genre by Chaucer. The audience of the Middle English romances is primarily a lower or lower-middle-class audience, a class of social aspirants who wish to be entertained with what they consider to be the same fare, but in English, as their social betters. It is a new class, an emergent bourgeoisie, whose tastes were assessed with professional expertise by the compilers of the Auchinleck MS.[3] By the end of the fourteenth century, this class, though it has not disappeared, has changed, and popular romance, which may be seen as the primary extant literary manifestation of the newly enfranchised vernacular, is no longer to its taste. This veneer of sophistication is partly Chaucer's doing, and is acquired more slowly in the north than in the south, so that as the century progresses we notice a northward shift in the provenance of romance.

Fifteenth century romance is thus significantly different from fourteenth century romance. There is, for one thing, a marked decrease in output, and the few verse-romances that are produced, such as *Generydes*, the *Squyr of Lowe Degre*, and *Partonope*, are evidently directled at a more sophisticated bourgeois audience, an audience more aware of social tone and capable of responding, on however simple a level, to the Chaucerian stylistic.[4] The ultimate resort of this enhanced sophistication is of course the prose romance of Malory and Caxton. But side by side with *Generydes* and *Partonope* there are other romances like *The Grene Knyght* and *The Turke and Gowin*, often crude debasements of earlier romances, which represent the regression of romance into oral tradition. This oral tradition we may take to have existed before the flourishing of romance and to have co-existed with it, the last crude residue when popular tradition had done its worst with courtly romance. It would be the property of the lowest classes of society, and by its very nature would not be written down and therefore would not be extant. Accidents of survival, likelier to occur later than earlier, have preserved the debased fifteenth century Gawain-romances for us, two of them unique in the Percy Folio, and thus enabled us to glimpse a substratum of literature usually hidden.

---

[3] Nat. Lib. Scot., Adv. 19.2.1. For a plausible account of the commercial provenance of this MS, see L. H. Loomis, "The Auchinleck Manuscript and a Possible London Bookshop of 1330 – 1340", *PMLA*, 57 (1942), 595 – 627. The MS is fully described by E. Kölbing in *Englische Studien*, 7 (1884), 177 – 191. See also Brunner, *op. cit.*, 219 – 220.

[4] In *Partonope* (ed. A. T. Bödtker, *EETS, ES*, 109, 1912) there is explicit reminiscence of Chaucer, especially of the *Knight's Tale*. Compare 11128 – 11145 and *KnT*, I, 2600 – 2618, 2636 – 2637. See B. J. Whiting, "A Fifteenth-Century English Chaucerian", *Mediaeval Studies*, 7 (1945), 40 – 54; also R. M. Smith, in *MLN*, 51 (1936), 320 – 322, and J. Parr, in *MLN*, 60 (1945), 486 – 487.

Fourteenth century romances continued to be copied in the fifteenth century — some, indeed, are extant only in fifteenth century manuscripts — but the adaptations are usually free enough to reveal the same two tendencies. The tendency to increased sophistication is illustrated by the fifteenth century rewriting of *The Seege of Troye* in Harley MS 525. This redactor omits minstrel material such as direct address to the audience and oral punctuation, and adds characteristically 'literary' material such as an expanded account of the building of the New Troy, a learned digression on Neptanabus, and a rhetorical amplification of the grief of Priam and Polyxena over Hector's death.[5] He also corrects gross errors in the text: he knows, for instance, that the three goddesses involved in the Idan beauty competition were Venus, Juno and Minerva, and not Saturn, Mercury and Jupiter, as the earlier version has it. The opposite tendency, what I have called the regression into oral tradition, is illustrated by a number of fifteenth century copies of fourteenth century romances, such as the text of *Sir Orfeo* in Harley MS 3810.

If 1240 – 1400 are accepted as working limits for this discussion, there is no need to make a point of excluding prose romance, which is a purely fifteenth century phenomenon in England, for reasons that have been suggested. Alliterative romance presents a slightly more difficult problem, especially as there is an important group of later northern non-alliterative romances which draw towards the alliterative tradition in sophistication of technique and social outlook. Even a strict formal distinction breaks down on a romance like the fragmentary *Song of Roland*, which is really an alliterative poem in rhymed couplets, though both alliteration and rhyme are loose and irregular. Stylistically, its affinities are with the alliterative tradition, the influence of which is clear in conventional contexts such as battle-descriptions.[6] However, alliterative romance has in general a strong enough formal and social identity to warrant exclusion from this study. It is not easy to talk of *Sir Orfeo* and *Sir Gawain and the Green Knight* in the same breath.

It would remain only to admit that the corpus of romance established by this process of elimination has no inviolate identity.[7] Some romances are

---

[5] See lines 306, 674, 1522.
[6] E.g. 336 – 339. See also 53, 202 – 205, 214 – 218, 237 – 238, 279, 305 – 309. The poem, which is edited by Herrtage for the *EETS* (ES, 35, 1880), is not included in the subsequent discussion.
[7] It comprises fifty pieces, though a different technique of computation might vary this convenient number slightly. They are listed here, with reference to the best available edition, in the order in which they are to be treated.

centrally typical of the form, while others are romances because they are more like romances than they are like anything else. At one point romance blurs off into history, and it would be hard, for instance, to decide, without some arbitrary line-drawing, what exactly the wretched *Arthur* is. This little piece occurs unique in the middle of a Latin chronicle of the kings of Britain, rather like the spurts of patriotic alliteration in the Anglo-Saxon Chronicle, as if the author felt that verse alone could match his mood of exaltation. *Arthur* is anything but exalted, however, and even its claim to be verse is tenuous. If it were less grotesquely inept one might

I. 1. *Havelok the Dane*, ed. W. W. Skeat, 2nd ed. rev. K. Sisam (Oxford, 1915).
    2. *Guy of Warwick*, ed. J. Zupitza, *EETS, ES*, 42, 49, 59 (1883, 1887, 1891). Includes the stanzaic continuation and *Reinbrun*.
    3. *Beves of Hamtoun*, ed. E. Kölbing, *EETS, ES*, 46, 48, 65 (1885, 1886, 1894).
    4. *Richard Cœur de Lion*, ed. K. Brunner, *Wiener Beiträge zur Englischen Philologie*, Bd. 42 (Vienna, 1913).
    5. *Arthour and Merlin*, ed. E. Kölbing, *Altenglische Bibliothek*, Bd. 4 (Leipzig, 1890). Includes the later *Merlin*.
    6. *Kyng Alisaunder*, ed. G. V. Smithers, *EETS, OS*, 227, 237 (1952, 1957).
II. 1. *Floris and Blauncheflur*, ed. A. B. Taylor (Oxford, 1927).
    2. *Ywain and Gawain*, ed. A. B. Friedman and N. T. Harrington, *EETS*, 254 (1964).
    3. *Lai le Freine*, ed. Margaret Wattie, *Smith College Studies in Modern Languages*, Vol. 10, no. 3 (1929).
    4. *Sir Landeval*. See IX. 3.
    5. *Sir Orfeo*, ed. A. J. Bliss (Oxford, 1954).
    6. *Sir Degare*, ed. G. Schleich, *Englische Textbibliothek*, Bd. 19 (Heidelberg, 1929).
III. 1. *Otuel*, ed. S. J. Herrtage, *EETS, ES*, 39 (1882). Includes *Roland and Vernagu*.
    2. *The Seege of Troye*, ed. Mary E. Barnicle, *EETS, OS*, 172 (1927).
    3. *Arthur*, ed. F. J. Furnivall, *EETS, OS*, 2 (1864).
    4. *Titus and Vespasian*, ed. R. Fischer, in *Archiv für das Studium der neueren Sprachen und Literaturen*, 111 (1903), 285 – 298, and 112 (1904), 24 – 45.
    5. *Ipomydon*. See X. 1.
IV.   *Laud Troy-Book*, ed. J. E. Wülfing, *EETS, OS*, 121, 122 (1902 – 1903).
V. 1. *King Horn*, ed. J. R. Lumby, *EETS, OS*, 14 (1866; re-ed. G. H. McKnight, 1901); ed. J. Hall (Oxford, 1901). The latter includes *Horn Childe*.
    2. *Sir Tristrem*, ed. G. P. McNeill, *Scottish Text Society* (1886).
VI. 1. and 2. Stanzaic *Guy* and *Reinbrun*. See I. 2.
    3. *Horn Childe*. See V. 1.
    4. *Amis and Amiloun*, ed. MacE. Leach, *EETS, OS*, 203 (1937).
VII. 1. *The King of Tars*, ed. F. Krause, *Englische Studien*, 11 (1888), 1 – 62.
    2. *Le Bone Florence of Rome*, ed. W. Vietor and A. Knobbe (Marburg, 1899).
    3. *Roland and Vernagu*. See III.1.

feel more certain about its literary status. At another point romance merges into epic, and although *The Seege of Troye* is certainly romance, and Lydgate's *Troy-Book* just as certainly epic, the Laud *Troy-Book* is somewhere between the two. At yet another point, didactic romance, pious legend and saint's life become difficult to distinguish, and formal criteria alone determine the inclusion of poems like *Sir Amadas* and *Sir Cleges* as romances.

With this inevitable blurring admitted, the homogeneity of the popular romance tradition still remains as a strong impression, though it has its diachronic as well as its synchronic aspect. In other words, it is possible to

4. *Sir Amadas*, (i) ed. H. Weber, in *Metrical Romances of the 13th, 14th and 15th Centuries* (Edinburgh, 1810), iii, 243–275; (ii). See XI. 4.

5. *Sir Cleges*, ed. A. Treichel, *Englische Studien*, 22 (1896), 345–389.

6. *Sir Gowther*, ed. K. Breul (Oppeln, 1886).

VIII. 1, 2. *Octavian*, *Octovian*, ed. G. Sarrazin, *Altenglische Bibliothek*, Bd. 3 (Heilbronn, 1885).

3. *Athelston*, ed. A. McI. Trounce, *EETS, OS*, 224 (1951).

4. *Sir Isumbras*, ed. G. Schleich, *Palaestra*, 15 (Berlin, 1901).

5. *Sir Eglamour*, ed. G. Schleich, *Palaestra*, 53 (Berlin, 1906).

6. *Torrent of Portyngale*, ed. E. Adam, *EETS, ES*, 51 (1887).

7. *Sir Tryamowre*, ed. Anna J. E. Schmidt (Utrecht, 1937).

IX. 1. *Emare*, ed. Edith Rickert, *EETS, ES*, 99 (1908).

2. *The Erl of Tolous*, ed. G. Lüdtke (Berlin, 1881).

3. *Sir Launfal*, ed. A. J. Bliss, *Nelson's Medieval and Renaissance Library* (1960). Includes *Landeval*.

X. 1. *Ipomadon*, ed. E. Kölbing (Breslau, 1889). Includes *Ipomydon*.

2, 3. *The Sege of Melayne* and *Rowlande and Ottuell*, ed. S. J. Herrtage, *EETS, ES*, 35 (1880).

XI. 1. *Libeaus Desconus*, ed. M. Kaluza, *Altenglische Bibliothek*, Bd. 5 (Leipzig, 1890).

2. *Sir Degrevaunt*, ed. L. F. Casson, *EETS, OS*, 221 (1949).

3. *Sir Perceval of Gales*, ed. J. Campion and F. Holthausen, *Alt- und Mittelenglische Texte*, Bd. 5 (Heidelberg, 1913).

4. *The Avowynge of King Arther, Sir Gawan, Sir Kaye and Sir Bawdewyn of Bretan*, ed. J. Robson, *Three Early English Metrical Romances* (Camden Society, 1842). Includes *Amadas*.

XII. 1. *Sir Ferumbras*, ed. S. J. Herrtage, *EETS, ES*, 34 (1879).

2. *The Sowdone of Babylone*, ed. E. Hausknecht, *EETS, ES*, 38 (1881).

XIII. *Le Morte Arthur*, ed. J. D. Bruce, *EETS, ES*, 88 (1903).

Sixteen of the above romances are edited, twelve of them complete, with the minimum of apparatus, by W. H. French and C. B. Hale in *Middle English Metrical Romances* (New York, 1930). The twelve are *Havelok, Floris, Orfeo, Degare, Horn, Cleges, Athelston, Emare*, the *Erl of Tolous, Launfal, Perceval*, and the *Avowynge*.

discern within the homogeneity of the tradition certain variations, certain patterns of growth and decline, certain interlockings of form and theme, which enable us to trace, as it were, a historical morphology of romance. The task is a complex one, involving as it does the assembling and reconciliation of evidence as to date, dialect, manuscript provenance,[8] metrical form, exact class of audience, type of source, type of story and range of art, and is made still more complex by the ambiguous or disputed nature of much of this evidence;[9] but it is a task which needs doing because of the inadequacy of the traditional classification according to the 'Matters' (of Britain, France, Greece and Rome, and England).[10] This classification, where it is not obviously useless, as it is in dismissing twenty-three of the fifty romances under discussion as 'miscellaneous', can be actually misleading where it lumps together quite dissimilar romances because of some superficial coincidence of plot-material. Stories are the property of everyone, but a formal tradition is the property only of its practitioners, and it is through its formal and stylistic aspects — in combination with the others — that the history of romance can be most objectively analysed.

The first broad division in the tradition is between the nineteen romances in four-stress couplet and the twenty-five in tail-rhyme. The remaining six are closely associated with the latter, either through partial anticipation of the full development of the form (*King Horn*, *Sir Tristrem*) or through subsequent variation upon it (*Octovian*, the *Sowdone of Babylone*, *Ferumbras*, *Le Morte Arthur*). This division is obvious enough, but it is a very real one, for it corresponds to a more fundamental division between 'epic romance' and 'lyric romance', the former more prosaic, realistic, historical and martial, the latter more emotive, more concerned with love, faith, constancy and the marvellous. In French, these different types also exist, but come in a series of waves, with much overlapping, as society gradually evolved the need for them: first the *chanson de geste*,

---

[8]   Much remains to be done in this particular field, especially now that Brunner (in the article cited, and another in *Anglia*, 76 (1958), 64–73) has opened it up. The main problem is one of fragmentation, for the 50 romances are found in 55 MSS and 25 exist in unique texts. But there are certain key MSS, such as the Auchinleck (which contains 15 of the romances, 6 in unique texts), Caligula A. ii, Egerton 2862 and Cambridge Ff.2.38.

[9]   Two useful handbooks, in addition to Wells's *Manual*, which help sift this evidence, are A. H. Billings, *A Guide to the Middle English Metrical Romances* (New York, 1901), and L. A. Hibbard, *Medieval Romance in England* (Oxford, 1924).

[10] This classification is used in virtually all the standard textbooks and bibliographies. Professor George Kane, in his chapter on "The Middle English Metrical Romances" in *Middle English Literature* (London, 1951), ignores the 'Matters', but the technique of classification he does use, one of aesthetic merit, is avowedly subjective and unhistorical.

romance a degree removed from epic, then the *roman d'aventure*, and finally its more refined, sentimental and ethereal derivative, the Breton *lai*. There are no such waves of development in English, but rather a more complex simultaneous layering, since by the time English was capable of absorbing the form, its full course had been run in the source-literature. Nor should the analogy of French be pressed too hard, since English romance, for all its great debt to French,[11] is more than merely derivative. A small group of non-epic romances in couplet (*Sir Orfeo*, &c.) are all early and may be regarded as the result of the powerful influence of French metrical form before the tail-rhyme tradition, with its mixed ancestry, had become fully established.

The first growth of couplet-romance is initiated by *Havelok* about 1280 and centres on *Guy of Warwick*, *Beves of Hamtoun*, *Richard Cœur de Lion*, *Kyng Alisaunder* and *Arthour and Merlin*, all five represented in part or whole[12] in the Auchinleck manuscript (c. 1330), and the last three forming a strongly marked south-eastern group. Typically, these are vigorously professional adaptations of French poems of the *chanson de geste* type, blunting the first keen edge of unsophisticated appetite with battles and heroic adventures strung in loosely climactic sequence over many thousands of lines. The first four have English heroes, and there are traces of patriotic feeling in Guy's fight against the Danish champion Colbrand and the outburst of anti-French prejudice in *Richard*,[13] but it would be the greatest mistake to regard them as any sort of national epic or significant outgrowth of germinally historic native tradition. Much has been made of the Matter of England, and certainly there is evidence for the growth of a considerable body of popular heroic legend in medieval England, some of it going back to the days of the Viking invasions (Horn, Havelok), or earlier (Wade, Weland), some to the days of resistance against the Norman conquerors (Hereward). A whole cycle of outlaw and exile

---

[11]   Of the 50 romances listed above, all but 12 would have a direct French source, extant or putative.

[12]   This phrase hints at a problem which this study, for the most part, will have to by-pass, the complexity of textual tradition in romance. It is not merely a matter of corrupt texts or incomplete texts but of related versions of a particular romance so different that it is questionable, for instance, whether we can talk about an English romance of *Beves* or whether there are not as many romances of *Beves* as there are texts (Kölbing's attempt to offer a critical text produces some extraordinary footnotes). Often the problem has to be explicitly recognised, as with *Guy*, where the texts need individual reference.

[13]   Caius *Guy*, 10579; *Richard*, 3849. The English versions of *Guy* add passages in which 'England' is used as a focus of national sentiment — Guy is fighting 'for England', 'to make England free' (Auchinleck, st. 248), and Athelstan declares that he has 'saved all England' (st. 271). *Beves*, on the other hand, is outrageously unpatriotic, ending as it does with Beves slaughtering 32,000 London citizens and the Thames running red with blood (4529 – 4532).

stories gave expression to re-emerging English spirit.[14] But this body of native heroic legend exists by hypothesis — usually from references or versions in French or Latin, paradoxically enough — and not in fact. Even the romances of *Havelok* and *Horn*, though their adaptations of the material owe something to memories of native versions of the stories, come to us strained through the medium of French romance.[15] It is possible to believe that such stories as these had wide currency in popular oral tradition, and at the same time admit that when such stories came to be written down, they would be written down as translations from available sources and not records of oral tradition. It would be easier for the hack to work from a source, and there would be prestige in it too. References to Athelstan and Anlaf in romances like *Guy* are evidence not of primitive historicity, but of the astuteness of the fabricators of these romances in scattering such names about so as to give the illusion of historicity.

The Havelok-story probably contains a germ of historical truth from Anglo-Viking tradition, but the English romance is a free reworking, about 1280, of some variant of the French poem (it is difficult to explain inconsistencies of narrative in the English except by derivation from the French), with contamination from local Lincolnshire tradition. *Havelok* is unique among English romances in its systematic realisation of the story in terms of humble everyday life. The midnight scene in Grim's cottage, the details of boat-building, fishing and trading, Havelok's work as a kitchen-boy,[16] all of them added or expanded from the French, are part of the very texture of common life. Havelok's qualities — his instinct for survival, opportunism, modesty, industry, lack of sentiment, practical good sense, love of children — are the virtues of common people. The fighting is savagely in earnest, the narrator's participation in the story full and intense, and behind the poem rises a respect for order and the rule of law which is deliberately emphasised in the opening description of Athelwold's ideal reign, in the juxtaposition of the two parallel episodes of the regent's betrayal of his trust, as if to drive home the enormity of the double outrage to justice, and in the scrupulously detailed punishment of

14   See R. M. Wilson, *The Lost Literature of Medieval England* (London, 1952), 16 – 19, 123 – 130; H. G. Leach, *Angevin Britain and Scandinavia* (Cambridge, Mass., 1921), 324 – 355; J. de Lange, *The Relation and Development of English and Icelandic Outlaw-Traditions* (Haarlem, 1935); C. E. Wright, *The Cultivation of Saga in Anglo-Saxon England* (Edinburgh, 1939), 31.

15   For full discussion of sources, see Hibbard, *op. cit.*, 83 – 92, 103 – 112; H. le Sourd Creek, "The Author of *Havelok the Dane*", *Englische Studien*, 48 (1915), 193 – 222; H. Heyman, *Studies on the Havelok-Tale* (Upsala, 1903); W. H. Schofield, "The Story of King Horn and Rimenhild", *PMLA*, 18 (1903), 1 – 84; W. H. French, *Essays on King Horn* (Oxford, 1939), 117 – 145.

16   Lines 565 – 648, 699 – 720, 749 – 784, 909 – 958.

the traitors at the end.[17] The manner of the poem is rough, but the handling of the story bears witness at every point to deliberate purpose, and *Havelok* has a claim, if any English romance has, to be regarded as the genuine expression of popular consciousness.

Guy of Warwick, by contrast, is hack-work, a flat recital of battles which increase only in length. Closely translated from the French, with some adaptations to suit less sophisticated taste, it is of great importance as a prototype of epic romance (and of lyric romance, as we shall see). In it the conventional techniques of narrative and description, especially battle description, long established in French romance, are naturalised and, with some modifications, converted to the English tradition. The story was well chosen to appeal to the new audience, both for its scrupulously detailed air of historical veracity and also for its theme, of the steward's son who achieves knighthood, marries his lord's daughter, and twice acts as the saviour of England, a theme which is the epitome of all those bourgeous narratives in which the hero breaks into a higher or more enviable social milieu through the exercise of innate merit. The story also has a strong pietistic undertow, which a non-aristocratic audience would have found very satisfying. Halfway through, soon after his marriage to Felice, Guy has a moment of spiritual illumination in which he sees the futility of mere knight-errantry, and so becomes an ascetic pilgrim-knight. The change makes precious little difference to the matter of the romance, except that Guy now fights in disguise (to display self-abnegation), but it makes a strong appeal to conventional piety, as does the sentimental ending. The shift to tail-rhyme stanza at the halfway point in the Auchinleck version, whether the work of a different continuator or not,[18] seems to be the result of deliberate policy which, recognising the affective nature of the new material — the wedding, Guy's moment of illumination, Felice's sorrow at his departure — adopts the more suitably lyrical and 'poetic' tail-rhyme stanza. The opening of the stanzaic *Guy* is certainly the best part of the poem, a repository and perhaps a primary source of classical tail-rhyme writing. A similar sort of professional adeptness, maybe that of the 'editor' of the Auchinleck manuscript, is displayed in the disentangling of the story of Guy's son Reinbrun from the last half of *Guy* so as to make of it a separate romance, though it is poor stuff when it comes.

Where *Guy* strains at uplift, *Beves of Hamtoun* makes every possible concession to popular taste. The story is a heady brew of outrageous

---

17 Lines 27 – 105, 286 – 337, 408 – 544, 2488 – 2511, 2808 – 2849.
18 R. W. Ackerman, in his essay on "The English Rimed and Prose Romances", in *Arthurian Literature in the Middle Ages*, ed. R. S. Loomis (Oxford, 1959), suggests that the commercial shop-hacks wrote in couplet and minstrels in tail-rhyme (p. 482).

incident, concocted *ad hoc* from many diverse sources, and culminating in a single-handed pitched battle against the massed citizenry in the streets of London. This and several other senational episodes are the work of the English adaptor,[19] as is the outright vulgarisation of Beves, who, stripped of crusading chivalry, becomes a saga or folk-hero, admired for his physical strength, bravado and low cunning. The whole fantastic pot-pourri is carried off with irresistible panache and a marked sense of the comic.[20] It is vivid, gross and ridiculous by turns, but never dull.[21]

Richard Cœur de Lion is most remarkable for the streak of crude physical brutality which it displays, as in the lion-heart episode and Richard's cannibalistic orgies at Acre.[22] These episodes, like the account of Richard's magical birth and early adventures in Germany, were added in an expanded second English version of the story,[23] and show the expertise of the romancer in recognising and satisfying new thirsts for stimulation which found heroic adventure in itself inadequate. Perhaps he helped create this taste, for it is characteristic of the purveyor of popular entertainment to run before his audience, to underestimate their capacity for the expected and to overestimate their need for new twists and gimmicks, perhaps because of his own wider acquaintance with the stock material. The technical skill of the author, the vigour and authenticity of the battle-scenes, do not, however, disguise the shapelessness of the narrative and laborious circumstancing of each incident, the real drama of history being rejected in favour of the sham of interminable Saracen-baiting.

If Kölbing is right, and *Arthour and Merlin* and *Kyng Alisaunder* are by the same Kentishman of the late thirteenth century as *Richard*,[24] then one

---

[19]   The Christmas-day fight against the Saracens (585–738) and the dragon-fight (2597–2910) are both new, and the Miles-Josiane episode (3117ff.), in which Beves's beloved strings up an unwelcome bridegroom on the curtain-rail of the marriage-bed (3220–3224), is richly expanded.

[20]   Notably in the farcical scene of the attempted baptism of the giant Ascopard (e.g. 2594–2596).

[21]   It is interesting that the Auchinleck text of *Beves*, the oldest if not the best MS, begins in tail-rhyme stanza, switching to short couplet at 1.475. Perhaps a different hack took over, or perhaps the English adaptor recognised the unsuitability of the more 'poetic' measure to this vulgar thriller.

[22]   Lines 1090–1109, 3077–3124, 3194–3226, 3409–3520.

[23]   Or there may have been two successive expansions of the original shorter version as it appears in the Auchinleck fragments. See Hibbard, 147–154; *Richard*, ed. Brunner, introd., 17–24. The French source is not extant.

[24]   This theory is advanced in the introduction to his edition of *Arthour and Merlin*, pp. lx–cv. It is accepted by G. V. Smithers in his introduction to *Kyng Alisaunder* (p. 41), along with the attribution of *The Seven Sages of Rome* to the same London (rather than Kentish) author.

would suspect that *Arthour* was written first. There is an assertiveness about the status of English in the very deliberate prologue —

> Of Freynsch no Latin nil y telle more,
> Ac on Inglisch ichil tel þer fore;
> Riȝt is þat Inglische understonde
> Þat was born in Inglond;
> Freynsche use þis gentilman
> Ac everich Inglische Inglische can —[25]

which suggests that this was one of the first attempts to fasten on the new audience, while the handling of the French story is cramped and the verse lacks the confident hard professionalism of *Richard*. On the other hand, in its more frequent use of the seasons-headpiece as a prestige-conscious form of narrative punctuation, *Arthour* is closer to *Alisaunder*. This device, the use of which provides interesting confirmation of the growing sophistication of the new audience, is employed only once in *Richard*[26] and elsewhere very sporadically in isolated romances, and is, with dialectal identity, an important part of Kölbing's thesis. For the rest, *Arthour and Merlin* is very much the stock-in-trade of this first growth of romance, an interminable catalogue of Arthur's first battles arainst the barbarians, preceded by some account of the marvels surrounding Merlin's birth and early career.[27] *Kyng Alisaunder*, however, is something different, technically by far the most accomplished of all the English popular romances. The poet seems conscious of the grandeur of his theme,

> Þis is nouȝth romaunce of skof (668).

and he elaborates the endless battles and fantastic marvels of the Alexander-legend with an abundance of detail, a richness of imagery and a full exploitation of the techniques of rhetorical amplification developed in the *chansons de geste*.[28] For this, the direct French source provides the bare bones, but little more. The appeal to a more sophisticated audience is suggested also in the full preservation of the courtly atmosphere of *fine amour* in the Candace episode, and in the novel and brilliantly effective

---

[25]   *Arthour and Merlin*, 19–24. Cf. *Richard*, 21–24.
[26]   *Richard*, 3755. Cf. *Arthour*, 259, 1709, 3059, 4199, 5349, 6595, 7397, 7619, 8657; *Alisaunder*, 235, 457, 795, 911, 1239, 1573, &c.
[27]   It is perhaps a mark of changed taste that the Lincoln's Inn *Merlin*, a hundred years later, has only the marvels and not the battles. This version is not a separate abridged recension of *Arthour* but a corrupt 2492-line text of the first 2162 of *Arthour*'s 9938 lines.
[28]   For suggestive analysis of these features, and excellent treatment of the romance as a whole, see the introduction by G. V. Smithers to his edition, especially pp. 28–40.

manipulation of the seasons-headpiece. There are twenty-seven examples of this device in *Alisaunder*, mostly of six lines, some of more, monorhymed, beginning as simple nature-descriptions but developing in complexity through the poem to accommodate sententiae and miniature evocations of courtly life. They are often finely rhetoricated, packed with metaphor, and function within the poem like illuminations in a manuscript, free-running arabesques of the literary imagination standing out by their perfect irrelevance in the narrative or by a subtle piquant contrast with it. This device alone would serve to set *Alisaunder* apart from the generality of English romance.

Meanwhile, simultaneously with this first growth of 'epic romance', there were some early ventures into French love-romance and the Breton *lai*. These poems, *Floris and Blauncheflur*, *Ywain and Gawain*, *Sir Orfeo*, the *Lai le Freine*, *Sir Landeval* and *Sir Degare*, are in short couplet, and cut across the broad formal distinction between 'epic' and 'lyric' romance drawn earlier, suggesting the predominance of French metrical form before the development of native tail-rhyme.[29] *Floris* is very early, about 1250, and the others are from the first quarter of the fourteenth century, *Ywain* being latest. All are from the London area except *Ywain*, written in the north, where tail-rhyme took longer to spread.[30] These romances are markedly more urbane and delicate than the last group, and were designed for a somewhat more sophisticated stratum of the audience, perhaps for women. They deal less in battle, more in love and the supernatural, and the narratives are shaped to a purpose. *Floris* is particularly successful in catching the idyllic sentiment of its French original, which the poet chose in preference to another French version padded out with fighting. Though some ornamental descriptive matter is omitted and some of the lengthier love-scenes curtailed, this story of tender calf-love loses nothing in translation and gains in humour and irony. Even the Saracens are treated with mild good manners. *Ywain*, an abridgement of Chretien's *Yvain*, is less interested in sentiment, and not at all interested in Chretien's psychological speculations,[31] though otherwise very faithful in outline to the French story. Nothing much of

---

[29] This epithet is not intended to pre-empt discussion of the origin of tail-rhyme but to suggest that tail-rhyme, whatever its formal origin, soon became a specifically 'English' form.

[30] It will be recognised, here and elsewhere, that these are necessarily broad statements, and that the evidence as to date and dialect is a good deal more ambiguous than these assertions make it sound. However, no evidence has been deliberately neglected or distorted, and the general context of time and place is fairly clear.

[31] For instance, Ywain's debate with himself about the possibility of his love (for the lady whose husband he has slain) being returned occupies 1428 – 1506 in the French text but only 893 – 902 in the English (the total proportions are 6818:4032). For further examples, see the *EETS* edition, xvi – xxxiv.

the special quality of Chretien's writing comes through, and in the absence of this dialectic of love the romance is bound to seem somewhat otiose, but it is far from being a travesty of its original and, like *Floris*, bears all the marks of carefully contrived professional adaptation for more popular consumption.[32]

The other four in this group are Breton lays, *Lai le Freine* and *Landeval* both being based on extant French *lais*. The former is fragmentary, but seems close in style and technique to *Sir Orfeo*. The two poems occur side by side in the Auchinleck manuscript, share a common prologue, and were perhaps the work of the same translator.[33] *Sir Landeval* is an undistinguished translation of the *Lanval* attributed to Marie de France, fairly close except for the usual vulgarisation of story-material. Some late texts of this romance, known as *Sir Lambewell* and *Sir Lamwell*, are so corrupt that they have often been mistaken for separate recensions of the story.[34] *Sir Orfeo* is probably derived from a lost French original, and represents a weirdly convincing Celticization of the classical Orpheus-legend with the addition of a happy ending. It is one of the most interesting of all Middle English romances,[35] partly for the perpetual fascination of the myth itself and partly for a rare economy and neatness which underlie the apparent naivete of style and handling. *Sir Degare* is stylistically close to *Freine* and *Orfeo*, with verbal imitation of the former, and may be an original English product designed to exploit the popularity of the form. The title, however, suggests a French original, a 'lai d'Egare', as the English text explains carefully (perhaps too carefully) at line 256. Whatever the case, *Sir Degare* is a remarkable comprehensive collection of typical *lai* motifs, and, though there are a few loose ends,[36] the patchwork is cunningly done and the whole thing is a not at all contemptible example of what the professional romancer could knock together when pressed.

---

[32] The *EETS* editors suggest "the sober, realistic audience of a provincial baron's hall" (p. xvii). This seems reasonable.

[33] See L. Foulet, "The Prologue of *Sir Orfeo*", *MLN*, 21 (1906), 46–50; G. Guillaume, "The Prologues of the *Lay le Freyne* and *Sir Orfeo*", *MLN*, 36 (1921), 458–464; *Orfeo*, ed. Bliss, introd., pp. xliv–xlvii.

[34] See *Launfal*, ed. Bliss, introd., 4–5.

[35] Recent signs of interest include J. Burke Severs, "The Antecedents of *Sir Orfeo*", in *Baugh Studies*, 187–207; D. M. Hill, "The Structure of *Sir Orfeo*", *Mediaeval Studies*, 23 (1961), 136–153.

[36] See G. V. Smithers, "Story-Patterns in some Breton lays", *Medium Aevum*, 22 (1953), 61–92; also C. P. Faust, *Sir Degare: a Study of the Texts and Narrative Structure* (Oxford, 1936); C. H. Slover, "*Sir Degarre*: a Study in a Medieval Hack Writer's Methods", *Texas Studies in English*, 11 (1931), 6–23. W. C. Stokoe, "The Double Problem of *Sir Degare*", *PMLA*, 70 (1955), 518–534, argues that some of the apparent confusion is due to the existence, hitherto unrecognised, of two separate recensions of the story, both textually corrupt.

The channelling of composing talent into tail-rhyme and the taste of an increasingly discriminating audience for something more than inventories of cloven heads and mutilated limbs lead to a sharp decline in short-couplet 'epic romance' after about 1320. The products of this second phase, the Auchinleck *Otuel*, the *Seege of Troye*, *Arthur*, *Titus and Vespasian* and *Ipomydon*, are uncompromisingly popular in tone, all crude abridgements of familiar pseudo-historical 'epic' material except for *Ipomydon*, a prosaic redaction for a popular audience of the important northern tail-rhyme *Ipomadon*. These poems are like a back-wash from the first surge of romance-writing, third-rate fumbling in an enfeebled tradition when the new points of growth are elsewhere. Late in the century the rhetorically elaborate epic manner of *Kyng Alisaunder* is imitated in the Laud *Troy-Book*, but in a bookish, laborious, pedestrian manner which the author tries occasionally to invigorate with infusions of alliterative phraseology, for instance in the interesting secondary prologue, where for twenty lines he writes in a strongly alliterative manner, as if to whip up flagging interest.[37] The Laud *Troy-Book*, which appears to be of north-west-midland origin, would thus provide another late fourteenth century link between the older tradition of rhymed romance and the poetry of the alliterative revival.

There was something of a revival of short-couplet romance in the fifteenth century, in a series of smooth, fashionable romances such as *Partonope of Blois*, the *Squyr of Lowe Degre* and *Eger and Grime*, designed for middle-class consumption. Chaucerian influence, which is explicit in *Partonope*, and which extends also to other romances in rhyme-royal, such as *Generydes* and the *Romans of Partenay*, is the main factor in this revival, which precedes the major fifteenth century development, the shift to prose.

Investigation of the tradition of 'lyric romance', to which we now turn, must begin with *King Horn*, a unique early (c. 1240) survival in which we see the first germination of the form. The story, with its exile-and-return motif, is of great antiquity, perhaps a legendary outgrowth from the era of the Viking conquests, though any historical authenticity has been obscured by romantic accretions. The geography and place-names, for instance, are unrecognisable, and *Suddene*, Horn's native land, has been plausibly identified as Sussex, Cornwall, the Isle of Man and Roxburgh as well as with the land of *Suðdene* in *Beowulf*. The English poem is related to the French *Horn et Rimenhild*, probably by indirect derivation, though with drastic abridgement and some contamination, as in *Havelok*, from native tradition. The French romance is an amalgam of *geste* and *courtoisie*, with courtly love-scenes, tournaments and a rich and luxurious

---

[37]   Ll. 3243–3256. Compare the battle-description in 16675–16686.

social setting, but in *Horn* the story is reduced to its bare essentials and the social background is non-courtly, though there is no sign of any deliberate attempt to present the story in terms of lower-class values, as there is in *Havelok*. In fact, despite the ultimate Anglo-Viking origin of the story and the occurrence of both poems in MS Laud 108, *Horn* needs to be carefully dissociated from *Havelok* and indeed from the whole 'Matter of England' group of epic romances, less for its differences of matter, which are considerable (love, trial and constancy are here as important as fighting) than for its complete difference of manner. *Horn* is the first narrative outgrowth from song or lay, and may be presumed to bear the same relation to pre-existent sung lay as the extant *contes* of Marie de France to the Breton *lais* which they claim as their source.[38] *Horn* is close to song:

> Alle beon he bliþe
> Þat to my song lyþe;
> A sang ihc schal ʒou singe
> Of Murry þe kinge;[39]

and the manner of the telling is ballad-like, with concentration on the dramatic moment, abrupt transitions, internally dependent repetition, and a cryptic allusiveness of episodic reference. There is little attempt at 'literary' or rational articulation of the narrative:

> Þe word bigan to springe
> Of Rymenhilde weddinge.
> Horn was in þe watere,
> Ne miʒte he come no latere.
> He let his schup stonde,
> And ʒede to londe. (1093 – 8)

These narrative techniques demand the heightened alertness of response which one associates with song, and often a subtlety, especially in the two scenes where Horn returns disguised to rescue his princess from unwelcome suitors,[40] that makes nonsense of the idea that a popular audience must of necessity be a crude one. The verse itself has the same breathless character, a pared-down economy of phrase in which the conventional formulae lie in embryo:

[38] See W. H. French, *Essays on King Horn*, 1 – 19.
[39] Ll. 1 – 4. Quotation of *Horn* is from the Cambridge text, with numbering from the convenient synchronised system used in the *EETS* edition.
[40] Ll. 1185 – 1298, 1577 – 1618.

He was briȝt so þe glas,
He was whit so þe flur,
Rose red was his colur, (14 – 16)

and a curt parenthetic indirection pregnant with meaning:

Murie lif he wroȝte:
Rymenhild hit dere boȝte. (1491 – 92)

The couplet of *Horn* is a unique non-alliterative derivative from the alliterative first-half-line, blended with the French trimeter to give a standard line of three stresses, though two and four occur in special contexts.[41] This development of alliterative verse is already well advanced in Laȝamon's *Brut*, and *Horn* thus stands midway between Laȝamon, the debt to whom is explicit in a number of borrowed phrases,[42] and the later couplet. Whether it was so or not (i.e. in terms of lost literature), *Horn* seems to us of crucial importance, for it embodies, partly by derivation from Laȝamon, a conventional technique and conventional phraseology in unalloyed form, like crude ore, from which later romances such as *Guy* or *Richard* drew extensively.[43] Where they modify the metre of the oldest text, the two later manuscripts of *Horn* (Laud 108 and Harley 2253) always move towards four-stress regularity, but the clipped, short-breathed lines of the Cambridge *Horn*, with their sparse, abrupt syntax and lack of articulation, are the perfect complement of the narrative's lyric quality and may be considered a deliberate choice.

Sir Tristrem is the second link in the chain. Written about fifty years later than *Horn*, it is, with its rapid transitions, allusive episodes and cryptic, staccato narration, another attempt to adapt lay-type conventions to the conduct of a longer narrative. Features such as the prologue, with its graceful comparison of past and present with summer and winter, and the hunting-scene (474), with its technical account of the breaking of the deer where Tristrem reveals his breeding, presuppose a less popular audience, and there is a more sophisticated attempt to find a metrical alternative, more lyrical, more musical, more 'poetic', to the plain, pedestrian four-stress couplet by now firmly established for more prosaic narrative. The result is a difficult eleven-line stanza, ^{3}ababababc'ac, based on a three-stress line of the *Horn*-type, with a 'bob' embryonically suggestive of tail-rhyme. Unhappily, the stanza proves unsuited to narrative, and the

---

[41] This analysis is not unanimously accepted. See J. Schipper, *A History of English Versification* (Oxford, 1910), 79 – 84; *Horn*, ed. Hall, xlv – l; W. H. French, *op. cit.*, 23 – 113; H. S. West, *The Versification of King Horn* (Baltimore, 1907).

[42] See, for example, the notes in Hall's edition of *Horn* to ll. 11, 411, 913, 1366.

[43] See Hall's notes *passim*.

whole poem, though thoughtful and carefully adapted to its audience,[44] lacks the vigour of *Horn*. There is a traditional association with Thomas of Erceldoune, a Scots poet of the late thirteenth century, but the extant *Tristrem* is probably a south-midland adaptation of a lost work by Erceldoune.[45] He and *Tristrem* are both mentioned, though not specifically associated, in a passage in Robert Manning's *Chronicle*,[46] which is very interesting for its contrast of Manning's own simple style and simple English with the artificial verse-forms and 'strange Inglis' of poets like Erceldoune and poems like *Tristrem*. Manning says that his own writing is intended to be clear and readily understood:

> I mad noght for no disours,
> Ne for no seggers ne harpours.

But others, out of vanity, write in such complicated schemes of 'ryme couwee or strangere or enterlace', and in such 'quaynte Inglis', that people can neither understand their poems nor recite them without errors. Whatever the *Tristrem* referred to, there is here clear confirmation of a distinction between the four-stress couplet (which Manning himself uses), with its 'ordinary' English and prosaic quality, and stanzas of the tail-rhyme ('couwee') type, with their musical associations, archaic and strongly alliterative phraseology, and definitely 'poetic' quality.

The developed tail-rhyme stanza, in which the formal problems of lyric romance are resolved and into which virtually the whole tradition is channelled from 1300 to 1400, is of twelve lines, typically $^4aab^3ccb^3ddb^3$ eeb^3. Whatever its origin,[47] it can be seen stylistically as an attempt to combine the clear articulation of the four-stress couplet with the musical and poetic quality of the native-based three-stress line.[48] There are differences of technique within the tail-rhyme tradition, but the basic

---

[44] There is a sympathetic reappraisal of *Tristrem* by T. C. Rumble in *Comparative Literature*, 11 (1959), 221–228.

[45] A southern provenance for *Tristrem* (which would associate it conveniently with *Horn*) is argued by B. Vogel in *JEGP*, 40 (1941), 538–544.

[46] Lines 71–128 in the edition of F. J. Furnivall in the Rolls series (London, 1887).

[47] It is usually assumed to be derived, through Anglo-Norman, from ecclesiastical sequences and responses. See Schipper, *op. cit.*, 296; M. Dominica Legge, *Anglo-Norman Literature and its Background* (Oxford, 1963), 250; A. McI. Trounce, in *Medium Aevum*, 2 (1933), 34–42.

[48] There seems to be something of this distribution in the *Brut*, where Laȝamon characteristically uses traditional formal alliterative verse for 'poetic' passages such as battle-pieces and sea-journeys and longer rhymed half-lines for more prosaic narrative. In Anglo-Norman, Nicole Bozon seems to have considered the couplet most suitable for narrative, and tail-rhyme stanza for "anything vaguely lyrical" (Legge, *op. cit.*, 231).

stanza is one of alternate movement and rest, the pressing forward of the narrative in the couplet contrasting with the pause in the tail-line for descriptive arabesque, emotive comment, exclamation or other conventional formula. Later poets, such as the author of *Athelston*, often set their material in quite subtle tension against this formal structure, running on from tail to couplet, for instance, or using the tail for *sotto voce* comment.[49] The musical or poetic satisfaction of the stanza is at once in the variety provided by the contrast between couplet and tail, and in the unity of the fourfold tail-rhyme. The ever-present danger of the form is that the tail-line, whilst fulfilling its musical function, will become a meaningless tag and eventually drop off like a mortified limb. The tail-rhyme romances maintain their identity further through the use of an extensive and elaborate conventional phraseology, often strongly alliterative and particularly heavily concentrated in the tail-line, which can thus become the poetic core of the stanza. The tradition is centred in the east-midlands but shifts northwards towards the end of the century, closely pursued by Chaucer's ridicule.

The first quarter of the century sees the establishment of the classical tradition of stanza technique and conventional idiom in the stanzaic *Guy* and *Reinbrun*, already mentioned, in *Horn Childe* and *Amis and Amiloun* (all are in the Auchinleck). *Horn Childe* is an independent reworking of the Horn-story, less primitive and more courtly in setting than *King Horn*, and closer to the French, though the pressure behind the native tradition is still strong enough for the story to throw out historical roots in the opening account of the heroic death of Horn's father Haþeolf at the hands of Irish raiders. This is a semi-historical north-eastern accretion to the story which has not been filtered through the French, and its spirit is stern, northern, unchivalric and powerfully authentic. Haþeolf's rallying call to his men,

> He bad þe harpour leven his lay:
> 'For ous bihoveþ anoþer play', (157 – 158)

and his death, surrounded like a boar by the Irish dogs who, frightened to approach, stone him till his legs are broken —

> He kneled atte last — (222)

---

[49] This is the term used by A. McI. Trounce, whose study of the tail-rhyme romances (*Medium Aevum*, 1 (1932), 87 – 108, 168 – 182; 2 (1933), 34 – 57, 189 – 193; 3 (1934), 30 – 50) is full of valuable material, though his attempt to force all the romances into a strictly east-midland tradition is unnecessary and has brought his work into disfavour. See A. R. Dunlap, "The Vocabulary of the Middle English Romances in Tail-rhyme Stanza", *Delaware Notes* (1941); also G. Taylor, "Notes on *Athelston*", *Leeds Studies in English*, 4 (1935), 47 – 57.

are among the most stirring passages in English romance. Much of this spirit is lost when Horn leaves for the south and his more familiar adventures begin, and the rest of the romance is rather commonplace. *Amis and Amiloun* is a thoroughly conventional adaptation from the French, a fine romance, beautifully shaped to the idealised illustration of friendship but never burdened by its didactic theme. The tail-rhyme form fixes the romance-convention absolutely, so that, with never a suggestion that the laws of romance are going to be violated, the poem can afford considerable elaboration of the genuinely affective parts of the story. In other words, though the events of the story are wildly improbable by realistic standards, the formal tradition is strong enough to inhibit any appeal to such standards, strong enough furthermore to allow a broadening and deepening of the area of human response, within the romance-convention, which makes of *Amis* a genuinely poetic experience. The handling of the narrative line is typical of tail-rhyme, flowering at times into a lyrically free expansiveness, as in the talk of Amis's excellence, or the spring-scene, or the battle,[50] where we feel we are at the very poetic heart of romance. At the climax of the narrative the poet passes out of the conventional phraseology into a pregnantly simple style which lies beyond art,[51] though only made possible by art, that is, by the establishment of a conventionally valid poetic context in which such a situation can be invested with deep narrative significance. *Amis* has some claim to be regarded as the typically best English romance.

English composers were not slow to exploit the didactic possibilities opened up by *Guy* and *Amis*, and a group of midland and north-midland tail-rhyme romances, the *King of Tars*, *Le Bone Florence*, *Roland and Vernagu*, *Sir Amadas*, *Sir Cleges* and *Sir Gowther*,[52] tap the rich vein of popular piety with varying degrees of success. The first two, both early (c. 1320), effectively combine a strong religious colouring with much traditional romance-material and a close adherence to classical tail-rhyme techniques. These romances are the bridge to the saint's legend, and contain much typically hagiographic material, such as the elementary exposition of Christian doctrine by the princess of Tars to her husband the Sultan, prior to his conversion.[53] A similar passage of exposition occurs in the roughly contemporary *Roland and Vernagu*,[54] which is included in this group because the chief motive in extracting it from the

---

50   *Amis*, 439 – 468, 529 – 540, 1297 – 1320.
51   E.g. 2281 – 2292, 2311 – 2316.
52   The last three, which are later, are significantly grouped in Nat. Lib. Scot., Adv. 19.3.1, along with *Sir Isumbras*, which has close didactic affiliations.
53   Lines 836 – 870. This passage was altogether too much for the scribe of the Vernon MS, who omits it entirely.
54   Lines 677 – 790. Vernagu proves more stubborn than the Sultan.

Latin chronicle of the pseudo-Turpin seems to have been pietistic. However, it is difficult to talk of motives with such a wretched piece of work. The handling of tail-rhyme is so crude and so feeble as to suggest that the form was, at the time of writing, still inchoate. *Amadas* and *Cleges* are somewhat later, short moral exempla with a homely bourgeois tone. Both derive from native folk-loristic motifs, and both have to do with money, poverty and debts, and the practical rewards of virtue. *Amadas* exists in two redactions, of which the later (in the Ireland MS) is the closer to popular romance.[55] The romance-setting of *Cleges*, however (at the court of king Uther), is the merest gesture, the real centre of the story being in its folksy wisdom. *Gowther* claims to be a Breton lay but it is really a sensationalised version of the popular legend of Robert le Diable, the repentant warlock. The tone of the prologue is earnestly religious, but the poem as a whole is an unscrupulous and highly professional exploitation of popular piety, credulity and love of sensation. The tail-rhyme affiliations of *Cleges* and *Gowther*, both late fourteenth century, are lame and sporadic.[56]

Meanwhile, the central tradition is embodied from 1340 onwards in a series of romances with a marked unity of plot-material, *Octavian*, *Athelston*, *Sir Isumbras*, *Sir Eglamour*, *Torrent of Portyngale* and *Sir Triamour*, all stories of rejection or exile, trial, constancy and reward. *Octavian* is the earliest and basic exemplar, a brisk and lively narrative, full of piety and pathos, with a humble gift for the dramatic realisation of the story which, anticipated by *Amis*, is one of the most striking achievements of later tail-rhyme romance. This is shown especially in the scenes describing prince Florent's life as a Paris butcher's adopted son, where there is not only development of the obvious comic line (e.g. 889) but also an effective presentation in terms of narrative of the real difference between knightly and bourgeois manners. These domestic scenes have a pungent authenticity which would have appealed strongly to an audience of lower bourgeois, and which fulfils, in however humble a way, the demand for 'some sort of substantial contents' which W. P. Ker saw as the necessary corollary of the development of romance.[57] There is another version of the Octavian-story, in an unusual tail-type stanza, ^{4}aaab^{2}ab^2. It is independently derived from the same original French source and is usually called the 'southern' *Octavian*, though it might be

---

55   Two stanzas are added at the end, for instance, to show *Amadas* recovering his original
      lands and rewarding his faithful steward, an archetypal romance-motif (ed. Robson, st.
      71 – 72).
56   One short-couplet piece, *Robert of Cicyle* (c. 1360), is closely associated with this group
      of tail-rhyme romances in theme, though it is doubtful whether it can be considered a
      romance itself.
57   *Epic and Romance* (2nd ed., Oxford, 1908), 354.

more convenient to call it *Octovian*. This version is throughout cruder and more popular in appeal, and develops the comedy of social situation with less concern for its narrative point than for its farcical possibilities.

The quality of dramatic realisation discernible in *Octavian* is fully developed in *Athelston*, a strict, sober tale shaped by its English author to a serious moral and religious purpose. It is a story of treachery, false accusation, ordeal by fire and the vindication of innocence, told with a strong sense of physical, historical and political reality. The relationships of Church and State, the conflict of king and archbishop, the interdict, as well as the ordeal by fire and the messenger's journey to Canterbury, are all described with powerful authenticity, and the tiny sub-plot of the messenger (whose name is also Athelston) is like a counterpointing of common imperfect reality against the figuration of reality in the main romance-plot. The annexation of new areas of experience to tail-rhyme in *Athelston* is matched by deliberate and highly effective innovation within the form.[58]

The other four romances in this group are composites of stock incidents, of the type that the professional romancer could turn out *ad libitum*. *Isumbras*, the legend of the man tried by Fate, has a strong religious colouring, like *Athelston* and the *Amadas*-group, as well as elements of prosaic realism which link it with *Octavian*.[59] Like many tail-rhyme romances of the mature tradition, it relies heavily on the carrying power of the tradition, beginning confidently and vigorously, only to decline as the narrative slips limply from the composer's grasp. *Sir Eglamour* is a mechanical shuffling-together of stock incidents, whisked vigorously and poured out at a pace that aims to provide little time for reflection on what rubbish it all is. Sheer multiplication of stimuli is the writer's recipe for success, and the existence of four manuscripts and five sixteenth century prints would seem to suggest that he knew what he was about. *Torrent* is, if such a thing can be conceived, a composite derivative of *Eglamour*, with further multiplication of stock incidents: where *Eglamour* had two giant-fights, *Torrent* has no less than five.[60] *Sir Triamour* is marked as late by a good deal of variation and transposition of the traditional tail-rhyme phraseology. The praise which this romance has received may be due in part to its inclusion of a faithful dog among its chief actors, but it is on the

---

[58] See Trounce's edition of the romance, 57–59, 95–96, 104, 122. Trounce's observations on the tail-rhyme style are sometimes over-refined, but he does at least give it a chance.

[59] E.g. the description of ironsmithing, 397–432. Isumbras's first 'trial' is to have his farm-buildings burnt and his beasts slain, 73–96. Cf. *Degrevaunt*.

[60] *Torrent* comes down to us in a single late 15th century MS in a state of advanced textual corruption, which may help explain its incoherence. Like *Triamour*, the original romance would date from the early 15th century.

whole a skilful rehash of conventional motifs with a quite intricate plot. There may not be much interest in what is going on, but at least there is always something going on.

The late fourteenth century saw a revival of interest in the Breton lay, as the *Franklin's Tale* bears witness, and three romances claim Breton origin, *Emaré*, the *Erl of Tolous* and *Sir Launfal*. Though all three share a mild refinement of tone which makes the claim not entirely pointless, only *Launfal* is authentic, *Emaré* being a slight, trivial, tinselly handling of the Constance-story and therefore associated with the *Octovian*-group, while the *Erl of Tolous* shows the growing taste of an audience surfeited with marvels for the potentially real and unmarvellous human situation, and thus represents a further stage in the growth of romance to accommodate some sort of 'substantial contents'. In *Launfal*, freely expanded by Thomas Chestre, who names himself in line 1039, from the earlier *Landeval*, the elements of fantasy and reality are held in uneasy suspension. Where earlier translators of Breton lays accepted the supernatural and irrational without question, Chestre makes a systematic attempt to obscure them with prosaic circumstance and rational motivation. The careful explanation of Launfal's poverty in relation to his disapproval of Guenevere's promiscuity, his polite fiction of a dying father, invented to save hurting Arthur's feelings when he leaves court, the embarrassed evasiveness of the mayor of Caerleon when Launfal asks for hospitality, the quiet irony later when Launfal's luck changes, all these and many other new touches show Chestre aware of simple dramatic interplay of character.[61] But much is lost that is more traditionally 'romance': Tryamowr receives less emphasis as a faery mistress than as a rich patroness who will help Launfal out of a tricky financial situation, while the Guenevere of romance is sadly smeared in the final episode. Chestre is something of a hack, and his handling of stanza and descriptive formulae is often uncomfortable, in the manner of a writer working towards the lag-end of a tradition. He is generally credited with two other romances, *Octovian* and *Libeaus Desconus*, in addition to *Launfal*, on the principle that when a shadowy figure emerges from the mist, it is a pity not to load him with as much responsibility as we can.[62] Such attributions, within a tradition so close-knit, are not susceptible of proof, though this one is plausible. *Libeaus Desconus* would be somewhat earlier (c. 1350) than the other two, a

---

61   *Launfal*, 44 – 48, 70 – 72, 73 – 84, 109 – 120, 400 – 415. The long tournament and giant-fight (433 – 636) are both added by Chestre to make Launfal more 'substantial'.

62   The poems were first associated by G. Sarrazin in his edition of *Octavian* (pp. xxv – xxxi). See Dorothy Everett, ''The Relationship of Chestre's *Launfal* and *Lybeaus Desconus*'', *Medium Aevum*, 7 (1938), 29 – 49; M. Mills, ''The Composition and Style of the 'Southern' *Octavian*, *Sir Launfal* and *Libeaus Desconus*'', *Medium Aevum*, 31 (1962), 88 – 109.

popular abridgement of some version of *Le Bel Inconnu* (the English title effectively conceals the derivation) by Renaud de Beaujeu. It is a good example of the way in which passionate erotic romance in French is emasculated into innocent knockabout in English. Metrically, it provides a link between *King Horn* and the *Degrevaunt*-group, having a tail-rhyme stanza based on three instead of four stresses.

The northward shift of tail-rhyme romance, which we have explained in terms of change of taste in the metropolis, is focussed in *Ipomadon*, a close translation of the late twelfth-century Anglo-Norman *Ipomedon* of Hue de Rotelande. There is little concession to popular taste here, for *Ipomadon* is courtly, witty, smooth, enormously leisurely, and technically highly gifted, and it opens up the tradition for a much more sophisticated audience. The heavy alliteration is a mark of the developing northern tradition, as are the freer handling of syntax and stanza and extensive non-popular vocabulary. These are the characteristics too of *Sir Degrevaunt*, the first of a group of three late fourteenth century romances in sixteen-line stanza, $^3aaab^2cccb^2dddb^2eeeb^2$, in which the triplet and tail lines are derived from alliterative first and second half-lines respectively.[63] In *Degrevaunt* can be seen the fullest and most successful attempt to place romance in a dramatically realised social setting, to merge the traditional knight of romance with the knight of reality, for Sir Degrevaunt is not only a knight of the Round Table and companion of Percival and Gawain but also a Yorkshire country landowner with his estates, gamekeepers, letters demanding compensation and prosaic responsibilities worlds away from romantic chivalry. The story of his love-affair with Melidor is realised in the same manner, with scrupulously detailed accounts of the feast she prepares for him and the room she entertains him in.[64] There is exaggeration, of course, but there is also knowledge: upper-class life as described here is no idealised fantasy. The other two poems in the group, *Sir Perceval of Gales* and the *Avowynge of King Arther*, share this quality of vivid dramatic realisation, but on a more popular level. Both are technically skilled, with full development of the stanza-linking hinted at in *Degrevaunt*. *Perceval* is an effective and very amusing exploitation of the theme of the ill-bred hero, the son of a Round Table knight who is brought up in the woods by his mother in ignorance of chivalry and knighthood, and of the impact of his rough-hewn heroism on the court of Arthur. The appeal of the situation is simple and obvious, simultaneously to the

---

[63] See the discussion of metre in Casson's edition of *Degrevaunt*, xxxi-xli, where further references are given.

[64] Ll. 1389 – 1520. *Degrevaunt* also states with bourgeois bluntness the need for strict pre-marital chastity (1533 – 1536), though 'bundling' is permissible (1557 – 1560).

audience's vanity (in that they recognise the breaches of decorum) and to the latent spirit of anti-chivalric mockery, but the poem has wit and skill. The episodic *Avowynge* is from still farther north, perhaps a little after 1400, and provides a link with the stricter Scots alliterative tradition of the fifteenth century.

Two vigorous offshoots of the *Ipomadon* tradition are the *Sege of Melayne* and *Rowlande and Ottuell*, the only effective treatments in English of the Matter of France. The choice of such material at a date when England must have been at war with France demonstrates the insatiability of appetite for new stories, but the theme is made palatable by a twist of patriotic feeling in which the *douseperes* become 'oure Cristen men'. The *Sege* is a splendidly stirring fragment which takes fire from the moment of Bishop Turpin's first appearance and thereafter maintains a stern, martial ardour (e.g. 1507 – 1512) which *Rowlande* lacks only by comparison.[65] The contribution of tail-rhyme tradition to the effectiveness of these two romances is best assessed by comparing the latter with the crude couplet *Otuel*, based on an identical source.[66] Where *Rowlande*, for instance, strives to subordinate detail to an overall narrative pattern, *Otuel* snatches at any sensational incident in order to exaggerate it, and where *Rowlande* can surround any situation with a rich accumulation of traditional detail, *Otuel* can only reel off statement after crude statement.[67] The two English versions of the Fierabras-story, *Sir Ferumbras* and the *Sowdone of Babylone*, also serve to throw into relief the accumulated strength of the tail-rhyme tradition, since both are late non-northern deviations from the tradition, the former in ballad-quatrain $^4ab^3ab^3$ and (from line 3411) six-line tail-rhyme stanza,[68] the latter in quatrain ^4abab. *Ferumbras* is metrically crude and shows little knowledge of traditional techniques or phraseology, though it is a faithful enough translation to convey something of the vigour and graphic detail of the original *chanson de geste*. The *Sowdone* follows a familiar pattern of popular abridgement and adaptation, but shows uncertainty of touch in introducing some peculiar passages of

---

65   The prologue to *Rowlande*, for instance, with its talk of adventures, of 'gamen and gle', should be compared with the imperious demand for attention to history and bygone chivalry, 'ryghte lele trouthe', at the beginning of the *Sege*. The two romances are still likely to be by the same author, and both occur unique in the same MS. It is worth remarking that all the Matter of France romances occur unique.

66   Ultimately, the French *Otinel*. There is a third version of the story in the 15th-century *Otuel and Roland*, in the Fillingham MS, which also contains a third version of *Firumbras*. Both are edited by Mary I. O'Sullivan, *EETS, OS*, 198 (1935).

67   Compare *Rowlande*, 614 – 624, with *Otuel*, 641 – 642; 466 – 468 with 461 – 463; 172 – 174 with 167 – 168.

68   Both metrical forms are disguised in the *EETS* print, as well as the enormous length of this romance, which in standard numbering runs to nearly 12,000 lines.

meretricious ornamentation, which may be sops thrown out to changing taste in the late century.[69]

Before its degeneration in the Gawain-romances of the fifteenth century, the sophisticated nothern alliterative tail-rhyme tradition threw off one poem which embodies all that is best in lyric romance. Though *Le Morte Arthur* is written in a difficult eight-line stanza, [4]abababab, and not in tail-rhyme, it is deeply indebted to the tradition for its conventional techniques and heavily alliterative phraseology. There is a fine response to the story, a knowledge of courteous and proper behaviour, little or no vulgarisation, and an elegiac quality which even Malory found hard to improve on.[70]

It remains only to admit that new evidence, and further evaluation of the more neglected romances, may affect the details of this historical morphology of Middle English romance. There are many blurs in it, and many assertions which lack of space alone has caused me to leave unqualified. But the main lines of the scheme, particularly the general formal distinctions, though only tentatively sketched out here, have at least some objective basis, and may serve as scaffolding for others to build on.

---

[69] E.g. a spring-prologue, 41 – 48; a spring-transition on love and valour, 963 – 978 (hinted in *Fierabras*); and an apostrophe by the Sultan to 'Mars Armypotente', 939 – 962 (cf. *Knight's Tale*, 1, 1982). Such passages could be 'Chaucerian' interpolations.

[70] For a full recognition of Malory's debt to *Le Morte Arthur*, see E. Talbot Donaldson, ''Malory and the Stanzaic *Le Morte Arthur*'', *SP*, 47 (1950), 460 – 472.

Plans, Predictions, and Promises: Traditional Story Techniques and the Configuration of Word and Deed in King Horn

ANNE SCOTT

Abounding in familiar characters and predictable scenes, the Middle English romance *King Horn* relates in a typical fashion what is, in many ways, a typical story of love and adventure. The young and beautiful Horn, expelled from Suddene by Saracens who have murdered his father, King Murry, journeys across the sea with his twelve companions to Westerness, where he is fostered by King Aylmar. The King's daughter Rymenhild falls in love with Horn and asks that he marry her, but Horn refuses, saying that he must prove his valour first. Horn does so by slaying numerous pagans, and he plights his troth to her afterwards, but the treachery of Horn's jealous companion, Fikenhild, stands in the way of Horn and Rymenhild's happiness, forcing Horn to depart from Westerness. Adopting the alias "Cutberd," Horn crosses the sea to Ireland, serves King Thurston for several years, and kills a Saracen giant, his father's slayer, in the meantime. When told that a certain King Mody seeks to marry Rymenhild, Horn leaves King Thurston's kingdom (refusing his daughter's hand in marriage), arrives in Westerness in the nick of time to foil Mody's attempt, and marries Rymenhild himself. Leaving Rymenhild behind once more, Horn restores Suddene to Christian leadership by ousting its pagan leader, returns to Westerness to save his bride from yet another treacherous marriage (this time to Fikenhild), and makes her his queen.

Such is a summarized version of *King Horn*, a romance written as early as 1225 and perhaps the oldest in Middle English.[1] Compared

---

[1] The romance exists in three manuscripts, printed in parallel columns in Hall's 1901

with the various romance and ballad treatments of the Horn story and with other medieval romances, the poem has been described as a "veritable catalog of traditional romance motifs"; it is "pure narrative, story for story's sake," "simple" and "plain," abounding with numerous stereotyped phrases, and "full of primitive touches centuries older than its language."[2] These descriptions are accurate in many respects, and yet they seem to strike a patronizing if not dismissive note, which provokes the main theme of this essay. As recent criticism has begun to show, *King Horn* is a fine poem appealing to readers of all levels of sophistication. Its story evokes profound archetypal images, and its style is spare yet beautiful and effective. It is the aim of this essay to relate the poem's achievement to its manner of proceeding — which is, indeed, unfamiliar to our modern ideas about what poetry should be like. In order to establish a more fruitful new approach to the poem we must recreate an earlier, different attitude to poetry so that we can understand it imaginatively and free ourselves from the modern prejudices we often bring to these apparently simple and unassuming works.

Perhaps the most essential point to grasp in approaching a work like *King Horn* is that there is a great difference between writing which is based in oral delivery and that which is purely literate. *King Horn* has its roots in a world and poetic sensibility much closer to Homer than to the poems of our modern print-culture. At the same time, the poem also has been modified by the literacy that has preserved it, and it is this unique mixture of orality and literacy which conditions the nature of the poem.

---

edition: British Library Harley MS 2253 (which I will term, following Hall, the London MS), Bodleian Library Laud Misc. MS 108 (the Oxford MS), and Cambridge University Library MS Gg. 4.27.2 (the Cambridge MS). This paper is based on a reading of the Cambridge MS version (as edited by Hall), although I will make occasional reference to variants in the other MSS. The Cambridge MS was generally thought to be the earliest (1240 – 60), although recent opinion suggests that both the Cambridge and the Oxford MSS date to about 1300 (see Rosamund Allen, "Textual Cruces," 73, 76 – 77, notes 1, 2). In her recent critical edition of the poem (*King Horn*, [NY, 1984], 3), Allen proposes that the Cambridge MS, if not the earliest of the three, at least presents "an earlier state of the text" than either the Oxford or London MSS.

2   Donald Sands, *Middle English Romances*, 15; A. V. C. Schmidt and Nicolas Jacobs, *Medieval English Romances* 1.2; Hall, *King Horn*, liii; and George McKnight, *King Horn*, xxi. For complete bibliographical information about these references and others, see "Works Cited."

There is much about the poem's language and style that suggests its affinities to orally composed or transmitted works. The short, alliterating couplets in the poem which occur in the Cambridge and Oxford versions and its terse, rhythmical style give the poem a songlike quality and have led both early and later critics to liken the poem to a ballad.[3] These aspects of the poem, along with the poet's own introductory lines — "Alle beon he blithe / that to my song lythe, / A sang ihc schal ʒou singe"[4] — very likely indicate that *King Horn* was a romance not to be read but to be listened to, written down, perhaps, by knight, cleric, or other court member to be recited in a hall. The textual divergences between the manuscripts also suggest an oral transmission for the poem. Many of the poem's synonymous variants might have arisen when a reciter would substitute similar words in place of those which had been forgotten or misremembered (see Allen, "Textual Cruces," 73). Sung or simply read aloud, changes might have taken place as acts of recomposition during the actual performance. The poem's numerous repeating phrases are also reminiscent of those formulae which recur throughout the orally-composed works studied by Milman Parry and Albert Lord.[5]

In the case of romances in general, however, as John Speirs notes, it is not always easy to distinguish "between poems which are written compositions and those which, though they have been preserved by having been written down, are none the less oral poetry" (*Medieval English Poetry*, 109). The theory that *King Horn* was an actual product of oral composition or recital is challenged by scholars who stress that romances arose as a "new written genre" (Walter Ong, *Orality and Literacy*, 159) and that *King Horn* in particular represents a "*literary stage*" in the transition from an oral to written culture (Allen, *King Horn*, 106 [note 29]). As Allen's detailed analysis of the variants in the three MSS demonstrates, *King Horn* is both a "carefully written poem" and a poem which has retained distinct traces of an oral tradition; Derek Pearsall also has remarked that the poem's variants could have been intellectual and imaginative reworkings by poet or scribe ("Textual

---

[3] See, for example, McKnight (xi – xii); A. C. Spearing, "Medieval Style," 5; and Derek Pearsall, *Old English and Middle English Poetry*, 114. Walter French, *Essays*, 8 – 10 remarks on the poem's "musical presentation of material." *Cf.* Maldwyn Mills's discussion of the ballad-like nature of the romance *Athelston* (*Middle English Romance*, xxii).

[4] Lines 1 – 3. All future quotations, taken from Hall's edition of the poem, will be included in the text.

[5] For an up-to-date bibliography of "oral-formulaic" criticism, see John Miles Foley, *Oral-Formulaic Theory and Research*.

Cruces," 73; "Editing Medieval Texts," 101).[6]

King Horn can best be seen as a work which was at least partly composed in writing but which was built upon an oral foundation. Derek Brewer, in a number of recent essays but most notably in *Symbolic Stories*, Anne Wilson in *Traditional Romance*, and Walter Ong in *Orality and Literacy* have provided useful discussions of oral-traditional story styles and techniques. Traditional stories such as the *Odyssey* contain high levels of redundancy, familiar patterns, and "flat," two-dimensional characters who "fulfill . . . expectations copiously" (Ong, 70, 151). *King Horn* makes use of many such features of repetition, patterning, and two-dimensional characters, as well as other techniques found in traditional narratives. A number of these techniques, and their relationship to the poem's aesthetic and didactic aims, will be looked at in more detail now.

* * * * *

Susan Wittig concludes in *Stylistic and Narrative Structures* that the style of *King Horn* and other romances is marked by "redundant, formulized patterns of speech" (14, 19). Redundancy in traditional narratives occurs not merely at a lexical level but also at a semantic level (A. C. Spearing, *Age of Chaucer*, 12). We can find numerous phrases in *King Horn*, which, although worded slightly differently from one another, convey the same general meaning (see, for example, the poet's expressions for Horn's being "dubbed knight" in 438, 447 – 48, 458, 479 – 81, 487, and 499 – 500). Wittig also notes that the poem is marked by the repetition of larger structural units such as episodes — e.g., "revenge" or "threatened marriage and rescue" — and linked episodes — e.g., "separation — adoption — love" (141).

Repeated patterns, especially patterns of twos, predominate throughout *King Horn*. For example, Horn serves not one king but two; he is exiled

6   The oral-literate transmission of texts, in general, and the terminology appropriate for labelling "transitional" works have been discussed by early articles on medieval literature (Ruth Crosby, "Oral Delivery," 88 – 110; Michael Curschmann, "Oral Poetry," 36 – 52; Ronald Waldron, "Oral Formulaic Technique," 792 – 804; and Albert Baugh, "Authorship," 13 – 28, and "Presentation," 1 – 31, in recent journals (*New Literary History* [1977, 1984]), and in books devoted to exploring the issues in larger political, sociological, and anthropological contexts (Jack Goody, *Domestication of the Savage Mind*; and Eric Havelock, *Preface to Plato*). See also H. J. Chaytor, *From Script to Print*; M. T. Clanchy, *From Memory to Written Record*; Pearsall, "Revival," 44; and James R. Hurt, "The Texts of *King Horn*," 47 – 59. Cathy Preston's "The Ballad Tradition and the Making of Meaning" (diss. University of Colorado, 1986) provides a summary of Parry's and Lord's ideas (141 – 46), as well as a useful discussion of the critical assumptions implicit in labelling a work either "oral" or "written" (15 – 19).

twice; two similarly-named women, Rymenhild and Reynild (King Thur-ston's daughter), seek to marry Horn; Rymenhild suffers two ill-conceived marriages and must be rescued twice by Horn. These repeated patterns and double movements are common in folktales and other traditional stories. Patterns of threes, also occurring frequently in traditional stories, occasion-ally surface in *King Horn*, Rymenhild asking for marriage three times and Horn encountering pagans in three major battles. Trounce, in discussing *Horn Childe* and other tail-rhyme romances, mentions the fondness for pairs, "either opposites or complementaries," shown in these types of romances.[7] The prevalence of opposites in folk narrative has led Axel Olrik to posit the "law of contrast" which these narratives follow (see Brewer, "Nature of Romance," 35) and such a law can be seen operating, as well, in *King Horn*: pagans are pitted against Christians, evil kings usurped by good ones, and bad marriages replaced by noble ones. Exile is followed by return, estrangement by reconciliation, and discord by harmony.

These kinds of patterns make the plot of *King Horn* predictable, as do the ways in which Horn is characterized. As in other traditional stories, the hero of this romance is a "heavy" character, one whose deeds are "monumental, memorable and commonly public" (Ong, 70). "Briʒt so the glas . . . whit so the flur" (14 – 15), Horn's beauty clearly distinguishes him from all other characters in the poem. His actions are courageous, and he customarily kills not one pagan during an encounter but more often hundreds. His heroic stature defined by these monumental deeds, Horn's "personality" issues, as Brewer says of characters in traditional works, from the poem's events — essentially from *what* Horn does (not *why* he does it) — rather than the other way around, as is most common in our modern novels (*Symbolic Stories*, 4, 35).

Like many other romances and folk tales, *King Horn* is also about the maturation of its hero. Horn leaves home, subjects himself to physical trials and tribulations, and gradually proves himself worthy to be the suitor of Rymenhild and the king of his native land. Critics have long noticed this element of "growing up" in medieval French romances, which tend toward more stylistically sophisticated and psychologically astute character presentations than their English counterparts.[8] There is

---

[7] "Tail-Rhyme Romances," 1.99. See also 2.51, and 3.34,44 for his comments on *Horn Childe*.
[8] See, for example, Erich Auerbach, *Mimesis*, 134 – 39, and Robert Hanning, *Individual in Twelfth Century Romance*. Both Georges Duby ("Youth in Aristocratic Society," 112 – 22 and *Medieval Marriage*, ch. 1) and Stephen Knight (*Arthurian Literature*) have approached the issue from historical perspectives, and have identified the subversive aspects of French feudal and marital law underlying the younger son's need (and not "romantic" desire) to undertake quests in order to ally himself with a woman of money and reputation. Susan Crane's *Insular Romance* provides a long-awaited companion of several Anglo-Norman romances and their Middle English versions, and discusses the pattern of "exile and return" underlying the poem's concern with dispossession and inheritance rights. For her comments on *King Horn*, see her chapter entitled "Romances of Land and Lineage".

an element of "growing up" in Middle English romances, but their authors prefer action-packed scenes, free from the distractions of detailed portrayals. Horn does appear to mature as the narrative progresses, but aside from this *Bildungsroman*-like aspect of Horn's portrayal, the poet of *King Horn* indeed shows no interest in what we call "character development," "development" used here with our accompanying assumptions about the realistic psychological complexity often depicted in the protagonists of modern novels. Horn's thoughts are not shown to us, and his actions remain unburdened by any introspection or psychologizing. With no attempt to display its hero's inner life, *King Horn* resembles other traditional works whose portraits of their heroes, for good historical and aesthetic reasons, elaborate on numerable, memorable feats of prowess but not on the possible motives or thoughts underlying them. Horn's beauty, prowess, and trustworthiness are designed to fit his heroic stature so well that it is only natural that we can predict the successful course of his growth and accomplishments.

Horn's character is, so to speak, "given." Our interest instead is drawn to the romance's plot and to Horn's actions. Such works based on an oral tradition direct their attention not to the "visual appearance of objects or scenes or persons" (Ong, 127), but to action instead. Horn is described briefly for us and we are shown glimpses of physical locations now and then, but the bulk of the poem concerns itself with Horn's deeds, the promises or predictions foreshadowing them, and the statements recounting them. As in other traditional narratives, Horn's deeds often involve "agonistic" encounters. The poem contains numerous battle scenes and verbal challenges, Horn taunted by pagan enemies on one occasion or returning the boasts and blows on another. As we shall see in more detail later, the numerous configurations of word and deed — of absolute promise and fulfillment — reinforce the singular way in which both narration and dialogue revolve around the hero's actions and uphold in the process such traditional values as truth and loyalty: Horn's deeds must confirm his word; promises should not be broken, and so on.

This kind of work, like so much folktale and traditional narrative, may seem to a modern reader to be "absurdly implausible" and lacking any rational cause (*Symbolic Stories*, 64). Why, it may be asked, must there be so many battle scenes, sea journeys, or departures from home, or why must there be two treacherous marriages involving Rymenhild, the first after Horn has betrothed himself to her and the second after he has already married her? Wittig comments on the oddity of this last repeated event (144, 203 [note 2]). If we find the many battles, journeys, and mismarriages baffling, we might explore profitably beneath the poem's literal level to uncover its underlying pattern of meaning. Wilson, who views the issue of "growing up" through the eyes of the protagonist, finds that the numerous journeys made by Horn correspond to his successive, and ultimately successful, dealings with conflicting wishes and desires (61). In other words, although there is no attempt at individual psychological characterization, the structure of the plot and the action in it may be seen as a mode of the mind, representing conflicting emotions and final integration of the protagonist's character.[9] A reading such as Wilson's adequately explains, in general psychological terms, the significance of a story structure that revolves around the improbable quests of its hero. Such a structure can also be explained in light of what we know about traditional story patterns: the "repetition of leaving home, adventure, victory, and the return home to recognition," a sequence of events which Vladimir Propp calls a "move," is an integral part of countless folktales as well (Wilson, 59).

King Horn is typical in that, like many other romances, it makes use of such features of traditional stories as repeated patterns, familiar characterizations, and striking but non-realistic series of actions which often give rise to a meaningful symbolism. Other traditional story techniques, as well, exist in King Horn. A kind of local realism, for example, appears in the form of the poem's numerous descriptions of coasts and sea voyages (Brewer, "Nature of Romance," 44, and Trounce, 1.103). These, coupled with the poem's sprinkling of place-names, add colour to the poem's possible Irish and Cornish sea-side setting, one which would have been familiar, perhaps, to the audience (e.g., 39 – 42, 131 – 36, 148, etc.). A number of critics of medieval literature have recognized the satisfaction derived from reading or listening to traditional narratives like King Horn.[10] There is, they note, something both compelling and reassuring about stories that describe and reiterate the familiar, and that confirm expectations for happiness or success. Hans Robert Jauss, who discusses the "alterity" or "otherness" of medieval literature, also concedes that works like romances have an enduring appeal, and he lists several factors contributing to our aesthetic appreciation of these works, among them being that romances satisfy our need for a fantasy world and also reaffirm our sense of the familiar ("Alterity," 184 – 85). In just these ways King Horn is satisfying to read — for both a modern and a medieval audience: the pleasure and security derived from a stable, predictable world are not merely quirks of a traditional society but are

---

[9] Wilson (61) and others (Speirs, 187 – 88; John Stevens, *Themes and Approaches*, 43 – 44; and Spearing, "Medieval Style," 6) have also discussed the symbolic significance of the net, fish, and ring which appear during in Rymenhild's foreboding dream, and also during the first instance of Horn's homecoming. Timothy O'Brien, ("Word Play," 110 – 22) also proposes a personification allegory suggested by the poem's use of puns.

[10] See, for example, Brewer, *Symbolic Stories*, 20; Crosby, 102; Mills, xiv – xv; Wilson, 4; and Wittig, 44.

also comforts a modern sensibility can appreciate. It is the genuis of *King Horn* to focus these fundamental appeals in a spare, taut, beautiful style that is arguably superior to the elaborated literariness of the Anglo-Norman version of the story.

These aesthetic considerations form part of another, more complex reason for *King Horn*'s appeal. By portraying a "world of extremes" which is enhanced by hyperbole — "Athulf wes the beste / ant fykenyld the werste" (29 – 30)[11] — and by thematic opposition — Christian strength and rectitude vs. pagan weakness and inferiority — *King Horn* presents its readers with obvious notions of right and wrong, correct and incorrect ways of acting. *King Horn* is replete with characters who are clearly good or clearly bad but never both simultaneously, like those found in many a fairy tale (Bruno Bettelheim, *Uses of Enchantment*, 9). Presented in this black-and-white world where good is rewarded over evil, Horn's courageous and righteous deeds, repeated in an "almost incantatory way," stand in obvious opposition to those of his pagan enemies; his actions suggest the inevitable triumph of good and capture the optimism that is a hallmark of many other romances and traditional works.[12] This optimism and world of extremes may lend the poem its "escapist" quality; real life, we may think, is never so happy, nor our choices ever so clear-cut. To this extent, all literature is escapist which concerns itself with the telling of success stories. In *King Horn*, evil is recognized (there is no shortage of villain figures) and suffering is admitted (separations are painful, as Rymenhild's swooning reminds us). More importantly the poem testifies, as our own experiences of life testify, that success is possible through repeated efforts.

King Horn, like all literature, attempts to persuade us, to convince us, though not by any modern mimesis. It is a commonplace that there is a strong affinity between romances and saints' legends.[13] *King Horn* shares with these other, more overtly persuasive works the goal to illustrate pious, upright behaviour through the presentation of its hero's character. It also stresses the rewards of Christian vengeance. Unlike saints' legends, however, *King Horn* has no religious axe to grind. We cannot call it a didactic romance like *Amis and Amiloun* or others which "appear much concerned with their lesson," and which, like *Amis*, have a hagiographic

---

11   Spearing, "Medieval Style," 10. Spearing's article draws attention to many of the fine points of *King Horn*'s style. See below for his comments on the poet's use of synecdoche.

12   John Ganim, *Style and Consciousness*, 46. The *Tristram* stories are a notable exception. We are led to expect failure and disaster, which eventually occur.

13   See Dieter Mehl, *Middle English Romances* (4 – 5, 17, *passim*); Diana Childress, "Between Romance and Legend," 311 – 12; Margaret Hurley, "Saints' Legends and Romance," 60 – 73; and Piero Boitani, *Narrative*, 18 – 19.

tradition underlying them (J. Burke Severs, *Manual*, 167). Nor can we call it "didactic" in the sense invoked by *Le Petit Jehan de Saintre*, a prose romance detailing many of the "do's" and "dont's" of courtly behaviour appropriate (or inappropriate) for a young squire. It is clear that no dividing line can easily be drawn separating romances with "didactic intent" from those without. *King Horn*'s condensed, unimpeded quality, derived from the purposeful way in which it sticks to its main point — that is, telling the story of its hero's growth and success — gives us a lasting impression of a psychological and imaginative cohesiveness that rings true to the experience of our own lives (we all grow or wish to grow up, and, in this sense, experience "success"). This cohesiveness encourages an identification with the hero that is both admiring and sympathetic,[14] one which allows us to reaffirm the human quality of Horn's actions as well as our own. We are encouraged in other words to view the poem's events through a kind of "transparent window,"[15] which does not in the least obscure the edification inherent in the nature of the story. Frequently presented with characters who are unambiguously good or bad, actions that are noble or ignoble, we can then "glean" the "rules of behavior," as Margaret Hurley says, "which could not fail to produce changes for the better" ("Saints' Legends and Romance," 62). Whether any literature can actually make us good may be doubtful, and so simple an approval of didactic intent risks patronizing the poem, but the fact does remain that the poem is heartening and encourages traditional virtues, however distasteful those may be to the modern sensibility.

Like other traditional stories, *King Horn* relies upon a world of extremes, an essential optimism, and especially a larger-than-life portrayal of its hero to assist in the task of teaching its audience about certain values. As Eric Havelock has shown, it is through the typical, or conventional and idealized, characterization of heroes that an "effective paradigm of social laws and customs" can be "preserved" (168). Ong strikes a similar note when he says that a traditional society "generates outsize figures . . . not for romantic reasons or reflectively didactic reasons but for much more basic reasons: to organize experience in some sort of permanently memorable form" (70). The poem's aesthetic appeal is strengthened, not undermined, by this kind of idealized character. Together with the poem's patterns and redundancy, the conventional,

---

[14] Robert Holub (*Reception Theory*, 78 – 81) provides a useful discussion of the predominating reader-character-author relationships existing in major literary genres. "Admiring identification [cultivated in such works as medieval epics] . . . involves a perfect hero whose actions are exemplary for a community or a segment of the community." Hanning, in "The Audience as Co-Creator," 1 – 28 treats the same issue as it relates to medieval authors, works, and audiences.

[15] Spearing, "Medieval Style," 4.

heroic aspects of Horn's portrayal contribute to our enjoyment of the poem's predictable qualities, for they delineate a mythological, larger-than-life hero whose idealized, repeated actions make him easily identifiable and provoke a timeless and enduring admiration.

Critics like Umberto Eco and Wittig claim that a work like *King Horn* conveys a "pedagogic message" which is "substantially immobilistic," and that its conventional and redundant language "cannot be a vehicle for new discoveries either about itself or about the nature of the world that it defines and describes" (Eco, 122; Wittig, 45). We should be wary of the condemnation implied in such statements, however, for they tend to assume that nothing reiterated or re-discovered is of any worth; that an imaginative re-working of that which was already known (but may not be known or felt now) is therefore valueless; that only change, variation, and innovation can be treasured. Critics often find romances intractable and frustrating because of their "highly codified" nature, as John Burrow has explained ("Alterity of Medieval Literature," 387). Wittig's descriptive analysis, pre-empted, in many ways, by her assumptions about the repetitive and therefore static nature of romances, often fails to comment significantly on variation when it does occur in the romances and tends to diminish any appreciation that could be cultivated for the artistic quality of their repetitive style. Such poems, she suggests, were created "rapidly according to patterns" and "slots," their "structurally homologous variants" merely a product of "conditioned reflexes" (37–41, 179–81).[16] Individual works, of course, may well be inferior in their execution, but one should not confuse that inferiority with the redundancy and "primitive" quality which are not in themselves inferior but are produced from the same world-view and orally-based techniques which are at the heart of such unquestionable verbal masterpieces as the Homeric epics and the Bible. The world is always open to re-discovery and the reaffirmation of beliefs, and *King Horn*'s celebration of this fact stands as a credit to the ways in which it has employed numerous traditional story techniques.

Thus far I have emphasized those fundamental characteristics of *King Horn* which can be related to its oral base (but not necessarily oral origin). The poem's excellence can also be seen in certain features stemming from a manuscript literacy which establish the poem's intriguing individualism of language and style. The unique position which the poem occupies between orality and literacy stands out most noticeably in the poem's treatment of dialogue and narration — of speech and action, word and deed. On the one hand, the poem's numerous fulfilments of promises and predictions chart an expected path for Horn's success against his pagan

---

[16] See, for example, her discussion of the "exile" scene in *Octavian*, 125.

46

foes, his many deeds aligned and executed in accordance with such cherished virtues as loyalty and honesty. Seen from the point of view of these paired words and deeds, the poem's overall cast is basically conservative, as it aims to preserve and protect received values, and to please through reaffirmation of the familiar and expected.

There is, however, a complexity and specificity in *King Horn*'s patterns, repetitions, and idealized portrayal of its hero which suggest the poet's awareness of their creative potential and which, in some ways, carries the romance beyond the boundaries of "traditional" works as we have defined them here. Much of the poet's precision of style and narration can be located, in particular, in his handling of word and deed. The poet controls the tale's suspense, reinforcing predicted outcomes on one occasion with an obvious display of paired words and deeds, but disrupting expectations on another with delayed promises and conditional statements. Although the romance depends ultimately upon underlying patterns rather than realistic cause and effect, the romance nevertheless displays a forceful causality which derives its strength from the careful manner in which the numerous promises or predictions are shown to be fulfilled through the course of the narrative. The romance, in addition, questions and defines the relationship between Horn's statements and fulfilments in a way that broadens, and individualizes, the presentation of Horn's heroic character. Exploring the binding power of promises, intentions, and desires, *King Horn* stresses the importance of self-made conditions, behaviour based on one's own experience rather than the imitation of paradigms, purposeful but not necessarily predestined actions, and the individualizing aspects of the promise itself.[17] As a poem transitional between oral and literate art forms, *King Horn* both reaffirms and challenges traditional narrative techniques, and the "immobilistic messages" implied through their use. The remainder of this essay will be devoted to examining configurations of word and deed in *King Horn* — first, as they reaffirm the poem's traditional values, and second, as they play an essential part in the poem's creation of a more self-conscious aesthetic and world view.

．　．　．　．　．

Nearly half of *King Horn* is devoted to characters' speeches, and in them numerous statements can be found which express plans for Horn's exploits: the promises made to accomplish them, commands enlisting

---

[17] See Hannah Arendt's philosophical discussion of promises and "self-made conditions" in *The Human Condition*, 9, 236, 244, and 245.

help for their completion, and predictions made to assure us of their success. That portion of the tale which is not taken up with these kinds of "future-oriented" statements is devoted to showing the ways in which the statements are fulfilled. Virtually every speech anticipates some future action, or, conversely, nearly every action completes or fulfills a prediction or promise. The long Anglo-Norman version of the poem contains numerous speeches as well and also makes one of Horn's oaths and its legal implications the subject of an extended scene (1937 – 2048) between Horn and King Hunlaf (i.e., Aylmar; see below).[18] The Anglo-Norman version, however, accords equal status to lengthy and detailed narratives about feasts, pageantry, and battles. *King Horn* is devoid of these elaborations. The Middle English poet systematically pairs word and deed, and, focussing in particular on specific statements and their fulfilments, builds a narrative structure that is economical, patterned, and predictable.

Paired words and deeds in *King Horn* play a natural role in the poet's handling of suspense and fulfilment. Showing a penchant for symmetry, the poet assures us that all that is wished or asked for, intended, or commanded will be resolved at some later point in the narrative. This symmetry, like the poem's frequent folktale-like doubling, fulfills expectations by creating, and resolving, suspense through a predictable pairing of events. Through the characters' predictions and promises, the poet gives his readers "continual occasions for forecasting" (Eco, 32, 34) but he does not require that we labour in our efforts to guess at the outcome of future events. Predictions are fulfilled: Horn's father is slain (61), Horn is knighted quickly (490), and pagans feel the strength of Horn's hand (607 – 08, etc.). Commands are executed: Horn plights his troth to Rymenhild (672) as she requests, and he serves King Thurston (780, etc.) after having been apprised earlier of his duties to him; as he is bidden, King Thurston pays Horn his wages (990 – 1000), and the Palmer tells Horn about Rymenhild's treacherous wedding (1029 – 50). And promises come true: Horn plights his troth to Rymenhild and marries her (672, 1253 – 54), proves his knighthood (607 – 20, etc.), and avenges his father's death (857 – 88, 1375 – 78).

---

[18]   The Anglo-Norman version was composed somewhat earlier than *King Horn* but was not a source for the English romance. For a comparison of the Anglo-Norman version and *King Horn*, see Mildred K. Pope, *The Romance of Horn* (ANTS vols. 12 – 13) 19 – 21 and "The Romance of Horn," 164 – 67; McKnight, viii – xvi; C. B. West, *Courtoisie in Anglo-Norman Literature*, 47; Dominica Legge, *Anglo-Norman Literature*, 98, 103 – 04, and "Rise and Fall," 5; and Pearsall, "Development," 24 – 5 above. Quotations are taken from vols. 9 and 10 of Pope's ANTS edition. All translations are my own.

Every utterance in *King Horn* seems to become the "cause" for some "effect," becomes the motivation and justification for some future narrative situation. The story as a whole thus acquires a kind of "energetic directness" (Hall, lvi) and a strong, forward-looking temporality that is infused in the poem's often non-realistic setting, what Piero Boitani might call its world "beyond space and time" (*Narrative*, 50). The narrative gathers a great deal of momentum when certain promises or plans are fulfilled immediately. Pagans, for example, assure Horn both with boastful words and with a quick execution of the deed itself that they will slay "alle that Crist luueth vpon" (43 – 46, 53 – 58). Rymenhild's prediction that Horn will be knighted within the week (447 – 48) moves quickly to its fulfilment, the prediction and the many events leading to its conclusion occupying scarcely fifty lines: Rymenhild tells Horn to bring tokens to Athelbrus (451 – 58); Horn does so, and relates "his nede" to Athelbrus (465 – 470), who promptly persuades King Aylmar of Horn's worthiness (473 – 82); the King replies that the knighting will occur "Bifore me this niȝte" (484 – 92), and then completes the task shortly thereafter (499). The poet, choosing not to gloss over the whole process leading to Horn's knighthood, but detailing instead each character's prompt compliance, purposively moves a sequence of events to an expected conclusion. The narrative gallops from suspense to fulfilment, as well, when Horn explains the foreboding significance of the fish in Rymenhild's dream (665 – 714), promises to slay the enemies of King Thurston single-handedly (833 – 883), and plans with Athulf to return to Westerness, saving Rymenhild from her marriage to Fickenhild (1419 – 92).

Numerous events in *King Horn* follow promises, predictions, or commands quickly in succession in a kind of "narrative confirmation": intentions expressed in dialogue are fulfilled in later events, and there is a "marked similarity between the vocabularies of narrator and character or of different characters in a relatively short passage," something which can be observed in other traditonal works such as Malory's *Morte Darthur*.[19] This process of confirmation, as Mark Lambert notes, works against the "individuality of the speaking voice" (13), and instead reaffirms traditional virtues or moral truths. Horn's honest deeds are repeatedly shown to confirm his honest words, his honest words and deeds project

---

[19] Mark Lambert, *Style in* Le Morte Darthur, 8. See also Mary Hynes-Berry, "Cohesion," 653 for a similar view.

honest intentions and desires.

The predictions and fulfilments concerning Horn's vengeance against the pagans emphasize most forcefully, perhaps, this exemplary quality of Horn's character. Horn's duty to avenge his father's death is fore-shadowed three times near the tale's beginning. The Emir, young Horn's adversary, states first that Horn must die, for if he lives, he "scholde slen vs alle. . . . With swerd other with kniue, / We scholden alle deie / And his fader deth abeie" (100 – 112). Sent across the ocean, Horn arrives safely in Westerness, and then sends word himself to the pagans that he is "hol & fer" and that they "schal fonde / The dent of [his] honde" (149 – 52). King Aylmar forecasts Horn's success a third time: "Horn thu lude sune / Bi dales and bi dune" (209 – 10); the pagans will feel the "strengthe of [his] honde" in "Eurech londe" (215 – 16). These predictions are fulfilled copiously. Horn beheads one group of Saracens with many a "dunte" (607, 609), and slaughters one hundred more shortly thereafter (613 – 20). After he identifies and slays his father's murderer during his stay with King Thurston (857 – 88), he then returns to Suddene, begins "his horn to blowe" so that "folk hit gan iknowe" (1371 – 72), and finally destroys the pagans who have ruled his country (1379 – 80). These numerous acts of prowess, coupled with Horn's renewal of his promise to King Aylmar and to his mother Godhild much later in the story (1283 – 84, 1369 – 70), confirm the poem's earlier predictions, reminding us of Horn's Christian righteousness. The frequent repetition of specific words in both dialogue and narrative — e.g., "dent" (or "dunte") and "horn" (his name and the musical instrument by which others know him) — make obvious the connection between the predictions and their fulfilments and point to the inevitability of Horn's success.

These predictions or prophetic statements and their fulfilments create what Robert Hanning might call a "Christian providential scheme," one which reinforces the romance's "hopeful, positive" dimension (*Twelfth-Century Romance*, 143). They also strongly imply that aspect of Horn's character which is public, community-oriented, and in a way inflexible. As the poet indicates, Horn's prophetic duty is common knowledge; persons both acquainted and unacquainted with Horn's past associate him with a task that is clearly meant to be performed for the salvation of his country and people. Addressing only Horn, the Emir and King Aylmar accurately predict Horn's success against the pagans, and assign the prophetic task to him alone. The poem's sharp focus upon Horn's personal election for the salvation of his people stands out in contrast to the vagueness with which Horn's objective is treated in the Anglo-Norman version. Unlike the Emir and King Aylmar, the pagan Rodmund discusses the possibility of Horn's vengeance in the third-person voice, directs his conversation not to Horn but to his fellow pagans, and makes the task a collaborative effort between Horn and his companions.[20] In the Middle English poem, Horn's prophetic task is dictated to but not chosen by him and is designed to make him appear as much a young saviour as an heroic knight. Horn, who is cast in an unyielding role through these paired predictions and fulfilments, reminds us of the traditional heroes we find in epics. Because his prophetic task is unchangeable, Horn is not "obliged to make meaningful choices between a variety of responses to [an] objective situation." In later, more literary medieval French romances, the opposite case — that is, many choices involving a subjective situation — appears much more frequently, as R. Howard Bloch has noted (*Literature and Law*, 232).

Tightly paired configurations of word and deed contribute greatly to *King Horn*'s traditional quality and its conservative message. Through repeated absolute promises or forecasts and their fulfilments, the poem upholds Christian rectitude and self-righteousness, the traditional virtue of loyalty, and the spectrum of activities or behaviour in which loyalty is found to be an important factor (see Brewer, "Archaic Mind," 109). Feudal relationships are honoured, Horn validating his promises to both kings with immediate, successful displays of martial valour. Other social hierarchies are preserved as well: Athelbrus and Athulf demonstrate their loyalty to King Aylmar's daughter or to Horn himself by helping to fulfill the predictions that have been uttered, or by complying quickly with the orders they have been given. The poem also highlights the importance of Horn's loyalty to received codes governing chivalric behaviour. Both seen and heard by others, Horn's words are subject to the public's scrutiny, provoking their judgment and reflecting the degree to which he has conformed to the knightly behaviour expected of him. "Kniȝt," says Rymenhild,

> nu is thi time
> For to sitte bi me:
> Do nu that thu er of spake,
> To thi wif thu me take.
> Ef thu art trewe of dedes,

[20] See Bloomfield, *Episodii Motivation*, 108: a "prophetic task," says Bloomfield, "is not chosen; it is forced on one." *Cf.* ll. 43 – 48 in the Anglo-Norman version. The pagan invader Rodmund knows that Horn will slay him if he lives, and he relates his anxieties to his pagan companions ("Ne-s pus fere perir ke jo-s seie esgardanz. / Si sai bien, s'il vivent, ke jo m'en ere pleignanz, / Kar j'ai ocis trestuz lur meillur partenanz, / E cil les vengerunt s'il remaignent vivanz" [44 – 46]; that is, if Horn *and* his companions live — "s'il vivent" — they will avenge their parents' death).

Do nu ase thu sedes. (533 – 38)

As Rymenhild's speech suggests, Horn's promises are spoken publicly, traditionally, for the preservation of public, community beliefs, each situation in which they have been spoken becoming a "general paradigm . . . of the loyalty which it both affirms and on which it depends" (Havelock, 75).

The importance, power, and also beauty of what is customary and beneficial for the community is suggested in this romance, as it is in other traditional works, despite — or in contrast to — the romance's primary focus on the speeches and actions of its sole protagonist. The poet sharpens this contrast, not by circumscribing Horn's heroic behaviour with expected pairings of absolute promise and fulfilment, but by structuring Horn's maturation around more subtly-phrased configurations of word and deed. Horn's promises and fulfilments, in particular his conditional promises, designate increasingly personal (not public) responses to specific situations. As such, they become the vehicles through which the poet elaborates upon his hero's intentions, and by which he both breaks and redefines patterns of expectation. The poem's conditional statements create a narrative complexity and sense of arbitrariness beneath the poem's predictable or transparent surface. These qualities, which add appreciably to the poem's suspense, enhance the poet's presentation of Horn's growth and experience, and invite our closer inspection of the poem's language and style.

• • • • •

As we have seen, absolute promises and fulfilments, unfailing predictions, commands quickly dispatched, and plans brought to fruition predominate throughout *King Horn*. These configurations of word and deed have the effect of hastening our reading experience by continually drawing our attention to the "fulfilling" events themselves (e.g., Horn's knighthood, defeat of the pagan giant, or triumph over Fikenhild). They also hasten the poem's resolution of suspense — in a sense *bond* resolution *to* suspense — by leaving no space, as it were, between promise or prediction and fulfilment in which the narrative might develop or expand.

These familiar, tightly-meshed words and deeds throughout *King Horn* form a kind of backdrop for the poem's more complex word-deed configurations. Taking the form of statements with delayed fulfilments, or statements dependent for their completion upon an executed condition or prerequisite — i.e., conditional statements — these configurations of word and deed complicate the poem's simple pairings of absolute promise and fulfilment, disrupting, in the process, its familiar patterns of suspense. *If* Horn lives (the pagans predict), they "scholden alle deie"

52

and Horn will "abeie" his "fader deth" (100 – 110). Horn does survive
his ocean journey, bidding his ship to tell the pagans that he is "hol & fer /
On this lond ariued her" (149 – 50). Horn, however, does not kill any
pagans until much later (607 – 20), nor does he avenge his father's death
until he resides in King Thurston's kingdom (857 – 88) and after he has
returned to, and departed from, Westerness for the second time
(1375 – 78). The "antecedent" portion of the pagans' prophecy — its
condition or prerequisite — is, in other words, fulfilled quite soon after it
has been uttered (leading us to believe that the whole prophecy will
quickly come true); but the actual completion of the prophecy's
"consequent" portion — the final fulfilment of the prophecy, Horn's
vengeful activity — is delayed until much later in the story. To take
another example: Rymenhild's request that Horn plight his troth and
marry her is repeated three times (once to the "false" Horn, Athelbrus),
each approximately one-hundred lines apart (303 – 08, 407 – 10,
531 – 40), but is only then fulfilled one-hundred and fifty lines after her
last request (672). Rymenhild's command is not actually dispatched until
three-hundred and fifty lines after it has first been issued. The numerous,
quickly-paired, and unelaborated configurations of word and deed
throughout the poem are interspersed throughout delayed promises,
commands, and predictions such as these. As a result, our forecasting
progresses somewhat lurchingly or unevenly, despite the plot's essential
linearity (see Ganim, 39). The outcome of the romance is ultimately
predictable, but our expectations are resolved intermittently, overlapping
with new expectations and provoking our curiosity about not how,
necessarily, but *when*, the next events will occur.

The temporal dimension created by these kinds of conditional
statements — a sense of relative time, of certain events taking place before
or after others — serves as an important function in the poet's
manipulation of suspense. The poet draws our attention not only to those
events which must *fulfill* an absolute promise or prediction but to those
upon which others are *dependent* and which must take place before the
story can progress. The poet holds our attention by asking that we keep in
mind both past, completed events as well as events-to-be. Our formulations or reformulations about the outcome of the romance thus alter
through a kind of imaginative parallax, as we envisage and continually
resolve both completed and uncompleted events into a single image
encompassing our current expectations for the poem's outcome. Delayed
or conditional promises and predictions give the poet of *King Horn* a
certain flexibility in maintaining the poem's suspense that he would not
have by relying entirely on expected and familiar pairs, say, of absolute
promise and fulfilment.

The sheer number of conditional statements in the poem indicates their importance as a structuring device in the story and suggests a more detailed examination of their significance. Seen in relation to one another and in the context of Horn's development, Horn's conditional statements raise issues concerning the complex relationships between a hero's public and private behaviour, between collective and individual actions, and between traditional and modern values. Carefully articulated, Horn's conditional statements determine the various times at which he will perform certain deeds (and in what order), and they suggest the relative importance or value which Horn assigns to the particular activities mentioned in them. Often inherently ambiguous, many of Horn's promises and conditional statements invite us to examine the texture of the poem's language, and to evaluate the poem's use of traditional styles and techniques.

Horn makes at least six conditional statements during the course of the romance. Generally speaking, each of them states the following, that Horn must prove himself before marrying Rymenhild. Horn answers Rymenhild's plea — ''Thu schalt haue me to thi wif'' (408) — not with marriage but with a request that she first help him to attain knighthood:

> Help me to kniзte
> Bi al thine miзte,
> To my lord the king,
> That he me зiue dubbing.
> *Thanne* is mi thralhod
> Iwent in to kniзthod,
> And ischal wexe more,
> And do, lemman, thi lore. (435 – 42; emphasis added)

Rymenhild, Athelbrus, and King Aylmar scurry to meet Horn's demand (the passage makes frequent use of the words ''sone,'' ''swithe,'' and ''bliue''), leading us to believe that Horn will comply promptly with Rymenhild's wishes. When Horn receives his ''dubbing'' and Rymenhild asks him again for marriage, commanding that he ''Do nu ase [he] sedes,'' he substitutes, in place of his actual compliance, his word that he will comply. He then follows with three more conditional statements that spell out in no uncertain terms the order in which he will perform certain actions — deferring, with more stipulations, the specific response she requires:

> 'Rymenhild,' quath he, 'beo stille;
> Ihc wulle don al thi wille.
> Also hit mot bitide,
> Mid spere ischal furst ride,
> & mi kniзthod proue,
> *Ar* ihc the ginne to woзe.

> We beth kniȝtes ȝonge,
> Of odai al isprunge,
> & of vre mestere
> So is the manere
> With sume othere kniȝte
> Wel for his lemman fiȝte,
> *Or* he eni wif take:
> *If* ihc come to lyue
> Ihc schal the take to wyue.' (541 – 60; emphasis added)

Before Horn woos and marries Rymenhild, that is, he must first "ride" to prove his valour, must joust with "sume othere kniȝte" on behalf of his "lemman," and must survive his ordeals. Lastly, when he has returned to Westerness, Horn clears himself twice of Fickenhild's charges that he has lain with Rymenhild (695 – 98). Horn first states, "Ne schal ihc hit biginne, / *Til* i suddene winne," and then concludes (with this sixth conditional statement):

> That lond ischal ofreche
> & do mi fader wreche.
> Ischal beo king of tune
> & bere kinges crune,
> *Thanne* schal Rymenhilde
> Ligge bi the kinge. (1277 – 78, 1283 – 88; emphasis added)

Horn's conditional statements, generally speaking, are spoken in a public context. Horn expresses his desire to establish his reputation through his bold, ostentatious displays of valour. He will perform his deeds both for public recognition and for the public's "consumption," fuelling their expectations of his success. His occasional remarks to both kings also stress the importance of his rapport with public figures and his duty to recognize their established positions of honour. Horn is careful to recount his martial success to King Aylmar twice (629 – 44, 1263 – 68); he invites King Thurston to witness his triumph over the pagan giants 845 – 48), and pays homage to him by stating that he will serve him. Not questioning or testing the inalterable relationship between king and subject, the poem protects certain feudal and political hierarchies. In contrast to the Anglo-Norman version of the poem, however, feudal and political relations and the reinforcement of knightly codes play a relatively minor role in *King Horn*. A brief look at the Anglo-Norman version will illustrate this point.

Numerous passages in the Anglo-Norman version continually point out Horn's desire to remain loyal to King Hunlaf. Refusing Rigmel's ring on the basis that he would risk the King's displeasure otherwise ("Vostre perre m'ad fair nurrir par sun comant. . . . Ja ne li mesferai, taunt cum serai parlant" [1114 – 16]),[21] Horn states conditions for wooing Rigmel that cater explicitly to King Hunlaf's wishes and to the mores of his court:[22]

> Mes quant sun pleisir iert ke seië adubez
> E joe iere en sa curt d[ë] armes bien preisiez
> Pur quantquë aië fait dedevant ses barnez,
> Si idonc m'aïdast k'oüsse mes regnez
> E vus donc par sun los autresi m'amissez,
> Dunc ne di joe ke tost ne fusse cunseillez
> De vus prendre les duns, d'afermer coe qu'offrez.
> Mes pur neent autrement, danzele, en parlerez,
> Kar, si pus, ja li reis vers mei n'iert corociez. (1172 – 80)

Horn's words are directed to Rigmel, and yet it is clear that his promises to her are paying homage to the King, and are "performed publicly to collectivise the relationship" (Knight, *Arthurian Literature*, 95), smacking "more of the authorial voice than of naturalistic characterization," as Burnley remarks ("Heroic Ethos," 385).

Horn's promises and deeds in the Anglo-Norman version are motivated by his adherence to such feudal relationships and to other traditional codes of behaviour, specifically to the kind of heroism exemplified by physical, agonistic displays. This can be seen in the conflict arising between Horn and King Hunlaf concerning the method by which Horn should disprove Wyckele's (Fikenhild's) slanderous statements (1920 – 79): he must support an oath either "par serrement," that is, by compurgation, or "par bataille" (Dannenbaum, "Anglo-Norman Romances," 604). For Horn, swearing an "oath rather than proving his innocence by battle would mean disparagement and betrayal of those [heroic] ideals" (Burnley, "Heroic Ethos," 389), and thus Horn chooses to display his martial valour instead. In later medieval French romances these oaths of compurgation displace the other, more customarily violent methods by which a hero proves his innocence. This shift from the

---

21 "Your father brought me up and I will never do him injury, as long as I can speak."
22 "But when it will be the King's pleasure to knight me, and when I will be well-praised in his court for my exploits, if it then helps me to have my kingdoms and through their renown you would love me, then I do not say that I would not be speedily minded to accept the gifts from you and to confirm what you offer. But you will not speak of this matter to any other purpose, for never will the King be angered against me, if I have any say in the matter."

physical to the verbal "battlefield" corresponds to the movement in the judicial domain from trials by combat to trials by inquisition, and to the movement from oral to written discourse.[23] By having Horn's conflict resolved with a physical proof of innocence, not with a passive, more verbal or literary showing, the Anglo-Norman poet substantiates Horn's behaviour within an older — an oral or a traditional — framework that supports such physical displays or agonistic encounters.

To return now to our English romance: Horn indeed demonstrates his knowledge of knightly, heroic, and feudal codes by performing physical acts of prowess, and by showing his allegiance to both kings. His conditional promises for marrying Rymenhild, however, unlike the analogous promises in the Anglo-Norman version, contain nothing specifically pertaining to his duties to the kings. Their primary focus appears to be not feudal or familial loyalty (the kings being his "surrogate" fathers) but rather his loyalty to the very conditions themselves — that is, performing certain deeds before performing others in the way he has specified. As Horn honours his self-made stipulations, he acts in a way that stresses the importance of his own decisions. Seen from this perspective, Horn's conditional promises create a personal, not public context, designed to bring to the foreground (and to fruition) the wishes and desires implicit in them. Unlike the Anglo-Norman poet in his treatment of Horn's proof "par bataille," the poet of *King Horn* does not explicitly draw our attention to a certain choice existing between what we are calling orally-based or traditional story techniques and more literary ones. And yet Horn's promises, his conditional statements in particular, register a certain shift from traditional values concerned with received codes and social structures, to individualized values, words, and deeds tailored to meet personal, not public, needs.

The conditional nature of many of Horn's promises aids the poet in his task to reveal the individuality of his hero, and points to the general psychological truths suggested through their repetition. There is something natural in a young person's need to leave home, to test himself, and to prove himself trustworthy *before* accepting, and settling down to, more mature responsibilities which involve others besides himself. Desire must be fulfilled before obligation. "Nu thu hast wille thine," Rymenhild says to Horn (539); now he has been knighted, and now he must be "trewe of dedes" and must "vn bind" her from her "pine" (537, 540).

The conditionality of Horn's promises also makes explicit a hierarchy of values which corresponds to his actions as he fulfills his promises. Horn reinforces the priority of his martial, over his marital, behaviour when he carefully fulfills his stipulations in a specified order. Horn's deeds of

---

[23]   Bloch, 206 – 07. See also pp. 16, 28, 125, 127, 139, 161, *passim.*

valour, which take place before his marriage with Rymenhild, earn a "special prestige" as they appear to "generate" or control subsequent events: betrothal or marriage cannot occur until certain conditions are first met.[24] Horn's valorous deeds, however, are represented as a *means* to his marriage to Rymenhild but not the end result of his entire actions. Having a marked temporal priority, his deeds nevertheless remain subordinate activities performed for the purpose of attaining his subsequent (and, in terms of his gradual maturity, more important) goal of marriage. Each step, in fact, leading to Horn's union with Rymenhild — his betrothal to her, his marriage, and his final act to make her his queen — becomes the culminating event which caps a particular performance involving Horn's prowess or valour. Postponed, but therefore highlighted, Horn's actions involving Rymenhild take on a prestige which, throughout course of his maturation, surpasses the importance of those valorous deeds which he has performed earlier

Like heroes in traditional works, Horn exemplifies traditional, community values such as honesty and loyalty by honouring his promises, by "do[ing] nu ase [he] sedes." As we have seen, however, the activities which Horn performs for the benefit of the public, his righteous battles against the pagans, for example, are placed in the service of his more personal wants and desires, and are directed toward his union with Rymenhild — the motivation of which seems distinctly personal, not public. Through his conditional promises, Horn both exemplifies and transcends community values. Although Horn's promises comprise a general paradigm of loyalty to certain received codes or feudal relationships, as Havelock might have it, they nevertheless express Horn's loyalty to his own ideal conception of himself (see Stevens, *Medieval Romance*, 75); they also define a personal framework of time within which his completion of certain prerequisite activities gradually leads to his fulfilment of a more private, more intimate goal.

Horn attains his heroic status paradoxically, it appears, by weakening the firm bond between absolute promise and fulfilment. By formulating conditional promises, repeatedly fulfilling their stipulated prerequisites (i.e., proving his valour), but postponing the fulfilment of their expected results (i.e., betrothal and marriage) Horn is able to accumulate a number of successes on the battlefield prior to each "romantic" move he makes. Horn effectively prolongs marital events by proliferating martial ones, by taking full advantage of the conditional statements he has proposed.

[24]   Patricia Dreschel Tobin, in *Time and the Novel: The Genealogical Imperative*, suggests an analogy of function between events in time and generations of families, where "events in time come to be perceived as begetting other events within a line of causality similar to the line of generations"; prior events earn a "special prestige" since they can be seen to "originate, control, and predict future events" (7).

The "elliptical character" of causal statements in general, as J. L. Mackie notes, invites our examination of such statements ("Causes and Conditions," 24 – 25). Confronted with statements that are " 'gappy' or indeterminate," we are encouraged to "confirm their causal relationships," to determine whether each portion of the conditions is fulfilled, in the order specified. Horn's conditional statements invite, and in many ways bear up under, this kind of close inspection. As noted above, Horn says (541 – 60) that he will: (1) prove his knighthood before beginning to woo Rymenhild ("Mid spere ischal furst ride, / & mi kniȝthod proue, / Ar ihc the ginne to woȝe"; (2) fight on her behalf before marrying her ("so is the manere / With sume othere kniȝte / wel for his lemman fiȝte, / Or he eni wif take"); and finally (3) marry her if he survives his exploits ("If ihc come te lyue / Ihc schal the take to wyue"). Horn first proves his knighthood by "smatting" the Saracens (607 – 08), then performs more exploits explicitly on behalf of "his lemman": "He lokede on the ringe, / & thoȝte on rimenhild. / He sloȝ ther on haste / On hundred bi the laste" (613 – 16), and finally survives his exploits to tell about them (629 – 44), plighting his troth to Rymenhild afterwards (672). Horn's actions prior to his vow to Rymenhild occur in the chronological order which he has specified in his conditional statements. After having performed the prerequisite acts of valour, Horn signals with his vow that he has begun to woo Rymenhild — indeed, has formally expressed his intention to marry her — and in this manner honours the conditional statements which he has made earlier to her.

Horn's actions generally bear out the order of events implied in his conditional statements. But when we try to pair every one of Horn's stipulations in his conditional statements with a specific event, we discover that there is often not a unique event that corresponds to each stipulation. Every marital gesture of Horn's is preceded by a number of valorous exploits: Horn wins *and* proves his knighthood before plighting his troth to Rymenhild; he kills numerous Saracens (including his father's slayer), *and* disrupts a treacherous marriage before celebrating his wedding with Rymenhild; then he slays more foes, wins back his country of Suddene, *and* foils a second treacherous marriage before making Rymenhild his queen. Horn fulfills, in excess, the prerequisites for his involvement with Rymenhild by performing feats of valour at every opportunity. There is not a precise one-to-one mapping between Horn's stipulations in his conditional statements and the events satisfying them. As we can see from the analysis above, however, the poet of *King Horn* attempts to play out a complicated sequence of stipulations to its logical conclusion. Being explicit both in his wording and in his ordering of Horn's conditional statements and deeds, the poet ties up any loose ends that might have been created had Horn not honoured his word. More importantly, the poet attempts to detail, and to distinguish from one another, the incremental steps proposed by Horn which lead him to marry Rymenhild.

An elliptical, indeterminate quality nevertheless persists in Horn's statements. The contractual nature of Horn's conditional statements is such that Horn need not honour them at all if their antecedent portions are not, for some reason, fulfilled. If, for example, Rymenhild does not "help [Horn] to kniȝte," then Horn is not bound by any agreement to marry her or even to plight his troth to her. Horn avails himself of just this option for marital postponement when he negates, in effect, the conditional statement which he has made to King Thurston concerning the marriage of his daughter, Reynild. "*Whanne* i thi doȝter ȝerne / Ne schaltu me hire werne [i.e., refuse]" (915 – 16). Clearly never yearning for her, Horn does not oblige himself to marry her, and therefore neither puts himself in a compromising situation by swearing oaths to two lovers, nor compromises his loyalty or honesty. The manner in which Horn handles his promise to King Thurston reminds us of a similar situation in Chrétien's *Yvain*, in which the hero's promise "to return [to the lord's castle at Pesme Aventure] 'if possible' " retains "the obscuring value of courtesy" but is "the height of white-lie politeness" (Knight, 92). We need not attach any pejorative interpretation to Horn's unfulfilled promise. It is instructive to notice, however, that Horn does indeed "bow out" of his agreement with King Thurston in the kind of clever way we often deem appropriate for the more psychologically complex heroes in medieval French romances.

The syntax and wording of Horn's promises contribute to their indeterminate nature, and to our impression of Horn's cleverness. Horn's request for knighthood allows him to remain uncommitted to any specific course of action involving Rymenhild. "Help me to kniȝte / Bi al thine miȝte," Horn asks; "*Thanne* is mi thralhod / Iwent in to kniȝthod, / And ischal wexe more / And do, lemman, thi *lore*" (435 – 42). The order of the statements obliges Horn to do Rymenhild's "lore" after he has attained knighthood. The activity, however, which is shown depending, and following most closely, upon his knighthood is not his duty to Rymenhild but rather his "thralhod" turning into "kniȝthod," clearly signalled by the temporal marker "thanne." Horn will do Rymenhild's "lore" after he attains his knighthood, but he will both leave his thraldom *and* prosper before he does so. A direct contingency between Horn's knighthood and his execution of Rymenhild's command has been twice removed. This syntactical postponement of Horn's marital activity mirrors the deferral which takes place at the narrative level. We can also propose that Horn's duty to Rymenhild has been vaguely worded in this promise. By substituting, in place of what is stated in Rymenhild's actual "lore" or bidding, a name for the activity itself, Horn moves further away from promising something concrete. The ambiguity of the word "lore" highlights the openendedness of Horn's promise, and remains consistent with the presentation of Horn as uncommitted to, or hesitant to begin, his marital endeavours. Because Horn's wishes are "bound" in some "definite, controllable form, such as a special word" or syntactical pattern, they are invested with a kind of power that enables him to proceed, somewhat leisurely, through a course of events which he controls himself (see Wilson, 55).

Any sense of certainty implied by Horn's promises is undermined, to a degree, through the poet's use of "wulle," which we notice especially in the Cambridge MS: Horn "wulle don all [Rymenhild's] wille" and he "wulle do pruesse" (542, 556). Used as an auxiliary, the verb "wulle" suggests a clear temporal reference to the future: Horn will, at some point in the future, accomplish certain tasks. In these contexts, however, the verb shows a degree of modality as well, conveying Horn's "volition, desire, or intention."[25] This volitional or intentional sense of the verb is drawn out especially in the first instance, where the verb has been paired with the related substantive, "wille" ("Ich wulle don all thi wille"). By contrast, the Oxford MS casts the first of these promises with "schal," and both the London and Oxford MSS write "sal" and "shal" (respectively) in the second promise, choices which reflect the tendency for this verb to be employed, in oaths especially, as modal auxiliary conveying "compulsion, obligation or inexorability" (Burnley, *Chaucer's Language*, 42). In employing "wulle," the Cambridge MS directs our attention both to future certainty and to Horn's desire, the latter connoting less certainty than possibility.[26] We detect with the verb "wulle" not the "mere assurance of the event" conveyed by the verb "schal," as C. B. Bradley expresses it, but rather a "stronger personal quality" instead ("Shall and Will," 19). Horn, who *intends* to accomplish an act, commits himself to a purpose, or to a direction *toward* a goal, not to the inevitable or compulsive achievement of the goal itself.

The poet of *King Horn* sketches out a kind of grey area that exists between absolute promise and expected fulfilment by elaborating upon Horn's intentions, desires, and motivations, along with his absolute

---

[25]   Burnley, *Chaucer's Language*, 42. See pp. 43 – 46 for further comments on "wille" and "schal."

[26]   See Mary Karen Wallum's useful chapter on "Willan" in her dissertation, "The Syntax and Semantics of the English Modal Verbs from the Late Tenth to the Fifteenth Century," (University of Michigan, 1973), esp. 182, 184, 191, 194, 199. I am grateful to Helen Kao at The Middle English Dictionary for directing my attention to this dissertation, and to Editor-in-chief Robert E. Lewis for allowing me to peruse the entry-in-progress for "schulen."

promises and fulfilments, in the presentation of his character. Through Horn's promises the poet gives an increasingly accurate, and individualized, voice to these intentions and motivations. Events conveying dubious motives earlier in the poem are given greater, more personal clarity later in the poem through Horn's direct dialogue. "Wel ofte," Fikenhild claims, has Horn lain with Rymenhild in the bower (698) — a sweeping condemnation of which Horn clears himself in his carefully-worded speech to King Aylmar (1277 – 88, quoted above). Horn greatly reduces the moral severity of his alleged promiscuity by denying the existence of any intimate encounter with Rymenhild — he had never "begun" to lie with her — and by making such an activity strictly contingent upon his martial endeavours. He also explains exactly *who* would be lying with *whom*, were the conditional statement to come true ("The wendest that iwroȝte . . . Bi Rymenhild for to ligge . . . Ne schal ihc hit *biginne*, / *Til* i suddene winne . . . / *Thanne* schal *Rymenhilde* / Ligge by thi kinge"). The pointed reversal of subject and object, the legitimizing of the activity itself (to lie with a *king* is surely an ennobling activity), the double occurrence of "ligge" (hearkening back to Fikenhild's original accusation), the precise phrasing of the entire statement — these aspects call attention to the statement itself as well as to the accusation it dismisses, in a way that creatively underscores the poet's depiction of his hero's growth.

We notice an increased precision, as well, in the wording of Horn's prophetic task as the poem progresses. Horn, we recall, foreshadows his vengeance by instructing his ship to relay the message "that hei [the pagans] schal fonde / The dent of myne honde" (151 – 52). Such statement shows the poet's preference for synecdoche, in which a part substitutes for a whole. The effect, according to Spearing, is one of cinematic "close-ups," where "dent of myne honde" stands for Horn's entire powerful physique and the injuries which he inflicts upon his enemies (see "Medieval Style," 11 – 12). This focused image of Horn's hand-as-weapon is a potent one that looks forward to the potentiality, or probability, of his success later on.

The formal, controlled phrasing of this early prediction lends it a boastful tone which hints at Horn's self-aggrandizement, but it also effaces Horn from the very statement he utters. Horn forecasts what the action will be — "the dent of myne honde" — and who will experience it, but he does not explicitly make himself out to be the agent of the action. Brief and depersonalized, Horn's prediction outlines a strategy of action in which he will play a part, but it does not bind him or commit him to an action in a manner demanded, for example, by an absolute promise. Like many of the oaths in *Havelok the Dane*, Horn's prediction here is "functional," an indirect "invocation of God into the affairs of men so as to seal and ratify the order of human society, rather than an affirmation of personal commitment'' (Jacobs and Schmidt, 1.12). Acting more as God's agent than as his own, Horn is barred, to a degree, from actually designing the course of his future.

Only after Horn proves his valour extensively does he then own, as it were, his promises and his decisions, boldly inserting into his speeches one first-person pronoun after another. Horn's second prediction of his vengeance, occurring much later in the story, is replete with many of these personalizing references:

> Thu kep hure [Rymenhild] a stunde,
> The while that ifunde
> In to *min* heritage
> & to *mi* baronage.
> That lond ischal ofreche
> & do *mi* fader wreche.
> *Ischal* beo king of tune
> & bere kinges crune. (1279 – 86; emphasis added)

Neither Horn's message to his ship nor this portion of his speech to King Aylmar is contained in the Anglo-Norman version of the romance, the former being omitted entirely and the latter apparently lost where the manuscript has broken off. These two passages in *King Horn*, framing but not punctuating the narrative account of Horn's exile, indicate stylistically the general movement of Horn's development and suggest the power he acquires from making promises and keeping them. The poet, by representing Horn's desires in an increasingly detailed fashion, turns a public issue into a private one — illustrates, in other words, that Horn has taken it upon himself to perform the tasks necessary to restore his homeland to Christian leadership.

King Horn appears to make use of a broadened or extended definition of traditional heroic behaviour to allow for a developmental, although not necessarily mimetic, presentation of Horn's experiences. Horn's promises, in particular his conditional statements, betray a certain process of self-discovery that is fed and modified by the hero's awareness of his goals, which alter to accommodate both personal desire and social obligation. Like other romance heroes, but much less like epic heroes, Horn's statements make explicit a selection of choices involving the order and execution of his valorous deeds and, just as importantly, his relationship to others, especially Rymenhild. Heroes born of a traditional or archaic mind, we might say, assert their predictable valour by pairing absolute promises with unquestioned fulfilments. Heroes like Horn, however, who are products of a developing, more self-conscious tradition, assert a conventional valour, but also their individuality, by making and fulfilling conditional promises — by making possible a range of acceptable heroic behaviour through carefully worded stipulations.

King Horn celebrates the growth of its hero with a firm sense of closure: an abiding symmetry underlies the poem's patterns of word and deed; Horn's repeated accomplishments support the poem's thematic expression of the adage "if at first you don't succeed, try, try again." Horn's behaviour, generally speaking, is not "calculating" or "calculated."[27] The loyalty he is called upon to exemplify is never undermined by vagrant displays of broken promises, what Knight might call a disturbing individualism (95).

The indeterminate nature of many of Horn's promises, however, suggests that no matter how certain Horn is to discharge the tasks which he has delineated in his promises, he will perform them, above all, in such a manner that keeps pace with his readiness to do so. Horn's promises imply his abundant willingness to execute his deeds satisfactorily, and yet, as Bradley notes, "it is not always that one can safely vouche for the willingness of another person" (19). There is, therefore, something calculating in the expression of Horn's words and deeds that provokes, in however gentle a way, our own calculations about Horn's motivations, and about the degree to which the poem's language extends beyond a codified framework to support an individualism of style and character. We are encouraged to believe that the power of speech for Horn (to adapt Carlo Ginzburg's observation about language and culture in general) "offers . . . a horizon of latent possibilities — a flexible and individual cage in which he can exercise his own conditional liberty."[28] The use of conditional statements in *King Horn* enhances its complex narrative patterns and the presentation of its hero's growth in a way which looks forward to more literary, self-conscious works but which neither compromises, nor conceals, the poem's traditional roots and appeal.

---

[27] Contrast the behaviour of Calcas in Chaucer's *Troilus and Criseyde*, a man expert, as Brewer remarks, "in calculating the position of the stars, in predicting the future and therefore in a position to know what will happen to Troy." Armed with this knowledge, Calcas's actions become calculating and self-serving. Calcas is a "traitor," Brewer continues, for "calculation destroys values such as loyalty" ("Arithmetic," 158).

[28] *The Cheese and The Worms*, xxi. Ginzburg offers a provocative account of a sixteenth-century miller's understanding of the cosmos. Ginzburg accounts for the miller's heretical views by describing the oral or archaic mentality which profoundly affected the miller's reading and assimilation of selected religious works and chronicles.

WORKS CITED

Allen, R. S. *King Horn: An Edition based on Cambridge University MS Gg. 4.27(2)*. New York: Garland, 1985.

——. "Some Textual Cruces in *King Horn*." *Medium Aevum* 53 (1984): 73 – 77.

Arendt, Hannah. *The Human Condition*. Chicago: U of Chicago P, 1958.

Auerbach, Erich. *Mimesis: The Representation of Reality in Western Literature*. Trans. Willard R. Trask. Princeton: Princeton UP, 1953.

Baugh, Albert. "The Authorship of the Middle English Romances." *MHRA* 22 (1950): 13 – 28.

——. "The Middle English Romance: Some Questions of Creation, Presentation, and Preservation." *Speculum* 42 (1967): 1 – 31.

Bettelheim, Bruno. *The Uses of Enchantment: The Meaning and Importance of Fairy Tales*. London: Thames and Hudson, 1975.

Bloch, R. Howard. *Medieval French Literature and Law*. Berkeley: U of California P, 1977.

Bloomfield, Morton W. "Episodic Motivation and Marvels in Epic and Romance." In *Essays and Explanations: Studies in Ideas, Language, and Literature*. Cambridge, MA: Harvard UP, 1970, 97 – 128.

Boitani, Piero. *Narrative in the Thirteenth and Fourteenth Centuries*. Trans. Joan Krakover Hall. Cambridge: Cambridge UP, 1982.

Bradley, Cornelius Beach. "Shall and Will — An Historical Study." *Transactions of the American Philological Association* 42 (1911): 5 – 31.

Brewer, Derek. "Arithmetic and the Mentality of Chaucer." In *Literature in Fourteenth-Century England: The J. A. W. Bennett Memorial Lectures*. Eds. Piero Boitani and Anna Torti. Cambridge: D. S. Brewer, 1983. 155 – 64.

——. "Malory and the Archaic Mind." In *Arthurian Literature I*. Ed. Richard Barber. Woodbridge, Suffolk: D. S. Brewer, 1981. 94 – 120.

——. "The Nature of Romance." *Poetica* 9 (Tokyo, 1978): 9 – 48.

——. *Symbolic Stories: Traditional Narratives of the Family Drama in English Literature*. Cambridge: D. S. Brewer, 1980.

——. *Tradition and Innovation in Chaucer*. London: Macmillan, 1982.

Burnley, David. *A Guide to Chaucer's Language*. Norman: U of Oklahoma P, 1983.

Burnley, J. D. "The 'Roman de Horn': its Hero and its Ethos." *French Studies* 32 (1978): 385 – 97.

Burrow, J. A. "The Alterity of Medieval Literature." *New Literary History* 10 (1979): 385 – 90.

Chaytor, H. J. *From Script to Print: An Introduction to Medieval Vernacular Literature*. Cambridge: Cambridge UP, 1945.

Childress, Diana T. "Between Romance and Legend: 'Secular Hagiography' in Middle English Literature." *Philological Quarterly* 57 (1978): 311 – 22.

Clanchy, M. T. *From Memory to Written Record: England, 1066 – 1307.* Cambridge, MA.: Harvard UP, 1979.

Crane, Susan. *Insular Romance: Politics, Faith, and Culture in Anglo-Norman and Middle English Literature.* Berkeley: U of California P, 1986.

Crosby, Ruth. "Oral Delivery in the Middle Ages." *Speculum* 11 (1936): 88 – 110.

Curschmann, Michael. "Oral Poetry in Medieval English, French, and German Literature: Some Notes on Recent Research." *Speculum* 42 (1967): 36 – 52.

Dannenbaum, Susan. "Anglo-Norman Romances of English Heroes: 'Ancestral Romance'?" *Romance Philology* 35 (1982): 601 – 08.

Duby, Georges. *Medieval Marriage: Two Models From Twelfth-Century France.* Trans. Elborg Forster. Baltimore: The Johns Hopkins UP, 1978.

——. "Youth in Aristocratic Society." In *The Chivalrous Society.* Trans. C. Postan. Berkeley: U of California P, 1977. 112 – 22.

Eco, Umberto. *The Role of the Reader: Explorations in the Semiotics of Texts.* Bloomington: Indiana UP, 1979.

Foley, John Miles. *Oral-Formulaic Theory and Research: An Introduction and Annotated Bibliography.* New York: Garland, 1985.

French, Walter H. *Essays on King Horn.* New York: Cornell UP, 1940.

Ganim, John M. *Style and Consciousness in Middle English Narrative.* Princeton: Princeton UP, 1983.

Ginzburg, Carlo. *The Cheese and the Worms: The Cosmos of a Sixteenth-Century Miller.* Trans. John and Anne Tedeschi. Harmondsworth: Penguin, 1980.

Goody, Jack. *The Domestication of the Savage Mind.* Cambridge: Cambridge UP, 1977.

Hall, Joseph. *King Horn: A Middle-English Romance.* Oxford: Clarendon P, 1901.

Hanning, Robert. "The Audience as Co-Creator of the First Chivalric Romances." *Yearbook of English Studies* 11 (1981): 1 – 28.

——. *The Individual in Twelfth-Century Romance.* New Haven: Yale UP, 1977.

Havelock, Eric A. *Preface to Plato.* Oxford: Basil Blackwell, 1963.

Holub, Robert C. *Reception Theory: A Critical Introduction.* New York: Methuen, 1984.

Hurley, Margaret. "Saints' Legends and Romances Again: Secularization of Structure and Motif." *Genre* 8 (1975): 60 – 73.

Hurt, James R. "The Texts of *King Horn.*" *Journal of the Folklore Institute* 7 (1970): 47 – 59.

Hynes-Berry, Mary. "Cohesion in *King Horn* and *Sir Orfeo.*" *Speculum* 50 (1975): 652 – 70.

Jauss, Hans Robert. "The Alterity and Modernity of Medieval Literature." *New Literary History* 10 (1079): 181 – 229.

Knight, Stephen. *Arthurian Literature and Society.* London and Basingstoke: Macmillan, 1983.

Lambert, Mark. *Malory: Style and Vision in Le Morte Darthur.* New Haven: Yale UP, 1975.

Legge, M. Dominica. *Anglo-Norman Literature and Its Background.* Westport, CT.: Greenwood P, 1963.

——. "The Rise and Fall of Anglo-Norman Literature." *Mosaic* 8 (1975): 1 – 6.

Lord, Albert B. *The Singer of Tales.* NY: Atheneum, 1974.

Mackie, J. L. "Causes and Conditions." In *Causation and Conditionals.* Ed. Ernest Sosa. Oxford: Oxford UP, 1975. Rpt. 1980. 15 – 38.

McKnight, George H. *King Horn, Floris and Blauncheflur, The Assumption of our Lady.* EETS. O.S. 14. London: Oxford UP, 1901.

Mehl, Dieter. *The Middle English Romances of the Thirteenth and Fourteenth Centuries.* London: Routledge & Kegan Paul, 1967.

Mills, Maldwyn. *Six Middle English Romances.* London: Dent, 1973. Rpt. 1982.

O'Brien, Timothy D. "Word Play in the Allegory of King Horn." *Allegorica* 7 (Winter, 1982): 110 – 22.

Ong, Walter J. *Orality and Literacy: The Technologizing of the Word.* New York: Methuen, 1982.

Parry, Milman. "Studies in the Epic Technique of Oral Verse-Making." *Harvard Studies in Classical Philology* 41 (1930): 73 – 147.

Pearsall, Derek. "The Alliterative Revival: Origins and Social Backgrounds." In *Middle English Poetry and its Literary Background: Seven Essays.* Ed. David Lawton. Cambridge: D. S. Brewer, 1982.

——. "The Development of The Middle English Romance." *Medieval Studies* 27 (1965): 91 – 116.

——. "Editing Medieval Texts: Some Developments and Some Problems." In *Textual Criticism and Literary Interpretation.* Ed. Jerome J. McGann. Chicago: U of Chicago P, 1985. 92 – 106.

——. *Old English and Middle English Poetry.* Vol. 1. London: Routledge & Kegan Paul, 1977.

Pope, Mildred K. "The *Romance of Horn* and *King Horn.*" *Medium Aevum* 25 (1955): 164 – 67.

Pope, Mildred K., ed. *The Romance of Horn, by Thomas.* Anglo-Norman Text Society. Vols. 9 – 10 and 12 – 13. Oxford: Basil Blackwell, 1955.

Preston, Cathy Lynn Makin. *The Ballad Tradition and the Making of Meaning.* Diss. U of Colorado, 1986.

Sands, Donald B. ed. *Middle English Verse Romances.* New York: Holt, Rinehart and Winston, 1966.

Schmidt, A. V. C. and Nicolas Jacobs, eds. *Medieval English Romances, Part One.* London: Hodder and Stoughton, 1980.

Severs, J. Burke, ed. *A Manual of The Writings in Middle English 1050 – 1500.* Vol. I (Romances). New Haven: Connecticut Academy of Arts and Sciences, 1967.

Spearing, A. C. "Medieval Narrative Style." *Poetica* 17 (Tokyo, 1984): 1 – 21.

Spearing, A. C. and J. E. *Poetry of the Age of Chaucer.* London: Edward Arnold, 1974.

Speirs, John. *Medieval English Poetry: The Non-Chaucerian Tradition.* London: Faber and Faber, 1957.

Stevens, John. *Medieval Romance: Themes and Approaches.* London: Hutchinson, 1973.

Tobin, Patricia Dreschel. *Time and the Novel: The Genealogical Imperative.* Princeton: Princeton UP, 1978.

Trounce, A. McI. "The English Tail-Rhyme Romances." *Medium Aevum 1* (1932): 87 – 108, 168 – 82.

——. "The English Tail-Rhyme Romances." *Medium Aevum* 2 (1933): 34 – 57.

——. "The English Tail-Rhyme Romances." *Medium Aevum* 3 (1934): 33 – 50.

Waldron, Ronald A. "Oral-Formulaic Technique and Middle English Alliterative Poetry." *Speculum* 32 (1957): 792 – 801.

Wallum, Mary Karen. *The Syntax and Semantics of the English Model Verbs from the Late Tenth to the Fifteenth Century.* Diss. U of Michigan, 1973.

West, C. B. *Courtoisie in Anglo-Norman Literature.* Oxford: Basil Blackwell, 1938.

Wilson, Anne. *Traditional Romance and Tale: How Stories Mean.* Cambridge: D. S. Brewer, 1976.

Wittig, Susan. *Stylistic and Narrative Structures in the Middle English Romances.* Austin: U of Texas P, 1978.

Breton Lais *and* Modern Fantasies

T. A. SHIPPEY

This essay is an attempt to extend the thesis of Derek Brewer's book *Symbolic Stories*[1] to two further bodies of material, the twelfth-century 'Breton *lais*' of Marie de France, and a small group of fantasy novels for children written within the last twenty years. Some will think that such an attempt would better not be made. Reviews of *Symbolic Stories* were often unconvinced or hostile; J. A. Burrow remarked (*London Review of Books*, 2 – 15 July 1981) that for all Professor Brewer's good sense, the main line of *Symbolic Stories* was 'an idea which I suspect few of his readers . . . would wish to see him pursue any further'. For another to pursue the idea a good deal further may be even more unwelcome. Still, *Symbolic Stories* did not receive an altogether fair trial. Part of the trouble may well have been that its central thesis was all too easy to grasp.

This was, in essence, that 'A very large number of traditional stories, though by no means all, are centred on the basic human experience of growing up'. Stories within this group, labelled by Brewer as 'family drama', furthermore have an irreducible plot existing in both a male and a female version. In the male version, the job of the protagonist, stated with deliberately 'crude brevity' on page 9 of *Symbolic Stories*, is to 'kill his father, dodge his mother, and win his girl' (and along with the girl, freedom, maturity, escape from the home). The female version meanwhile both reverses the sexes, so that it is the father's love which has to be avoided, and also for cultural reasons allows the heroine only a less active role: she has to show herself to Prince Charming and then wait for his advances rather than running boldly after him. Corollaries of this theory are that all the characters in such traditional narratives are (apart from the idealised sexual partner) father-figures, mother-figures, or 'splits' and

---

[1] Derek Brewer, *Symbolic Stories: traditional narratives of the family drama in English literature*, Cambridge and Totowa N.J., 1980.

'repeats' of the protagonist; and that the extreme emotions aroused by the plot, including guilt, anxiety and remorse, lead to quite unusual levels of displacement and symbolic disguise all through.

A strong argument for this thesis is that its applicability can immediately be recognised for one story after another. *Cinderella* is no doubt the *locus classicus*. It is a story with which everyone is familiar, so familiar that its logical gaps and hiatuses are immediately ignored. Nevertheless once attention is drawn to it as a 'family drama', it becomes clear, for instance, how ambivalent Cinderella's father is (for he seems both too strong to be rebelled against and too weak to protect his own daughter). The 'wicked stepmother' and 'fairy godmother' of Perrault also come over very plausibly as split aspects of a child's-eye view mother, at once loved and hated, relied on and resented. The Ugly Sisters take more interpreting, for they could be images of 'sibling rivalry', or alternatively 'repeats' of the protagonist herself, there to express the heroine's self-doubt, or self-admiration, or conceivably both at once. However they, like Prince Charming, have no life of their own; all are there only to reflect the heroine. Finally one may remark that the distinctive appeal of Perrault's plot may lie in the powerfully ambiguous images of the ashy hearth — warm, dirty, central — and the glass slipper, inflexible, undeceivable, rigidly exclusive.

Cinderella, together with *Snow White* and *Sleeping Beauty* and a few similar tales, may persuade even a sceptic that there *is* such a category as 'family drama'; while even a sceptic could accept that this is a category extending much further than fairy-tale, and always liable to be spontaneously re-invented. It is not one of Brewer's examples, but few could deny that the opening chapters of *David Copperfield* encapsulate 'family drama' in an extreme form; for there the rivalry and hatred between David and Mr. Murdstone are not (though they pretend to be) the result of rivalry between a boy and his father's supplanter. They are between a boy and a strongly negative image of his own genuine father. Peggotty may say to David, as they return from Yarmouth, 'You have got a Pa! . . . A new one'. But the horror behind Mr. Murdstone is not that he is a 'new Pa' but that he is the old one come back from the dead, like Lazarus (of whom David is deeply frightened) from beneath the gravestone. Mr. Murdstone is white-skinned and clean-shaven, but his black beard shows all the time, like a washed corpse whose hair has continued to grow. The first words his friends at Lowestoft say to him are 'Halloa, Murdstone! We thought you were dead!' One could argue that *David Copperfield* from then on is populated by a variety of father-figures, to be crushed or killed, and of mother-figures, to be rejected or revenged on; David certainly shows signs of becoming a Murdstone himself in his relations with his first wife Dora. However the main point is just that the notion of 'family drama' can be applied persuasively to many tales, romances and novels; this multi-applicability makes out a case for the notion's truth.

Nevertheless there is also a case against it, partly generated (as has been said) by the very ease with which the thesis can be grasped. To put it bluntly, is it not tedious, disappointing, even frustrating, to have one story after another reduced to the same basic set of manoeuvres? Is there any room for variety in 'family drama'? And if there is — as surely there is from even the few examples already cited — does this not prove that the really interesting things even in traditional narratives are not their underlying elemental structure but the surface variations which readers and listeners and critics have all for centuries united in enjoying? Professor Burrow puts it well, in the review already cited, when he remarks that the real difficulty with theories of 'latent significance' has always been 'to develop those perceptions into analyses of particular works which can rival the subtlety and flexibility of the best non-Freudian criticism'. To this one can only reply that the methods of 'the best non-Freudian criticism' were not developed all at once; 'subtlety and flexibility' in explaining traditional narrative may also take time to develop. Still, it is a fair point that one should no longer be content with spotting new examples, nor with reducing plots as soon as possible to skeletons. One has also to consider the possibilities for creativity within the bounds of 'family drama'; and to ask what pleasure or value readers get (if they do) from reading one permutation after another of the same basic form. For answering these questions the twelve *lais* of Marie de France seem particularly well-suited.

One may begin with *Guigemar*, the first *lai* both in Harley MS 978 (the only complete manuscript) and in the two other most nearly complete manuscripts or early translated collections surviving. It was probably intended by its author to be the first *lai* read; it is striking that it is the most obvious and least distorted example of 'family drama' in the set of twelve. Its basic plot is as follows. Guigemar is a noble and handsome knight, with all the virtues, but one regrettable fault: 'To such an extent had Nature wronged him that never did he care for any kind of love'.[2] He refuses all offers of ladies' love, so that he is thought in the end by everyone to be *peri*, 'a lost one' or, seemingly, a homosexual. He is in service at court, but decides one day to return to his lovingly-described family, father, mother, and sister Noguent. Once home, though, he goes hunting; and in the forest, while chasing a great stag, comes upon a hind and a fawn — a strange, white, androgynous hind with stag's antlers. He

[2]   The translation is that of Rupert T. Pickens, 'Thematic Structure in Marie de France's *Guigemar*', *Romania* 95 (1974), 328 – 41.

shoots it, but the arrow rebounds and strikes him in the thigh. The stricken hind then says that his wound will be incurable except by a woman, who will suffer as much pain for him as he for her. The hind concludes: *'Va t'en de ci! Lais m'aver pes!'*[3]

Guigemar rides painfully away, comes to the sea, finds a boat, and is magically transported by it to an *antive cité*, ruled by an old, jealous lord who keeps his lady locked in a bower above a harbour. To this harbour, though, the boat comes; and the lady proves to be the one who heals Guigemar's wound. In the end the lovers are discovered, and Guigemar is despatched in the boat again — though not before he has put a clasp on the lady's girdle, and she has tied a knot in his shirt, and each has promised to grant love to no-one who cannot undo them. Guigemar returns home, where his knot becomes famous. The lady is imprisoned, till she resolves to drown herself — at which resolve she finds all locks open and the boat waiting for her. It takes her, though, not to Guigemar, but to the castle of a lord called Meriadus, who falls in love with her but cannot undo her buckle. Strangely, Meriadus remembers Guigemar's knot and calls him to a tournament: but (even after the two have recognised each other *and* undone clasp and knot) refuses to give the lady up. Guigemar therefore besieges his castle and kills him, returning with the lady to his own land.

The meaning which Marie de France intended this story to carry is clear enough. It is a panegyric on the power and necessity of true love, full of extensive descriptions (the anti-Ovidian picture within the lady's bower, the long account of Guigemar's sleeplessness after he has fallen in love), and of scenes which seem to encapsulate lovers' aphorisms: love is a wound, only the true love can heal it, love is distinct from lechery, true love cannot be confined. Yet the impulse to go beyond this perfectly conscious and deliberate level of significance, and reinterpret *Guigemar* in terms of 'family drama' is irresistible. It rescues so many features of the story from being mere accidents, or mere redundancies. The setting at the start is one example. Guigemar, we are told, has left home and gone to court — but has then gone home again, to what seems to be an ideal family, his valiant father, his loving mother, his beautiful sister, all of whom *mult l'aveient desiré*. Why not let Guigemar go hunting from the court where he is in service, and where his basic lovelessness has been exposed? Surely, we must feel — and the mere juxtaposition of home and hunt must have made many readers feel this, even though they had never heard of 'family drama' — it is because his lack of love for women has *something to do* with his overpowering attachments at home. He has not yet cut the apron-strings, as the folk saying has it.

[3]   All quotations of Marie are from Marie de France, *Lais*, ed. A. Ewert, Oxford 1944.

But then what is the strange hermaphrodite deer which he shoots? It has been suggested that this represents Guigemar's *destinee*, the state of 'perfect union' and 'sexual wholeness' he will one day reach in marriage.[4] But if so, why shoot it? Why, furthermore, should the shooting of it lead so very directly to Guigemar's immediate exile and ultimate success? These questions, it should be noted, are very near the surface of the narration and positively provoke some interpretation of the deer itself in any but the naïvest reading. The answers given by the rules of 'family drama' are strikingly apt, but not particularly recondite. In brief, it has to be remembered first that nearly all characters in 'family drama' are either 'splits' of the protagonist, or else father or mother figures: while second, the ultimate plot of male-oriented family drama is that of killing the father and avoiding the mother. Can the hind-with-antlers not function, according to rule 1, as a joint father-and-mother figure? In which case, one might add, its totally redundant fawn would function very neatly as an image of Guigemar's equally redundant sister Noguent. Meanwhile Guigemar has not exactly *killed* it, in spite of rule 2 (of which more later), but he has wantonly if innocently hurt it. Paraphrase is always a danger in quasi-Freudian interpretations, but it is very tempting to say that this scene says that to break the ties of home, one has to hurt one's parents. The rebounding arrow meanwhile points out that the same process hurts oneself — as Guigemar is hurt on being driven away from his cosy, supportive upbringing to an unknown destination from which, this time, he cannot lightly return. As for Guigemar's wound, this seems to bear a double meaning. It is a kind of awakening. It also, being in the thigh, threatens a kind of impotence. Guigemar was impotent before, at court. Now, however, he knows it, he desires a cure, he has left home in a sense more than merely physical.

It makes no difference to the scenes with the lady in the *antive cité* whether one reads them as 'family drama' or as 'love story'. The former suggestion works much better however with that (again) otherwise redundant character Meriadus. Here rules 1 and 2 above need once more to be invoked. There is little difficulty in seeing the old *gelus* as another father-figure whose role is to lock the lady up and prevent her from gaining sexual freedom; nor in seeing her desperate decision to drown herself once her lover has gone as a counterpart to the scene with the hind (for true independence is only achieved by abandoning security — it is interesting that once her decision is formed she finds all locks mysteriously open). However it is odd that the story does not end happily with the reappearance of the magic boat. Could it not have taken her to

---

[4] See Pickens, op. cit. Despite my disagreement with it here, this is a valuable article, especially in pointing out *Guigemar*'s symmetry of structure and social point.

Guigemar as easily as to Meriadus? Clearly something still needs to be done to make the story complete, though it is *not* anything to do with concealment; Meriadus in fact finds Guigemar for the lady. A convincing answer is to propose Meriadus as yet another father-figure. But while the deer was ambiguous, and also perhaps only wounded, and while the *gelus* was only (by the lady) 'dodged' and left, by the time the tale comes round to Meriadus the hero has perhaps been worked up to taking a final step, disguised though it is, of actually *killing* the powerful, aggressive and dominant figure who keeps the heroine from him. This step is heavily justified, for Guigemar makes Meriadus a generous offer, only to be turned down flat: '*Jeo la trovai, si la tendrai/ E cuntre vus la defendrai.*' After this it is fair, but also completing and satisfying, for Guigemar to take his lady by siege and storm, kill his rival, and lead her, not home, but *out*:

> Le chastel ad destruit e pris
> E le seignur dedenz ocis.
> A grant joie s'amie en meine;
> Ore ad trespassee sa peine. (879 – 82)

Guigemar in short follows the rules of 'family drama' quite as well as *Cinderella*. All its characters can be taken as hero, heroine, father or mother figure (apart, that is, from the doubtful case of the fawn-cum-sibling). It describes with some force the difficulty of leaving home except through scenes of pain. It has a strongly symmetrical structure, moving from home to an idealised bower through a kind of borderland (the forest), and then returning back again, though not quite all the way, via another neutral territory (the castle of Meriadus). Perhaps most evidently, its very clear and unmistakable point is that Guigemar cannot be considered a whole man till he has left home and won his lady; and once he has started winning his lady, we hear no more of his social ineptness, his status as *peri*, nor indeed of the father, mother and sister so strongly present at the beginning of the story. Everyone agrees that *Guigemar* has to be taken as a story about the development of maturity. The present interpretation merely urges that rejection of one kind of love should be seen as equally essential to the *lai* as gaining another.

Could *Guigemar* (the first *lai* in the set) have been seen by Marie as a kind of basic form? And would she have recognised in any way the category of 'family drama', with its rather un-courtly endocentric hostilities? On the last question, one of authorial consciousness, opinions have varied. S. Foster Damon for instance claimed that Marie's *lais* were indeed very like fairy-tales in their treatment of elemental 'human desires and interests', except that 'fairy-tales do unconsciously what Marie's lays do consciously. We have her word' [sc, Damon's reading of the *Prologue* to the *lais*] 'for their consciousness'.[5] Other scholars have preferred to see Marie as a story-teller innocent of theses, indeed one liable (like Dickens) to get into a muddle when trying 'to deal intellectually with a problem'.[6] Nearly everyone has agreed however on an answer to the first issue raised: there is a strong consensus that the *lais* are in some way or other patterned and repetitive, and many efforts have been made to disentangle or decode the pattern. Foster Damon, in the article already cited, went furthest in this direction, with the claim that 'the lays fit together into distinct couplets or quadruplets, as though one suggested the next by the simple process of inverting the situation or the characters' — a process so schematic, in his view, as to be readily reducible to a chart. Few have since accepted the chart. Many scholars, however, have taken the easier step of proposing one *lai* as a match or transposition of another: thus *Equitan*, has been proposed as an 'Anti-*Guigemar*', *Bisclavret* and *Lanval* have been *rapprochés*, *Bisclavret* and *Equitan* have been put together as villainess-*lais*, *Guigemar*, *Equitan* and *Le Fresne* have been seen as a sequence on a single theme (a sequence which leads through all the *lais* to their 'perfect conclusion' in *Eliduc*), and so on.[7] 'Coupling' has furthermore been proposed as the basic principle of the whole collection; the image has been proposed of a *kaleidoscope* (the same objects continually shaken into new patterns): another scholar writes of *kongruente Figuren eines dramatischen Grundrhythmus*.[8] It need hardly be said that in recent years the ideas of 'narremes' and 'mythemes' have been floated, if not very successfully.[9] Leo Spitzer perhaps put the general feeling most forcefully when he wrote (my translation) that: 'the whole interwoven system of the Lais is an expression of the interlacement of all the questions of love into one whole: therefore the stories also seem to me to have to be read not singly , but as a whole which had been

[5]   See Foster S. Damon, 'Marie De France: Psychologist of Courtly Love', *PMLA* 44 (1929), 968 – 96.
[6]   So John Stevens, 'The *granz biens* of Marie de France', in *Patterns of Love and Courtesy*, ed. J. Lawlor, London, 1966, 1 – 25.
[7]   For these ideas, see respectively: Rupert T. Pickens,'*Equitan*: Anti-*Guigemar*', *Romance Notes* 15 (1973 – 4), 361 – 7; Judith R. Rothschild, 'A *Rapprochement* between *Bisclavret* and *Lanval*', *Speculum* 48 (1973), 78 – 88; Ruth Morse, 'The *granz biens* again', *NM* 81 (1980), 361 – 5; Emanuel J. Michel jr., 'A Reconsideration of the *Lais* of Marie de France', *Speculum* 46 (1971), 39 – 65.
[8]   For these ideas, see respectively: John A. Frey, 'Linguistic and Psychological Coupling in the Lays of Marie de France', *SP* 61 (1964), 3 – 18; Lise Lawson, 'La Structure du Récit dans les *Lais* de Marie de France', in *Court and Poet*, ed. Glyn S. Burgess, Liverpool, 1981, 93 – 9; and Kurt Ringger, *Die Lais: zur Struktur der dichterischen Einbildungskraft der Marie de France* (Beihefte zur Zeitschrift für romanische Philologie), Tübingen, 1973.
[9]   As by Lawson, op. cit.

conceived as a unity.'[10] The *lais*, to Spitzer, are 'a coherent work on the problem of love': but (important reservation), the work as a whole is a labyrinth, with each individual tale in it a *Sackgasse* or 'dead-end'!

It is certainly bold to offer to find a thread through this labyrinth, but it is almost a majority opinion that there must be one. How much can be learned by taking the basic principle of the *lais*, the underlying figure of all their congruencies, to be 'family drama'? Several tales provoke one to try out the notion, though none is as uncomplicated as *Guigemar*.

The third *lai* of the series, *Le Fresne*, can for instance be convincingly read as a female version of 'family drama' (*Guigemar* was male), or a sort of delayed *Cinderella*. *Le Fresne* also begins with a cruel, rejecting mother, and a father completely unconcerned with his daughter because he has no idea of her existence: what has happened is that the heroine's mother has declared publicly that twins are the result of adultery, and then had girl-twins herself. She accordingly abandons one of them as a foundling, wrapped in a rich cloth. The heroine is then fostered and grows up, to be called 'Le Fresne' after the ash-tree in which she was left, and to have a young man fall in love with her and take her away. She seems, then, to have reached the normal climax of 'family drama', finding a mate. But she bears no children; the young man's tenants insist on finding him a fertile wife; he is betrothed unwillingly to Le Fresne's unrecognised sister La Codre, 'the hazel-tree'. In a gesture of generosity Le Fresne, on the wedding-night, spreads her only possession, the rich cloth in which she was wrapped, on her supplanter's marriage-bed. The mother sees it; recognises it and Le Fresne's story; confesses her fault to her husband, for him to forgive her, the archbishop to annul the wedding, and the way to be left clear for Le Fresne to marry her lover with a proper dowry.

As with *Cinderella*, several features of this story defy sense. Why should the girls end up with related names? If the opposition is of fertility/sterility — you get nuts from the hazel, the ash bears no fruit, as the *chevaler fiufé* so unchivalrously say — then what diffrence does it make for Le Fresne to be recognised? She will still be barren. However all these carpings seem mean against the story's central image of self-sacrificing generosity, the one rich possession spread out for the partner's honour and the rival's pleasure. True love, this scene declares, even casts out jealousy. Yet *Le Fresne* is like *Cinderella* also in the way the despised and unfortunate protagonist wins out over her rich and favoured sister (though this sister is later awarded a good marriage too, like the Ugly Sisters in Perrault). The tales are again similar in having cruel mothers, powerless fathers, and objects which serve as emblems of the 'real (and valuable) me' in coverlet

[10]   Leo Spitzer, 'Marie de France — Dichterin von Problem-Märchen', Z.f.r.Phil. 50 (1930), 29–67.

and slipper. Where *Le Fresne* is unlike *Cinderella* is that its object is not to get a mate and leave home, but to retain a mate already won after both parental home and foster-home have been left. The motif of leaving home twice is even stronger in *Le Fresne* than in *Guigemar*. It is as if the *lai* were saying that dangers continue long after the wooing stage: partners have not only to be won, but held.

The *lai* of *Les Deus Amanz* shows a similar mixture of normality and unexpectedness, if read as 'family drama'. Nothing could be more conventional than its start: once upon a time there was a king, whose wife had died, and who loved her daughter so much that he could not bear to part with her. The motif of 'dodging the father' is in this tale completely explicit, and even the danger of incest is very close to the surface.[11] Furthermore the test which the king sets to all potential suitors is unusually appropriate to a man aging and self-doubting: the king declares that only a man who can carry her without stopping to the top of a nearby mountain may marry his daughter. He sets, in other words, a test of strength in order that it will be failed, and in order that he can continue to regard younger men as inadequate, not serious rivals. This generation-hostility is incresed by the heroine's final choice of a partner: she falls in love with a man, or boy, described as a *damiseus*, whose youth and weakness are stressed even by the girl. Her father, she remarks, will consider him an *enfant*, while she herself is sure he cannot pass the test at all, '*N'estes mie si vertuus*', 'You are not at all strong enough'. Her solution is for him to go to the story's one other character, a female relation who lives in Salerno. She is described as an *aunte*: but it is hard not to see her as yet another mother-figure, this time benevolent like Cinderella's godmother, but benevolent — though this rather goes against the scheme as laid out by Brewer, see pp. 68 above — because of the deep female wish to see the generations kept in their place and a potential rival for the father's affections allowed to leave home. The *aunte* in any case supplies a potion of strength. Once he has drunk this the boy will be able to pass the father's test.

So far *Les Deus Amanz* has stayed very close to the theme of 'family drama'; but the test goes strangely wrong. The boy gives his potion to the girl to hold, picks her up and sets off at great speed. 'For the joy which he had in her he did not remember his potion.' She feels him tiring and urges him to drink. But he refuses:

'Bele, jo sent tut fort mun quer:

---

[11]   Harley MS 978 tactfully eliminates eight lines pointing in this direction, see Ewert, p. 178.

Ne m'arestereie a nul fuer
Si lungement que jeo beüsse,
Pur quei treis pas aler peüsse.
Ceste gent nus escrïereient,
De lur noise m'esturdireient;
Tost me purreient desturber.
Jo ne voil pas ci arester.' (189 – 96)

She keeps urging him to drink, but he refuses, carries on, reaches the top of the mountain — and then falls dead from exhaustion. She too dies, of heartbreak. The king, grief-stricken, buries the two lovers together.

As 'family drama' this has to be reckoned abortive; though it should be noted that other seemingly abortive tales are known, for instance (to take an example from Brewer) the strongly male-oriented *Jack and the Beanstalk*, in which the hero appears to escape his mother's control, climb repeatedly up the beanstalk (which almost all interpreters see as somehow phallic), and rob a very evident father-figure in the ogre — only, at the end of it all, to kill the 'father', but simultaneously destroy the beanstalk, and then retire contentedly to live with his mummy! Could *Les Deus Amanz* be seen as a withdrawal from sexuality of a similar type, but this time female-oriented? The maiden does indeed urge the *damiseus* to drink the potion, and all the blame for not drinking it falls on him — he had no *mesure*, remarks Marie forbiddingly. It is interesting, though, that before the test the maiden not only strips to her shift to lose weight, as if she doubted the potion, but also fasts for a long period. In modern times this is notoriously a menarche-retarding device of female adolescents rejecting maturity. Are the heroine's motivations not perhaps as ambivalent as her father's? To put it another way, the *damiseus* could be seen as a self-pleasing female fiction: he is a highly un-threatening lover, and one who allows the romance to stay on the level of pleasantly-contemplated 'fine feeling', with no risk of matters progressing further or the heroine's essential reluctance being exposed.

However at this point it is as well to remember Professor Burrow's remark about the lack of 'subtlety and flexibility' in criticism of this type; for there can be no doubt that 'non-Freudian criticism' would have no trouble at all with the central problem of this tale, the refusal to drink the potion.[12] The core of *Les Deus Amanz* it would say, is neither the hero nor the heroine, but the mountain: a symbol of reality, of a harshly material world, of a quality in life repeatedly identified by commentators on the *lais* as *médiocrité, méchanceté*.[13] To this the love of 'the two lovers'

---

[12] See for instance Stevens, op. cit.

[13] As by J. Ribard, 'Le lai du *Laostic*: structure et signification', *Le Moyen Age* 76 (1970), 263 – 74; and J. C. Payen, 'Structure et sens d'*Yonec*', *LMA* 82 (1976), 263 – 87.

functions as an opposite at once powerful and impotent. It cannot succeed in passing the test — or rather it can (for the boy does reach the top of the mountain) but only at a self-defeating price. Yet in another way material reality is defeated by fine feeling, for before she dies the heroine hurls the useless potion down the mountainside — and the mountain changes, becoming ever after *mut amendez*, a plot for *Meinte bone herbe*. In this view the moral of the tale is not what Marie rather dully says, namely that even in love moderation is advisable; it becomes instead a powerful statement about the evident weakness and not-so-evident strength of human emotion.

What such an interpretation would leave out, though, would be the dynamics of the setting. The loving king and the strangely helpful *aunte* would be relegated to mere devices to get the lovers on the mountain. Furthermore there seems no reason why an interpretation based on 'family drama' should not take in the non-Freudian interpretation above just as that interpretation might note and appraise the 'moderation-moral' of Marie herself. In this view, Marie would be seen as inserting an 'official' moral into her tale, and believing it, regardless of the sympathy she and all her audience would simultaneously feel with the lovers, even with the boy-lover's immoderate but noble desire to win his lady all by himself and in privacy. At the same time, the *dénouement* of the story provokes exactly the flow of 'fine feeling' and 'intense inner experience' which so many critics have seen in it; but, conceivably (and this is the addition created by the context of 'family drama') that very flow of feeling might contain, even for courtly contemporary readers of Marie, something of self-indulgence to which the story itself mutely points. Most of the time *Les Deus Amanz* seems to be a story about hero, heroine and *aunte* joining forces to circumvent the king. When it turns out it is not, the other characters in a sense diminish. They have failed, on one level or another, and the 'fine feeling' of them and their sympathisers cannot avoid a hint of escapism. This hint is only pointed out by the contrast with more normal 'family dramas'. Many listeners must have felt, without consciously thinking of *Cinderella*-tales at all, that Marie was not 'ransack[ing] the common store of fairy-tale',[14] but reversing it; many must also have felt that it would be a 'better' story, in some way, if it had led to consummation and not remained stuck at the stage of pubescent romance.

Guigemar, *Le Fresne* and *Les Deus Amanz* may be seen, then, as respectively male 'family drama', very close to basic type; female 'family drama', but oddly postponed; and female 'family drama', but rendered abortive. Seeing the three *lais* this way does no great violence to the

---

[14]   Stevens, op cit.

traditional or 'non-Freudian' interpretation, though it may change the tales' emphasis or give different explanations to particular details. There is no space here to consider Marie's nine remaining *lais* in detail, but my suggestion would be, first, that all nine may be read in a similar way, but second, that they are at increasing removes from the basic pattern, extending in the end almost to parody.

Lanval and *Eliduc*, for instance, are nearly as close to *Guigemar* as the other two tales already discussed. *Lanval* could indeed be seen as a reversed *Guigemar*. Whereas *Guigemar*, at the start of this story, is popular with everyone, apart from his one fault, Lanval is very much *Hume estrange descunseillez*, a man who is neither at his own home nor welcome at Arthur's court. Love saves him, as it did Guigemar, but puts him, in the middle of the tale, in a position very like Guigemar's at the start of his: he is now extremely popular, but his rejection of the advances of Guinevere (quite convincing as a thwarting mother-figure) leads to his being accused of homosexuality, as of treachery. He is saved from this accusation and goes away with his supernatural lady to another land: but unlike Guigemar he does not come back. The relationship between the two tales is almost that of a diagram; they are *kongruente Figuren*, in Kurt Ringger's phrase:

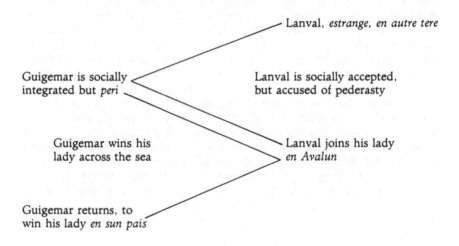

The end and centre of *Lanval* correspond to the centre and start of *Guigemar*, but the one ends with social integration, the other with rejection. If there were a 'familial' moral, it might be that when children grow up and 'cut the apron strings', a certain proportion of them will do so for good, never to return.

Eliduc meanwhile looks like a version of *Le Fresne* in which the centre of attention has been moved to La Codre. In it a protagonist already married falls in love with a maiden, only for this very unpromising situation to be saved by the self-sacrificing generosity of his wife, who brings the maiden back from death and then retires to a convent to let him marry again. The generosity of the wife recalls that of Le Fresne; but the effect of focussing the tale on her supplanter is to make her seem more of a mother-figure who has to be 'avoided', or as in *Guigemar* hurt, for the protagonists to reach consummation. The stress of the tale seems to fall on the sufferings which have to be undergone by others for heroines to get what they want. If *Lanval* is an anti-*Guigemar*, *Eliduc* could be described as a *Cinderella* seen from the viewpoint of the stepmother, or even one of the (allegedly) Ugly Sisters — who might have a different tale to tell.

Milun and *Yonec* for their part are clearly tales about 'killing the father'. The former has a strikingly apposite scene where a fiercely envious father challenges his son, but is overthrown, only for the latter to hold his hand as he sees the older man's gray hair and beard beneath the visor. However both these *lais* are complicated by the presence in them, seemingly, of two tales each, of different generations, so that the protagonist of one half becomes the father-figure in the other;[15] this makes them especially hard to read. By contrast three of the five remaining tales, all short, look like 'aborts', in each of which a relationship is crushed almost before it starts, either by a tyrannous husband (*Laüstic*), by King Mark of Cornwall (*Chevrefoil*), or by incurable crippling of the lover (*Chaitivel*). But what is one to make, finally, of the two 'villainess'-*lais*, *Equitan* and *Bisclavret*, stories which have tended to block most 'all-purpose' or generalising interpretations of Marie de France?

Once again one does not wish to do violence to the evident or superficial meanings of these tales, which are warnings about treachery in love or against love. Nevertheless it is striking how very close the 'villainess' of *Equitan* comes to the image of the infantilising, emasculating mother. Almost the last words Equitan says to her in his wooing are *'Vus seiez dame e jeo servant'*: he means 'you shall be the lady and I the servant', but *dame* can mean 'mother' as well. Later, after the relationship has lasted for some time, we are told that Equitan has been made unpopular (like Lanval and Guigemar) by his lack of apparent *talent* for women. To retain him in this state, the 'villainess' uses evident moral blackmail: *'Femme prendrez, fille a un rei . . . Pur vus m'estuet aver la mort'*. Jealousy against a

---

[15] Constance Bullock-Davies, 'The Love-Messenger in *Milun*', *Nottingham Medieval Studies* 16 (1972), 20 – 27, points out that the list of titles in the Shrewsbury MS seems to include two for *Milun*, 57 *Milun* (father), and 25 *Le Numper* (son), and two for *Yonec*, 24 *Mil de Mereth* (father), and 61 *Yonech* (son).

daughter, one of another generation, and insistence that 'it will be the death of me', sound as much maternal as romantic; the correct response has already been indicated by Guigemar's arrow. But Equitan does not give it, preferring instead to be 'bled' repeatedly — his highly suggestive pretext for privacy — and stay with his *dame*. In the terms of 'family drama', *Equitan* appears as an image of the fate all proper male protagonists try to avoid: it is a story about the 'mother' trying to kill her husband, the 'father', in order to be allowed to absorb and devour her 'son'. It is fortunate indeed — though it makes for a very un-courtly tale — that her plot does not succeed. As for the werewolf-*lai* of *Bisclavret*, this seems if anything to be a story about a 'father-figure' (the king) intervening to rescue a 'son' from the entrapments of a designing female, a reversal of pattern which goes well beyond *Jack and the Beanstalk*, but is still a good deal more familiar in family sentiment than in the ideals of courtly romance.

Deliberate and parodic transformations are not unknown in the history of fiction.[16] However at this point several scepticisms should be allowed to air themselves. Is it likely that Marie de France should have set out to write *Guigemar* as (whatever she called it to herself) a 'family drama'? Could she then conceivably have set out to write eleven further 'variations on a theme', excluding tales that did not fit, and deliberately choosing others so that she would have so many male, so many female, so many parodic, thwarted, minatory or abortive versions of the basic category available in her collection? No doubt the answer to both questions is 'No'. But then one has to remember that 'family drama' is rarely deliberate. Even Dickens (one can be fairly sure) had no clear idea of what he meant when he started writing *David Copperfield*; while it is in our day an absolutely normal experience to have writers — perhaps especially fantasy writers — not rejecting explanations put to them, but expressing surprise (sometimes gratified surprise) that they had built in more than they realised. There is no difficulty in thinking the same of Marie. The striking points with which to counter scepticism are, first, that her collection of *lais* has given so strong and general an impression of thematic unity; but second, that this derives so much from a sequence of motifs which have little or nothing at all to do with *amur*, but everything to do with parents and children — the abandoned child, the defeated father, the loving father, the man who cannot marry, the home that

---

16   In 'Breaking a Culture: a theme in science fiction', *Alta: the University of Birmingham Review* 9 (1969), 123 – 32, I remarked on a science-fiction story which took the basic pattern 'man saves girl from monster' (ABC), and worked carefully through the various permutations, BAC (girl saves man from monster), ACB, (man saves monster from girl), CAB (monster fails to save man from girl), etc.

cannot be penetrated, the locks that fly open, the female who cries '*Jo sui ocise!*', but turns out not to mean it.

There is no space here to make the evident comparisons with Marie's sources, analogues and successors in Old French and Middle English. However the briefest survey of the former group suggests how much Marie had to do to make her tales even as unified as they are; the latter group by contrast (for all its 'stragglers' like *Sir Gowther* or *The Erle of Tolous*) looks as if the unconscious force of Marie's collection had made an indelible if second- or third-hand imprint. *Sir Degaré* has been convincingly explained by Brewer in his own terms.[17] *Sir Orfeo* and Chaucer's *Franklin's Tale*, complex as they are, all but cry out to be read as masculine versions of *Le Fresne*, in both of which a once-achieved but subsequently-lost partner is rescued from a dominant and possessive rival by an act of supreme generosity. A certain symmetry is visible also (of a *Lanval/Guigemar* type) between *Sir Orfeo* and *Les Deus Amanz*. It is not unreasonable then to conclude that Marie de France consciously or unconsciously realigned her chosen stories, whatever their sources, along the no-doubt ancient patterns of 'family drama'; while she and her readers further enjoyed, as we do, the faint if persistent sense that there is more in them than meets the eye, and that apparent contradictions may turn out to be disguised similarities or alternatives.

* * * * *

Scepticism nevertheless may still not be entirely allayed. Nor must one forget the query raised by Professor Burrow (see p. 70 above) as to why anyone would ever *want* to read story after story droning wearily around the same old 'latent significance' or theme? But here, if analysis will go no further, comparison may be pressed into service. It is odd — but, since the authors are contemporaries of ours, very much more demonstrable and less deniable — that a set of stories exists in our own time which carries out a closely similar set of 'transformations' to those of Marie, does so without at any time losing the patience of thousands of readers, and does so while repeating, apparently spontaneously, many even of the detailed motifs of Breton *lai*. These stories give an especially good guide as to how 'family drama' is actually read and understood.

The four chosen here are fantasy novels written for children or teenagers within the last twenty years. The feature which connects them is that they are all in a sense 'window stories': in two of them — Ursula Le Guin's *The Beginning Place* (1980, later republished as *Threshold*) and William Mayne's *A Game of Dark* (1971) — the protagonists find

see p. 70 above

---

17   Brewer, op. cit., pp. 66–71.

themselves able by some unexplained process (gate and dream respectively) to enter and return from another world. Meanwhile in Robert Westall's *The Wind Eye* (1976)[18] the transit is more like time-travel, with the protagonists using the preserved boat of St. Cuthbert to pass to and fro between now and the seventh century. Finally, in Alan Garner's *Red Shift* (1973), there is no transit for the characters at all: instead, three sets of adventures are related, dating from Roman times, the seventeenth century, and the present, but all taking place in the same area and connected by the 'thunderstone' or votive stone axe which all the characters handle. All four stories in short fit quite implausibly well into Jean Frappier's characterisation of the Breton *lai* as *opposition entre le monde vulgaire et le monde idéal*, where *le plus souvent l'aventure se produit dans des régions intermédiaires;*[19] 'thresholds' are as important to *Guigemar* as to Ms. Le Guin, while even the 'window' image has been seen as central to the *Laüstic lai*, with its *fenestre* through the *haut mur* that the heroine dare not pass.[20] However the unmistakable point of the modern stories is that all four depend perfectly consciously on structural parallelism. Even the most inexperienced reader of them realises that events in one world or time have to be explained by reference to those in another.

Moreover a further strongly connecting feature of the four modern stories is that in their real-world strands all are beyond question 'family drama' in the most literal sense. In all four the children, or young adults (their ages are guessable at fourteen to twenty) are at odds with their parents in ways as bitter as commonplace. His mother's first words to Donald, the protagonist in *A Game of Dark* are 'Now, Jackson, what's the matter?' She calls him 'Jackson' because she is a teacher at his school, and cannot be maternal for the sake of discipline; still, her 'official' behaviour slips over into 'unofficial' moments. Jackson indeed finds himself wondering before long whether she *is* his mother, or his father his father. If they were not, then he would have 'no need to feel guilty for no longer loving them as parents'. The male protagonist in *The Beginning Place* is in a similar situation. At one moment in the book he says, appealingly, 'Mother'. She replies, 'There's no use you calling me that'. Meanwhile the Studdard family in *The Wind Eye* are almost like the Peggotty household in *David Copperfield*: they look like a nuclear family, but aren't. Instead Beth is the daughter of Bertrand, Michael the son of Madeleine.

---

18 Westall is well aware that 'window' derives from early forms of 'wind eye'.
19 Jean Frappier, 'Remarques sur la structure du lai: essai de définition et de classement', in *Du Moyen Age à la Renaissance: Études d'Histoire et de Critique Littéraires*, Paris, 1976, 17–35.
20 Ribard, op. cit.

Bertrand and Madeleine are both in second marriages, however, so that each child has a step-parent, and neither child has any blood relation to the other. So, like Ham and Little Emily, Beth and Michael are possible sexual partners, but have to play the role of siblings. All this looks as if it might be taken from a psychological textbook — one notes the 'grouping by initials' of the Studdards, reminiscent of Dickens once more — and indeed in *Red Shift* Tom, the male (modern) protagonist remarks that the trouble with his parents is 'they're not in a textbook'. He even refers at one point to memories of Freud's 'primal scene', the first awareness of parental copulation, though it is explained with perfect naturalism: he has lived all his life in a caravan, and observes gloomily that even if you wear headphones, caravans *move*.

There is no doubt then, that all four stories spring from child-parent tension, and from adolescent sexual tension, while they also share a closely similar structure. They vary a great deal within these established limits. Yet all four, besides being so clearly 'family drama' are also fantasies or romances: and it is the relation between these two elements which makes them generically interesting.

There is perhaps most doubt about the fantasy/reality relationship in *A Game of Dark*. In each of this book's eleven chapters Jackson finds himself both in this world and in another one; and in the latter it slowly transpires that it is his duty to become a lord and kill a 'worm' which has terrorised his dimly-imagined city not only by devouring people and cattle and reducing them to hair and rags, but also by its harrowing cries and nauseating stench. In the end Jackson fails in open, St. George-like combat, but kills it by digging a pit in its icy trail and stabbing it from beneath. What, though, we cannot help asking, does this recurrent dream of the 'worm' have to do with his daily life?

The answers are not difficult. The worm has something to do with his father. This is not (apparently) because of any phallic associations, but because its cold, its horror, its sheer repulsion suggest both that it is a representation of the disease that is killing his father, and even more powerfully that it represents the guilt Jackson feels — and which, we come to realise, he has consistently been *made* to feel. Jackson's case-history is too neat to be true. He is a second child; the first child, a daughter, was killed the day he was born; in the same accident his father was crippled; Jackson is seen by his parents as a deep disappointment, for not being the dead daughter come back. Jackson's father all but calls him 'Cecily' at one point. Half a dozen naturalistic incidents show Jackson being given both more responsibility and more blame than he can bear.

From this real world, it is abundantly clear that the fantasy-world is an escape. The worm is nauseating, but it can be killed. In the real world Jackson cannot even hope that his father will die (though he does die, seemingly, at the very end, just after the worm has been destroyed). The fantasy world is also full of hunger, duties, beatings and disobedience, but at least it is clear cut. One could well say that the horror of reality, for Jackson, in the *monde vulgaire*, is the weight of social expectation which comes down against all his deepest feelings. He is not supposed to like the Anglican vicar, Berry, who acts as his surrogate father; he *is* supposed to like his real father. He is not supposed to want to get out of his home all the time; but it is a cold home, unlike the strange, disorderly, but friendly homes he observes his acquaintances living in. A final observation is that *A Game of Dark* obeys a basic rule of family-drama very carefully, in that all major characters can be seen as either father-figures, mother-figures, or 'splits' of the protagonist — this latter including the 'knight' in the other world who refuses battle and rides away from the worm, as also Miral, his other-world rival, and Nessing, his this-world friend.[21] It has however very little sense of any potential sexual partner.

What good does it do Jackson to indulge his 'escapism' and kill the fantasy-worm? This question is barely answered in *A Game of Dark*, except on the last page, where there is a moving parallel of Jackson abandoning fantasy to start again 'where reality was', and Mr. Jackson apparently dying, with the words of the *Nunc dimittis*. It seems as if Jackson has confronted a fear, shed a guilt, done an easier task to make himself better able to do a hard one. However the parallels point in this direction much more sharply in *The Beginning Place*: a work which furthermore makes very clear statements about the function of fantasy.

It too is a book about dragon-slaying. In it Hugh and Irene both find their way independently from an American city to a pastoral world of forest and mountain. The force which drives them is again unmistakable. Hugh, in particular, leads a life of strongly-realised horror in his perfectly naturalistic home. He is the only child of a 'single-parent family', whose father deserted them years before. His mother accordingly has a terror of being left alone, and insists on having Hugh present all the time, watching television, when he is not at his totally tedious job as a supermarket cashier. Yet while she demands his presence, she also resents it. What she resents, Hugh realises, is the fact that he is male and nearly twenty-one: 'it was his deep voice, his size, his big feet and thick fingers, his heavy sexual body that she couldn't stand, that drove her to the edge'. She responds therefore with various devices of psychological castration: keeping him at home, belittling him, overfeeding him, nagging, and

---

[21]   Miral, we are told, is literally a bastard; Berry says at one point, jokingly, 'Nessing's a bastard, tell him from me'. The point seems to be that Jackson would *like* to be a bastard, i.e. fatherless. But he sees this also as an evasion. Miral, Nessing, and Sir Percecoeur all represent escape-routes for the protagonist, which he must not take.

acting on the assumption that he is totally incapable. Hugh in other words does not have to 'kill his father'; but he *does* have to 'dodge his mother'. Irene meanwhile has in a perfectly literal way to dodge the sexual advances of her stepfather (and of other men in a sexually aggressive society). Both protagonists also have to avoid repeating the errors of their same-sex parent, running away, in Hugh's father's case, abandoning independence, in Irene's mother's.

Is their flight into the other world from the *méchant monde*, this *monde vulgaire*, not a running-away? In a sense it is. But one should note that there are further potential false escapes even in that world. Irene for instance feels strong rejection for Hugh, strong attraction to one of the characters in it, Master Sark. But Sark, we realise, is an appeaser. When the dragon came to his world before, his grandfather took what he sees as the sensible decision to give it a girl, his own daughter, as sacrifice. Sark himself cannot face the dragon, or open the roads it has blocked; Irene will not reach 'the City' with him. He represents for her a false choice, a fixing of the emotions on a 'father-figure' who, like Lear or Agamemnon, sees daughters only as creatures to be used. The true road forward in the other world is for Hugh and Irene to face and kill the dragon.

It is however a *female* dragon. And the whole weight of the structural parallelism of *The Beginning Place* goes towards equating the dragon with Hugh's mother.[22] Both project panic; both are themselves hungry and in pain; when they come to the dragon's den, Hugh seems for a moment to be venturing inside, but instead Irene draws the dragon out. She knew, she says later, that if Hugh went in he would not come out again; the parallel is not only with images of the womb, but with the shut-in suburban houses in which Hugh and his mother have been lurking companionless ever since his father left. If he went back to *that*, he would not escape psychological castration or devouring. But he needs Irene to save him from the dragon, the 'mother-figure', just as Irene needs Hugh to save her from Sark, her 'father-figure'.

Finally, it is a temptation for Hugh at one point just to dismiss the other world as fantasy, 'kid stuff'. His reasoning is that he has no father; also no mother ('There's no use you calling me that'); so he can't be a 'kid'; and since the other world is 'kid stuff' he should abandon it. All the logic here, we can see, is diseased, but the conclusion he comes to, namely that fantasy is 'kid stuff' or mere 'escapism', is one with which many adults would agree. It would lead, though, via worship of hard realism, to a life of hard realism as a supermarket cashier trapped in a house with a neurotically resentful recluse. Ms. Le Guin is in fact putting forward a double argument for fantasy as beneficial: in the first place, she says,

---

[22] Very near the end Hugh is called 'dragonkiller, child of the dragon'.

carrying out the fantasy task of killing the dragon gives Hugh the nerve for his real task, breaking with his mother. So, fantasy is a game of instruction by analogue. In the second place, mere realism prepares the mind only for what an economist's model of society would indicate, namely a life as passive consumer. So, fantasy broadens horizons which have been artifically narrowed. *The Beginning Place* is remarkable above all for the clarity with which it sees a utilitarian relation between its fantasy world and its real one.

It also, and once more, fulfils very nearly ideally the basic rules of 'family drama'. It is about growing up; its basic theme is dodging/killing the mother; all its characters are father-figures, mother-figures, or 'splits' of the protagonists, i.e. images of how the protagonists would if unsuccessful end up. It ends with sexual consummation, Irene abandoning her 'kid's job', Hugh starting a career, the two of them finding a home together. Like Jackson, though, they cannot go back to the other world: it was for them a 'beginning place', a *stage*, if a necessary one. Yet in this highly naturalistic work one still cannot avoid seeing a whole sequence of parallels with Marie de France, and not only on the basic level of Frappier's *mondes* and *régions intermédiaires*. The two protagonists wandering on the desolate, hostile mountain are very like 'les deus amanz'. The world they find themselves in has no sun or moon, like the fairies' *cuntray* of *Sir Orfeo* or the *hoge-* world of *Yonec*.[23] Most strikingly, Hugh's wound, after killing the dragon, is a great bruise from his own sword-hilt, strangely like the rebounding arrow of *Guigemar*. In both the twelfth-century and the twentieth the moral seems the same: you have to hurt your mother when you leave home for good; but hurting your mother ought to hurt you too.

The two remaining 'window' novels further confirm the category of 'family drama', extend the parallels with Breton *lai*. In *The Wind Eye* one might note that the differing dangers of mother to son and father to daughter are seen with special clarity, the former leading to a fierce possessiveness (as in *Equitan*), the latter towards a false and static security. In Beth's time-travels St. Cuthbert — oddly enough for a misogynist saint — rescues her from a half-intention to retire into a nunnery which we see as created by the desire to stay safely asexual. Meanwhile *Red Shift* observes with odd scrupulosity for a modern novel the 'rule' that family drama is protagonist-centred:[24] Tom's father and

---

23 It has to be said that Ms. Le Guin has an academic qualification in French literature, having written an MA thesis in 1952 on the poetry of Ronsard. The 'twilight world' could well be a direct borrowing from Marie, or from *Sir Orfeo*. I think this is less likely of the other and more arcane resemblances cited.

24 See Brewer, op. cit., p. 83.

mother are never seen talking together when he is not there (or very close by) any more than *Sir Gawain and the Green Knight* will give us private conversation between Sir Bertilak and his wife. However both novels also raise a further question, which is how far 'growing up' *is* a 'basic human experience', and how far it is moulded by cultural pattern. Both in fact use their 'time-travel' structures to create a certain sense of modernity, in each case rather regretful.

The Wind Eye is for one thing populated by 'single parents' and stepchildren, an old motif now increasingly returning. This makes for special tensions between Beth and Michael, and also tends to 'halve the plot': neither child has a real same-sex parent to overthrow, while rebellion against a step-parent carries far less guilt and anxiety. More poignantly, *Red Shift* shows a set of new anxieties perhaps peculiar to this century. Tom and Jan are strongly presented as placeless, homeless in a literal sense. What they long for is not physical union, but a home of their own, outside his parents' caravan or her parents' sequence of transient houses; much of the time they are simply looking for a place to sit down in other than Crewe railway station! Here the extended adolescence and dependency of the modern teenager, in training or college for years after puberty, reinforces the ancient urge to get out. But now there is a dangerous stage *beyond* the parental home for protagonists to get stuck in. Tom in fact seems almost to destroy the relationship by selling the 'thunderstone' to a museum. Jan valued it above all because it was permanent, like nothing else she knew, and letting it go — as the two earlier pairs of lovers who possessed it did *not* — seems ominous both for their love and for feelings about family stability in modern times more generally. And yet the scene in which Tom sells it, one has to say, is curiously analogous to the refusal of the *damiseus* to drink the potion in *Les Deus Amanz*! In both cases a young man destroys the probability of long-term future happiness for short-term peace and quiet. Tom meant to use the money from the 'thunderstone' simply to buy more time with Jan in a place where they could be alone, where indeed *Ceste gent [ne] nus escrïereient, De lur noise [ne] m'esturdireient.*

There are differences as well as similarities between twelfth- and twentieth-century patterns. *Red Shift* generates with special power a sense of present-day sexual pressure. In earlier days (it suggests) women might be raped. In the 1970s Jan is obliged in a way to violate herself, to give herself to an older man simply from loneliness and fear of being 'abnormal'. As a result she too comes very close to destroying her relationship with her true partner. But this is only to repeat that modern adolescents have found themselves yet one more uneasy march or borderland to inhabit, after reaching sexual maturity but before they can hope for its financial or domestic equivalent. In these circumstances, one has to say, the 'father-figure' becomes especially insidious to the young woman, and dangerous to the young man. *Red Shift* and *The Beginning Place* point together to a shift of emphasis away from the theme of killing the same-sex parent, and towards the theme of dodging the opposite-sex parent (whether real or disguised). Yet the major utility of these 'window' stories lies not in their hints of cultural difference, but in their strong demonstration of how tales of fantasy are commonly read.

The argument by analogy is simply this. The four modern novels are clearly 'family dramas'. They are also unmistakably fantasies. The delight which modern readers take in them must come very largely from the sheer pleasure of relating the one to the other, observing the transformations of reality to fantasy and vice-versa. This can of course be done at subtle or at elementary levels. However many readers of *The Beginning Place* must certainly have said to themselves, 'Ah, I see now that the dragon is the same as Hugh's mother'; many readers of *The Wind Eye* must have reflected that what St. Cuthbert had taught Beth was that she needed to get away from her father, and *not* by going into a nunnery. Many more who did not say or reflect these things must nevertheless have realised them. Interpreting fantasy, in short, is rather like interpreting dreams: people take pleasure in working out parallelisms, but also in feeling themselves thrust away from too easy formulations. This is commonplace, and not confined to literary critics.

If this can be so for modern readers, could it not have been so for the audiences of Breton *lais*? No doubt much was dissimilar. Still, it is odd that so many images should recur — the twilight world, the hostile mountain, the rebounding weapon, the disastrous urge to privacy, the window, the *région intermédiaire*. But if modern readers can 'decode' these, why should medieval ones not have done the same? Furthermore, the comparison does suggest how medieval audiences (like modern ones) could cheerfully put up with the experience of reading one transformation after another of the same story. It is true, as Professor Burrow says, that there is something frustrating in having all one's favourite stories reduced to the same set of 'latent significances'. That does not mean they all have different significances. It means only that the critic's decoding has stripped away the levels of transformation which were always an essential part of the pleasure of reading.

The audience of Marie de France, in other words, might have pondered the relation of *Equitan* to *Guigemar*, or of *Le Fresne* to *Eliduc*, in much the same way as a modern reader might brood over the links between the two worlds of *A Game of Dark*, or the three layers of *Red Shift*. Their pondering might further have taken the form of generalisations about *amur* or *mesure*, just as a modern reviewer is liable to draw morals about 'broken homes' and 'single parents'. Such observations would however miss the point that the true force of the stories, medieval or modern, came from the tension with which one follows the protagonists' struggle for independence, the efforts of all those around them to hurt, shame, or seduce them back to childhood and subservience.

I have only to add that the modern 'window' stories seem to me clearly superior didactically, in explaining to children nowadays how to cope with the unfair pressures society puts on them. On the other hand the Breton *lais* seem a more adult and mature form. They recognise disturbing notions, as: that mothers have rights too (*Eliduc*); that finding a mate is not the end of growing up (*Le Fresne, Sir Orfeo*); that not everyone wants to grow up (*Les Deus Amanz*); that you cannot always expect to win, or to return (*Laüstic, Lanval*); perhaps in an extreme case, that it is rather pleasant to give up trying and relapse into mere masculine *camaraderie* (*Bisclavret*). Such morals are a long way from the overall, or official, thesis of 'family drama'. Yet they have been achieved by relatively simple narrative transformations.

The Folk-Tale Element in
Sir Gawain and the Green Knight·

CLAUDE LUTTRELL

Even since Kittredge published his fundamental study of *Sir Gawain and the Green Knight* and its analogues in 1916, discussion of the models for this romance has been almost entirely conducted in terms of the beheading and the temptation themes, which he held to be the chief narrative components that have been brought together in it.[1] Undoubtedly the Beheading Match originates in an Irish epic pattern that passed to Arthurian romances, but for the theme of temptation no such clear descent has been shown. We shall see that the resemblance of *Sir Gawain* to a particular folk-tale type illuminates this feature of the romance.

The stay at the castle in *Sir Gawain* is related to an international popular tale that is widely distributed, particularly in Europe and Asia, and so ancient that it was adapted in the story of Jason and Medea. The earliest proper records of it are in literary collections, first in eleventh-century Sanskrit and then in the Italian Renaissance. Tales of this type tell the following:

> *The Tasks.* The hero is at the castle of an evil being (a demon, devil, troll, giant, supernatural old man, sorcerer, etc.), who on each of three successive days imposes on him an impossible task on pain of death. The hero manages to achieve the tasks because the evil being's daughter, who has magic powers like her parent, is secretly in league with the hero and gives him aid.
>
> *The Flight.* She elopes with the hero, and outwits her pursuing parent in a magic (transformation or obstacle) flight.

· Reprinted, with minor alterations and additions, from *Studies in Philology*, LXXVII (1980), 105 – 27.

[1] G. L. Kittredge, *A Study of Gawain and the Green Knight* (Cambridge, Mass., 1916), pp. 137 – 9, 196 – 7.

What I have here described is the kind of tale known as Type 313 according to the classification in Aarne and Thompson, *The Types of the Folktale*.[2]

In England there has been little report of this tale-type, but few folk-tales of the *Märchen* kind have come to light in England, although from literary references it is evident that many of the international popular tales were once known here. Type 313 is very popular in Ireland, and good illustration of it has been found in Scotland.

The pattern of *The Tasks* typically has the evil being leaving at dawn (sunrise), with the day's impossible task having to be achieved by the hero before the master's return at nightfall (sundown). He may have gone hunting, from which he comes home "as usual".[3] I take the Scottish-Gaelic tale "Bodach Glas" as illustration of this. The master specifies in the morning that "I am going a-hunting to the mountain"; if the hero has not got the task ready "when I come home from the mountain on which I go to hunt", he will lose his head. The task is done "before the 'Bodach Glas' returned from the mountain on which he had been hunting on that evening". Later on in the tale his daughter reminds the hero several times of how on each day she had accomplished a task for him "before the 'Bodach Glas' came home from the mountain on which he was hunting".[4] In *Sir Gawain*, we have the host urging an arrangement by which he himself will go hunting while the hero remains at ease in the castle, and on the return from the hunt there is to be an exchange, the host giving whatever he has gained and Gawain providing "*quat chek so ȝe acheue*" (1107), i.e., whatever feat he achieves; this, in the castle life proposed for him, will obviously not be of the same nature as those in

---

2   There is a general description of Type 313 in S. Thompson, *The Folktale* (New York, 1951), pp. 88 – 90. The analysis of Type 313 in A. Aarne and S. Thompson, *The Types of the Folktale* (FF Communications, 184, Helsinki, 1961) is an abstraction on a high level. Of analyses in closer touch with folk-tales, for my purpose the following proved to be the most useful: H. Holmström, *Studier över svanjungfrumotivet* (Lund, 1919), pp. 17 – 18, 133 – 6; the section on Type 313 in P. Delarue, *Le conte populaire français* (Paris, 1957); R. Th. Christiansen, *Studies in Irish and Scandinavian Folktales* (Copenhagen, 1959), pp. 81 – 108. Since the picture of any folk-tale type does not emerge properly without extensive study of actual examples, I have collected, examined, and compared a large number of published stories of Type 313 in order to be guided in my descriptions by direct knowledge.

The Greek myth of the Argonauts utilises Type 513B (which has a wonderful ship and a band of wonderful companions) for the introduction, the fusion of the two kinds of tale resulting in the necessary modification of both. See K. Jackson, *The International Popular Tale and Early Welsh Tradition* (Cardiff, 1961), p. 73.

3   For example, J. F. Campbell, *Popular Tales of the West Highlands* (Paisley and London, 1890 – 3), i.53; J. Curtin, *Myths and Folk-Lore of Ireland* (Boston, 1890), p. 32. Here and elsewhere I cite by the first page of a tale.

4   *The Celtic Magazine*, XII (1887), 12, 57.

Wars of Alexander 3098: *And cheued him of cheualry chekis out of nombre.* On three successive days the host is out hunting in the hills from sunrise to sunset, and in the meantime at the castle, through an act performed by the host's wife, Gawain achieves a feat.

In the international popular tale, while the master is away his daughter comes and talks privily with the hero on each of the three days, and on her own initiative she enables him to get each day's task done. And since she acts against her father in helping the hero, we may find her requiring him to keep their dealings secret from her father. This, in any case, is implied. When the master returns, the hero shows him on each of the three days that the task has been accomplished; and, if it is an object that has to be obtained, he delivers it to him. Then the master of the castle makes some comment which expresses suspicion that his daughter has helped the hero, e.g., "You've not sucked this knowledge out of your own breast".[5] The young man, however, gives nothing away. For instance:

> He says, "Wha's helpin' ye, Jack?" He says, "Nobody's helpin' me." He says, "Somebody's helpin' ye, Jack." Jack says, "No!"[6]

In the romance, while the host is away his wife comes on each of the three days to Gawain's bedroom for intimate conversation, and it is by her initiative that he receives a kiss on the first day, two on the second, and three on the third; these kisses enable him to fulfil the arrangement made with his host by giving the kisses to him on his return to the castle each evening. In addition, on the third occasion the lady makes a present of a girdle to Gawain, asking him to keep it secret from her lord. On the first day his host remarks that what Gawain has given him in the exchange may be the better prize — so hinting that the kiss may have been taken from his wife, in whose care he has left Gawain — and inquires where he has managed to obtain this valuable possession. But Gawain refuses to disclose the source, saying that it was not part of the agreement to do so:

> "Hit may be such hit is þe better, and ȝe me breue wolde
> Where ȝe wan þis ilk wele bi wytte of yorseluen."
> "Þat watz not forward," quoþ he, "frayst me no more."
> (*Sir Gawain and the Green Knight* 1393 – 5)[7]

---

[5] In the classic example of Type 313 in P. C. Asbjørnsen and J. Moe, *Norske Folkeeventyr* (2nd ed., Christiania, 1852), p. 278, translated as "The Mastermaid" by G. Dasent, *Popular Tales from the Norse*, p. 71 (in my copy, 3rd ed., Edinburgh, 1888).

[6] From "The Green Man of Knowledge", printed and discussed by H. Hamilton in *Scottish Studies*, II (1958), 47 – 85.

[7] Citations from *Sir Gawain and the Green Knight* are taken from the edition by J. R. R. Tolkien and E. V. Gordon, 2nd ed., rev. N. Davis (Oxford, 1967).

On the second day, the host comments that Gawain will soon be rich if he does such business. And on the third day he observes that Gawain is becoming very prosperous with the profit from this merchandise, if he bought on favourable terms: *"ʒe cach much sele In cheuisaunce of þis chaffer, ʒif ʒe hade goud chepez"* (1938 – 9). Gawain brushes off the implication, quickly answering, in the same vein as his host, that the terms on which he bought do not matter, the essential being that the acquisition has been promptly handed over in discharge of his obligation:

> "ʒe, of the chepe no charg," quoþ chefly þat oþer,
> "As is pertly payed þe [porchaz][8] þat I aʒte."
> (*Sir Gawain and the Green Knight* 1940 – 1)

However, as desired by the host's wife, Gawain keeps her present of the girdle secret.

So both in Type 313 and in *Sir Gawain* we have the three successive days on which the master of the castle is out from sunrise to sunset, engaged in hunting, while the young lady comes to the hero and holds privy discourse with him. As regards the task elements, in both accounts — though there is considerable disparity between them — as a result of the young lady's initiative the hero is provided with feats which, in discharge of the obligation that has been laid on him by the master of the castle, he renders to him on his return. Again, in both tale-type and romance she requires the hero to keep their secret from the master of the castle, and he does so. The master hints that the source of the hero's achievement is the young lady — who is the daughter in Type 313, the wife in *Sir Gawain* — but the hero will not betray that she has provided him with it.

The resemblance between *The Tasks* and the events at the castle in *Sir Gawain* is not coincidental, for there is also correspondence between what leads up to them. The Green Knight makes a challenge to a game, and by saying that it is a game for the Christmas season he emphasises the idea of play. That the Beheading Match is here termed a game has been said to be a rather bizarre notion of the poet's.[9] For although there is a *jeu* in Arthurian analogues, it is a *jeu parti*, i.e., a choice offered between two parts in a contest, the opponent receiving whichever happens to be the other part: in the case of a beheading match the hero is given the choice of being either the first striker or the first receiver of the decapitating blow.[10]

---

[8] For *porchaz* instead of the cited edition's *chepez*, see the editor's note.

[9] *Two Old French Gauvain Romances*, ed. R. C. Johnston and D. D. R. Owen (Edinburgh, 1972), ii.173.

[10] The offer of the choice is set out most clearly in a German romance, *Diu Krône*, 13104 – 7, ed. G. H. F. Scholl (Bibliothek des literarischen Vereins in Stuttgart, XXVII, Stuttgart, 1852.

And naturally he chooses to be the first striker of it. It has been suggested that this so-called *jeu parti* may be responsible for the conception of a game in the English romance, but in fact there is no *jeu parti* in the episode in *Caradoc* (part of the First Continuation of Crestien's *Li Contes del Graal*) which is the closest analogue of all to the Beheading Match in *Sir Gawain* and apparently its main source: in both, the challenger simply proposes to have his head cut off and to return the blow a year later. Again, the Green Knight requires Gawain to discover his place and present himself there in a year and a day, whereas in all other versions of the Beheading Match the return blow is to be received by the hero at the spot at which he decapitated the challenger. In the features of a challenge to a game and the requirement that the hero should undertake a quest for the stranger, before whom he is to present himself in a year and a day, *Sir Gawain* corresponds to a typical introduction to *The Tasks*.

Of the regular introductions, the oldest recorded is that of the hero pursuing a bird to the demon's castle. Many a folk-tale pattern of sufficiently wide distribution to indicate great age is recorded no earlier than the nineteenth century, when the collecting of popular tales became a scholarly occupation. This is when we know of Type 313 with a Swan Maiden episode preceding *The Tasks*, a form of the story which occurs throughout Europe, and in which the hero has set out in quest of the castle because he is under an obligation to go there.[11] Especially in the eastern parts of Europe and in Denmark, the hero is promised before his birth to a stranger, who is the Devil, etc.[12] Typical of Western Europe is another kind of introduction to this form of Type 313, in which the hero comes into the evil being's power through getting into debt to him and having to pay it by going to his castle. It may happen in more than one way, but what Holmström specifies as the mark of this branch of Type 313 is the pattern we require: Youth plays game with stranger, loses, promises to come to his castle in a year and a day, sets out on the way there.[13] This game-introduction is a favourite in Ireland, where it occurs, as Christian-sen has shown, in half of the great number of accounts recorded there

---

[11] On this form of Type 313, see Holmström (note 2 above).

[12] Holmström's motif H2.

[13] Motif H1. Of the tales that Holmström assigns to this branch of Type 313, I find that the following have H1 or a close variant: German GT 42, Breton KB 4, 7, Irish KI 2, 4, Italian RI 15, 25, Rhaeto-Roman RL 4, Portuguese RP 1, Brazilian RP 5, Spanish RS 1, 2, 3, Welsh Gypsy ÖZ 3, Jamaican Am 2. To be distinguished, but as a closely-related group, are the versions in which the hero loses riches gambling and then meets the stranger, who imposes the condition of coming to him at his castle (in a year and a day) in return for receiving riches (Breton KB 8, French RF 5) or the means of winning (Flemish GH 1, Walloon RF 3). Further removed are the versions in which the stranger imposes the condition in return for giving the hero riches, but the gambling motif is lacking.

which belong to Type 313. A distinctive feature here is the laying of *geasa* on the Gaelic hero to compel him to carry out the quest.[14] According to Christiansen, the occurrence of the game-introduction elsewhere may, with some reason, indicate Irish influence. Outside Ireland and Scottish-Gaelic he cited only a few examples in Europe,[15] but there are many other instances on the Continent, with the distribution suggesting that France has been another centre of the game-introduction to Type 313.[16] With this opening a folk-tale leads up to *The Tasks* with matter of this kind:

Introduction. The hero is offered a game by a stranger which he loses, typically winning the first two but losing the third of three games; whereupon the stranger requires him to present himself within a year and a day at his castle, but leaves the hero ignorant as to its whereabouts.

Quest. The hero sets out on a quest for the stranger's castle.

The Swan Maiden. The quest is accomplished when the hero comes upon a Swan Maiden bathing, whom he asks for aid in return for letting her have her feather-coat back, and who helps him to reach the castle of the evil being, her father.

---

[14] Christiansen (note 2 above), pp. 17, 101 – 2, (Scottish-Gaelic) 106. Geas (pl. *geasa*) in Gaelic folk-tales is a kind of spell, spoken to the victim in some formula of traditional pattern, that lays him under a compulsion, usually to carry out a task. Christiansen had 50 tales of Type 313 in Ireland available for his survey in 1939. Since then, the activity of the Irish Folklore Commission has brought to light a mass of folk-tales, and S. O Suilleabhain and R. Th. Christiansen, *The Types of the Irish Folktale* (FF Communications, 188, Helsinki, 1963), record for Type 313 about 450 versions (plus by-forms), which are largely in manuscript. These should provide a great abundance of tales with the game-introduction.

Some examples with the game-introduction available in English are: P. Colum, *The King of Ireland's Son* (New York, 1916), p. 5; J. Curtin, *Irish Folk-Tales* (Dublin, 1943 = supplement to *Béaloideas*, 11, 12), p. 24; his *Myths and Folk-Lore of Ireland* (Boston, 1890), p. 32 (Holmström's KI 2); *Folk-Lore*, XXVI (1915), 191; *Folk-Lore Journal*, I (1883), 316 (Holmström's KI 4); A. P. Graves, *The Irish Fairy Book* (London, 1938), p. 182; M. F. MacGeehin, *The Long-Tailed Hen* (Dublin, 1934), p. 31; S. MacManus, *The Bold Heroes of Hungry Hill* (London, 1952), p. 15; his *In Chimney Corners* (New York, 1919), p. 259; P. Mullen, *Irish Tales* (London, 1938), p. 47.

[15] On some instances of Type 313 with the game-introduction in Norway and Sweden, see Christiansen, pp. 82, 91, 96, 226 – 9.

[16] Under Type 313 in Delarue (note 2 above) the complex of motifs A (Un jeune homme), A2 (perd tout ce qu'il a en jouant), B (le héros tombe ainsi au pouvoir du diable), C (Il doit se rendre chez lui dans un an et un jour), D (II part) is shown as occurring in the introduction of several tales: (Nivernais) 10, 11, 13, 16, 22, (Breton) 33 (Holmström's KB 4), 49 (Holmström's KB 7), (Limousin) 66, (French Canada) 89, 92, 93, (Antilles) 106, 109. In a related group of tales, the hero loses riches gambling (A2), then meets the stranger and is given riches (7, 8, 40, 44, 46, 50, 51, 53, 54, 55, 57, 59, 60, 62, 64, 79) or the means of winning (83, 84), thus falling into his power (B) and having to go to him at his castle (C). In another group of tales, the stranger imposes the same condition in return for giving the hero riches, but the gambling motif is lacking. Cf. note 13 above.

For example, in both Ireland and Brittany we have a version in which a prince out hunting meets a stranger and plays cards with him, eventually betting head for head. He loses, and is required to pay the debt in a year and a day at the stranger's castle.[17] Similarly, Gawain has to go to the Green Knight's place in a year and a day to surrender his head. The Breton hero asks "Mais, quel est votre nom et où demeurez-vous?", rather like Gawain:

> "Where shulde I wale þe," quoþ Gauan, "where is þy place?
> I wot neuer where þou wonyes, bi hym þat me wroȝt,
> Ne I know not þe, knyȝt, þy cort ne þi name."
> (*Sir Gawain and the Green Knight* 398 – 400)

In the Breton folk-tale the answer is "Mon nom est Barbauvert, et quant au château que j'habite, vous le chercherez et ferez en sorte de le trouver". Or the strange name given in the reply may be that of the place to be discovered. Thus, in an Irish version, the stranger says, "Within a year and a day from this you're to find out my castle, where I live when I'm at home"; and the hero asks, "And who are you?", receiving the answer "I'm the Giant of Band-Beggars' Hall".[18] Similarly, the Green Knight instructs Gawain that "*þou schal seche me þiself, where-so þou hopes I may be funde vpon folde*" (395 – 6), and hardly throws light on his identity with the information that he is the Knight of the Green Chapel.

For our purpose, a striking feature of the game-introduction to *The Tasks* in the British Isles is the existence of a tradition in which the challenger to the game is green. The Gypsy tale from Wales, noticed by Kittredge in his study of *Sir Gawain*, in fact belongs to Type 313. In this a gentleman comes and challenges Jack, a great gambler, to a game of cards; Jack first wins, but then he loses; and the stranger tells Jack that his name is the Green Man Who Lives in No Man's Land, and that unless Jack finds his castle in a year and a day he will be beheaded.[19] To Type 313 also belongs the Irish-Gaelic tale that Kittredge referred to, *Curadh Glas an Eolais*, "The Green Knight of Knowledge" (*glas* "green; gray"). Here the King of Ireland's son is challenged to a game of cards by a stranger who arrives in a skiff. The prince wins the first two games, but loses the third, and the Green Knight of Knowledge imposes on him the obligation

---

[17] Curtin, *Myths and Folklore*, p. 32; F. M. Luzel, *Contes populaires de Basse-Bretagne* (Paris, 1887), ii.355.

[18] MacManus, *In Chimney Corners*, p. 259.

[19] A more modern edition than that used by Kittredge is J. Sampson, *XXI Welsh Gipsy Folk-Tales* (Newtown, 1933), p. 17.

of discovering his abode in a year and a day, or else he will lose his head.[20] In 1958 the folk-tale scholar Hamish Hamilton published a Lowland Scots version of Type 313 from Aberdeen in which Jack, a proficient card-player, goes to an inn and joins in a game of cards with a man dressed in green from head to foot. Jack here wins. Before leaving, the stranger answers Jack's inquiry about him by saying that he is the Green Man of Knowledge (cf. *Curadh Glas an Eolais*), and lives East o' the Moon and West o' the stars. Jack sets out to find the place where he lives.[21] This tale was compared by Hamilton with another Lowland Scots version which follows the familiar pattern, and where the challenger is called Green Sleeves. The King of Scotland's son delights much in gambling, chiefly skittles. A strange old man appears one day and challenges him. The old man wins, and commands the prince to discover his name and abode before that day twelve months, or to suffer death.[22] Hamilton further cited a Scottish-Gaelic version *Fear Uain Oraid*, where the King of Ireland's son is challenged by a strange horseman to a game of cards. The prince wins twice, but loses the third game; and the stranger, who says that his name is the Green Man of Speech, puts him under the obligation of discovering where he lives, before a year is out.[23] As also noted by Hamilton, the name of the challenger in two Irish versions is Green Leaf and Green Levery.[24] I may add another Scottish-Gaelic version, which has already been mentioned to illustrate the hunting activity of the imposer of the tasks. A king's son habitually goes to the top of a knoll to play shinty and one day finds an old man there who challenges him to a game. The stranger, who is called Bodach Glas (*bodach* "churl; old man", *glas* "green; gray"), wins all three games, and lays on the prince the obligation of seeking him through the world until he is found.[25]

Hamilton showed that the nomenclature in the Welsh Romany tale betrays an English origin, and observed that the presence of a Green Man in a Lowland Scottish tale, and also in a Gaelic one, does not necessarily mean that Gaelic nomenclature has come over into Scots; it could mean the reverse. He suggested that an unrecovered English folk version of Type 313 is one of the sources of *Sir Gawain*. His view concerning the significance of the colour green with the challenger in the folk-tales has much in common with the view of the Green Knight held by John Speirs, who explained him from a Vegetation myth supposed to be represented in

---

[20]   J. M. O'Reilly, *Curadh Glas an Eolais* (Dublin, 1905).
[21]   See note 6 above.
[22]   *Transactions of the Buchan Field Club*, IX (1906 – 8), 170; summary in K. M. Briggs, *A Dictionary of British Folk-Tales* (London, 1970 – 1), A.i.296.
[23]   Summaries in Henderson, p. 71, and Jackson (note 2 above), pp. 11 – 12.
[24]   Listed in *Béaloideas*, II (1930), 189.
[25]   See note 4 above.

England by Jack-in-the-Green (the walking bush of the May festival), by the foliate head of medieval church ornament, and by the folk play (belonging to Christmas), where the central episode is a mock beheading or slaying followed by a revival or restoration of life.[26] Hamilton's inclination was to suppose that

> in certain versions of 313 the figure of the adversary has at some stage, and for some mysterious reason, become identified with the Green Man of the pub signs, the mummers' plays and the church roof bosses. One might hazard an explanation along the following lines: when the "playing episode" or "beheading game" attached itself as a lead-in to versions of the 313 tale-type, the decapitation motif, with its overtones of death and resurrection, *may* have led by association to the identification of the adversary with the Green Man of the fertility rites, who (like John Barleycorn) is killed and springs up again.

However, the mummers' plays have no Green Man, there is no evidence in England for such a figure being killed in fertility rites, and the term was not used of Jack-in-the-Green, which took part in an eighteenth-century practice of begging by chimney sweeps. Traditionally a Green Man is a figure dressed in green, whether in leaves or in a green costume, and this was reflected in inn signs. The term has been applied to the foliate head simply by modern convention; here the foliage, sprouting from mouth, etc., may be decorative rather than significant.[27] Hamilton's tentative theory about the Green Man in Type 313 is thus even more speculative than it sounds.

Let us look at a version of Type 313 told by a soldier in western Germany and printed in the middle of the nineteenth century. The King of Eiland's son Jacob, who plays cards day and night, comes across a man in the forest who is dressed in green and offers to play with him: if the hero loses, he will be his. When the prince asks him his name, he says that it is Grünus Kravalle. Prince Jack first wins, but then he loses, and the stranger gives the hero a year and a day to find him. With this he disappears, and the prince now realises with whom he has been dealing. The challenger, we should note, wears the green coat of a huntsman, being described as *ein Jägersmann im grünen Rock*.[28] Such a figure is a

---

[26]   J. Speirs, *Mediaeval English Poetry: The Non-Chaucerian Tradition* (London, 1957), pp. 219–20.

[27]   See J. Larwood and J. C. Hotten, *The History of Signboards* (3rd ed., London, 1866), pp. 366–8, and plates x, xiv, xv; F. W. Hackwood, *Inns, Ales, and Drinking Customs of Old England* (London, 1909), p. 296; K. Basford, *The Green Man* (Ipswich, 1978), pp. 18–21; R. Judge, *The Jack in the Green* (Cambridge, England, 1979, pp. 68–77.

[28]   J. W. Wolf, *Deutsche Hausmärchen* (Leipzig, 1851), p. 286.

commonplace of German folklore, as a phantom huntsman, the huntsman of the Wild Hunt, or the Devil. Dressed in green from head to foot, the Devil is said to be *ein grüner Jäger* (a green huntsman), also *ein grüner Mann* (a green man), and comes to be called *der Grüne* (the Green One), as well as being termed *Grünrock* (Greencoat).[29] How widespread this representation of the Devil once was in western Europe may be judged from Chaucer's *Friar's Tale*, in which the green dress of the huntsman is worn by the fiend who assumes the guise of a forester and finally makes off with the summoner, who has fallen into his hands, and by Pierre Bercheur's comment, in the middle of the fourteenth century, that *diabolus* habitually wears the green clothes of a huntsman in the stalking of his victims.[30]

The Devil entices a man into a contract with him in order to lead him to perdition. When the hero is playing a gambling game, the Devil may come as a huntsman and challenge him, eventually proposing to play soul for soul. *Der Grüne* plays against the gambler at the inn, and identifies himself only by some odd pseudonym.[31] If people are playing cards when they should be at church, they are joined by an unknown forester in green attire, a stranger in green hunting clothes, or wearing a long, green mantle, who is *der Teufel*.[32] Identical with this gambling scene is that in the tale from Aberdeen, "The Green Man of Knowledge", Scottish folklore having preserved the Devil's green clothes into modern times.[33] Jack hears the bells of a village, "like a church-bell ringin' awa", enters the inn there

[29] *Handwörterbuch des deutschen Aberglaubens*, ed. H. Bächtold-Stäubli (Berlin and Leipzig, 1927 – 42), iii.1182; J. and W. Grimm, *Kinder- und Hausmärchen*, No. 43; J. Jegerlehner, *Sagen und Märchen aus dem Oberwallis* (Basel, 1913), i.45, 90, 195; C. Kohlrusch, *Schweizerisches Sagenbuch* (Leipzig, 1854 – 6), p. 60; R. Kühnau, *Schlesische Sagen* (Breslau, 1910 – 13), ii.636, 646, 665, iii.43; E. Meier, *Deutsche Sagen, Sitten und Gebräuche aus Schwaben* (Stuttgart, 1852), p. 168; E. L. Rochholz, *Schweizersagen aus dem Aargau* (Aarau, 1856 – 7), ii.203; F. Schönwerth, *Aus der Oberpfalz: Sitten und Sagen* (Augsburg, 1857 – 9), i.370; I. V. Zingerle, *Sagen, Märchen und Gebräuche aus Tirol* (Innsbruck, 1859), p. 287. Cf. the Devil as *l'homme vert* in E. H. Carnoy, *Littérature orale de la Picardie* (Paris, 1883), p. 48; *Mélusine*, II (1884 – 5), 321 (Rhaeto-Roman).

[30] Noted in Berchorius by D. W. Robertson, "Why the Devil wears Green", *MLN*, LXIX (1954), 470 – 2.

[31] Zingerle, p. 269; the poem "Der Karfunkel" among the *Alemannische Gedichte* by J. P. Hebel (1760 – 1826).

[32] N. Gredt, *Sagenschatz des Luxemburger Landes* (Luxemburg, 1885), p. 315; Kühnau, ii.609; A. Meiche, *Sagenbuch des Königreichs Sachsen* (Leipzig, 1903), p. 474.

[33] Recorded in Scottish witch-trials during the 16th and 17th centuries; see M. Murray, *The Witch-Cult in Western Europe* (Oxford, 1921), pp. 36, 37, 43, 113, 229. A green hunting coat is worn by the Devil (under a pseudonym) in J. Hogg, *The Private Manners and Confessions of a Justified Sinner* (1824), ed. J. Carey (London, 1969), pp. 208, 223.

and finds a card-playing group, of whom one is dressed head to foot in green, "O a very cunnin'-lookin' man", the stranger with whom he plays in a game-introduction to *The Tasks*.

One version of Type 313 has been collected in England, from north-country gypsies, under the title of "Daughter Greengown". A young man, fond of playing cards, is challenged to a game by an old gentleman. The young man first wins, but then he loses, and is required to search for the stranger for a year and a day. The adversary is defined by the variants as: definitely the Devil; the Devil or some other high mulo;[34] not the Devil, but somebody much the same.[35] His devilish quality is thus sufficiently evident. And in the array of Type 313 in France the evil being is typically called *le diable*. I conclude that the greenness of the challenger to the game in the folk-tales stems from a tradition in which he is the Fiend in the green dress of a huntsman. With this figure we are to compare the challenger to the game in *Sir Gawain*, in his green costume, who later is an active huntsman in his other role, as Gawain's host.

These parallels between *Sir Gawain* and the tale-type I have been considering are much more convincing than the rather general analogues for the temptation theme in the romance, and indicate that the structure of *Sir Gawain* rests on a combination of the Beheading Match with a form of Type 313. The scenes where the young wife tempts the hero, in the romance, constitute a transformation of the privy dealings between him and the daughter in the international popular tale. It should be observed that the situation of a young lady coming to the hero's bed is typically Arthurian and that it was variously treated, with love-making often prevented, sometimes by the hero himself.[36] The exchange of winnings links this new treatment in *Sir Gawain* with the hero's obligation to render an achievement to the lord on his return at nightfall.

The combination with a form of Type 313 has introduced features which contribute a good deal to the unique power of *Sir Gawain* as a Beheading Match romance. A medieval popular tale, shaped by a process akin to Darwin's "natural selection", presented a model of what had been particularly effective with a very wide range of audience over large tracts of time and space. The connection between folk-tale and *Sir Gawain*, however, does not amount to an equivalence. The romancer is neither giving a version of the international popular tale nor properly following it

---

[34] Gypsy term for a supernatural being.
[35] "Daughter Greengown" is in *Thompson Notebooks* at the Institute of Dialect and Folk Life Studies, University of Leeds. The Director, Mr. S. F. Sanderson, kindly supplied photocopies of the variants. There is a summary in Briggs, A.i.202.
[36] There are some instances in C. Luttrell, *The Creation of the First Arthurian Romance: A Quest* (London and Evanston, 1974), pp. 111–12, 131–2, 268.

as a source, but exploiting it, by selection and adaptation, for his own sophisticated ends.[37]

A Green Man occupying the role of the supernatural challenger to the beheading match raises the question of his devilish nature and suggests that the challenge is the instrument of enticement into his power. However, when the Green Knight arrives at Arthur's court, this suspicion is not brought out. We are told merely that the phenomenon of a green man is there considered to be an illusion (*fantoum and fayry3e*); and that after he has gone, carrying away his decapitated head, Arthur and Gawain, although it is agreed that an extraordinary event has taken place, laugh it off. The king finds it possible to suppress his amazement and take what has happened as a natural part of Christmas festivities:

> "Wel bycommes such craft vpon Cristmasse,
> Laykyng of enterludez, to la3e and to syng,
> Among þise kynde caroles of kny3tez and ladyez."
> (*Sir Gawain and the Green Knight* 471 – 3)

This attempt at a rational explanation is connected with an English medieval custom which has points of contact with the game-introduction to Type 313. It was often banned, and so we find references to it in local records. Two of the passages in the orders of the city of London read:

(A.D. 1334) Also, we do forbid, on the same pain of imprisonment, that any man shall go about at this Feast of Christmas with companions disguised with false faces, or in any other manner, to the houses of the good folks of the City, for playing of dice there . . .

(A.D. 1418) . . . þat no manere persone, of what astate, degre, or condicioun þat euere he be, duryng þis holy tyme of Cristemes be so hardy in eny wyse to walk by nyght in eny manere mommyng, pleyes, enterludes, or eny oþer disgisynges with eny feynyd berdis, peyntid visers, diffourmyd or colourid visages in eny wyse.[38]

This custom was raised to the splendour of a royal occasion of which we have a detailed description. Masked men, disguised and excellently

---

[37]   I have already examined such operation of an Arthurian romancer, on a form of Type 400, in "From Traditional Tale to Arthurian Romance: *Le Chevalier au Lion*", *Nottingham Mediaeval Studies*, XXII (1978), 36 – 57. There I note that variants collected in the modern period can hardly present a true picture of a traditional tale as it was in medieval times, but that nevertheless light is thrown on its plot structure (pp. 36 – 7).

[38]   H. T. Riley, *Memorials of London and London Life* (London, 1868), pp. 193, 669. E. K. Chambers, *The Mediaeval Stage* (Oxford, 1903), p. 394, note 1, cites similar orders at Bristol and Chester. This last shows that the custom existed in the north-west midlands.

arrayed and mounted on horseback, after the fashion of such figures as an emperor, a pope, cardinals, and legates "with black vizards like devils appearing nothing amiable", visited Richard II for his entertainment in the feast of Christmas before his accession in 1377. They rode by night to Kennington, entered the hall on foot, invited the prince and his lords to dice, and discreetly lost, handing over rich presents as the stakes. To the prince they set three jewels, one after the other, which he won at three casts.[39]

The challenger in *Sir Gawain*, whose hair and beard cover the upper part of his body like a cape, who is not only magnificently attired in green but also bright green all over, even his eyebrows shining green, who rides a green horse with a green mane, and seems to belong to the realm of art rather than nature (236: *Þen grene aumayl on golde glowande bryȝter*), in Arthur's pretence is only a figure of the same kind as that going with mask, coloured visage, or feigned beard to people's houses at the time of Christmas festivities to offer the game of dice, and whom we have seen entering a royal hall in some fancy dress, including devilish masks. When the interrupted banquet is resumed in *Sir Gawain*, joy fills the hall, in contrast to the corresponding point of the Beheading Match in *Caradoc*, where anxiety so weighs on the banqueters that they can hardly eat. In the English romance, the conception of a Christmas game gives some refuge from the prospect of the hero's fate, and *Gawan watz glad to begynne þose gomnez in halle* (495). However, the court eventually has to face the truth. What game there has really been consists of Gawain staking head for head on the Green Knight not being supernatural, and losing, with the payment of his head put off for a year. When the time comes for Gawain to set out in order to keep the appointment and receive the return blow, the court recognises well enough what destiny is in store for him, to be beheaded by a supernatural man (681).

Where Gawain has to go for the return blow is a mystery, absent from other versions of the Beheading Match, which focuses attention upon the enigma of the adversary's identity. Instead of the challenger returning to the court, as in the analogous episodes in Irish epic and *Caradoc*, the hero has to set out to discover the location of a person whom no one knows. The apparently hopeless inquiry after his whereabouts is a folk-tale feature:

> Day after day he wandered asking everybody he met if they had seen the man he was seeking — he described him, of course — but nobody had. No matter where he went, nor how far, he could hear nothing.
>
> ("Daughter Greengown")

[39]   Chambers, i.394, note 4.

And ay he frayned, as he ferde, at frekez þat he met,
If þay hade herde any karp of a knyȝt grene,
In any grounde þereaboute, of þe grene chapel;
And al nykked hym wyth nay, þat neuer in her lyue
Þay seȝe neuer no segge þat watz of suche hwez
of grene.
(Sir Gawain and the Green Knight 703 – 8)

A quest in folk-tales is often pursued in conditions of hardship, and the Welsh Gypsy story, ''The Green Man of No Man's Land'', with its hero journeying in frost and deep snow, presents a parallel to Gawain travelling in sleet and ice.[40] By emphasising in this manner Gawain's devotion to his word, the poet underlines the quality that a Beheading Match is calculated to bring out in the hero; at this point, in other versions, the prospect of the return blow is his only, though sufficient, discomfort.

There is no equivalent in the romance to the aid asked for and received by the folk-tale hero from the Swan Maiden, who conducts him to the castle, unless it is Gawain's prayer for harbour, answered by the appearance of the castle in the forest. The Swan Maiden episode, however, may be omitted in the folk-tales, as in ''Grünus Kravalle'', in which the hero comes upon a great castle with soaring walls made of huge stone blocks (*himmelhohe Mauern von mächtigen Steinen*), even as Gawain sees before him a splendid castle where

Þe walle wod in þe water wonderly depe,
Ande eft a ful huge heȝt hit haled vpon lofte
Of harde hewen ston vp to þe tablez. . . .
(Sir Gawain and the Green Knight 787 – 9)

With his arrival at this castle Gawain has found the adversary, as the folk-tale hero does, but Gawain has done so unwittingly. Whereas Grünus Kravalle, for instance, is there and in his green hunting coat, not only are

---

[40] This may raise the question of whether *Sir Gawain* has fed back into folk tradition. Observe, however, that this time of the year for the quest has some parallel in Irish versions of Type 313. The hero sets out after the snow comes in *Béaloideas*, I (1928), 270. In *Curadh Glas an Eolais* we have a passing of the seasons to compare with that in *Sir Gawain*: spring comes, then the season passes, and the next, and we come to autumn, the hero leaving after harvest (at each season the folk-tale hero's departure has been postponed at his mother's urging). The differences between *Sir Gawain* and Type 313, although explicable in terms of the artistic use of the latter in the former, are so substantial that a very obvious common ground, apparently necessary for feedback from a literary text into the originating folk pattern, is hardly present.

105

the inmates of the castle strangely unnamed in the romance — while, in pointed contrast, Gawain's name is made known to them — but it is not yet revealed that the Christmas host is identical with the Christmas adversary. While the mystery of identity is thus increased by the poet, at the same time the suspension of the quest for the Green Knight (when Gawain is told by the lord of the castle that the Green Chapel lies nearby and he is persuaded to stay until the day appointed for him to be there for the return blow) lets implications sink in about the host himself. He comes to Gawain's view as a huge man with a *Felle face as þe fyre* (847), like the sun-god in *Wars of Alexander* 4922, whose burning intensity seems to be a reason for Alexander's perception that he is not of human kind. This quality in the host, along with his energetic maintenance of festive mirth and hunting, makes him dominate the scene as much as the huge Green Knight does Arthur's court by his vigorous and overwhelming presence.

At the castle Gawain sees a host who is well preserved for his years (844: *of hyghe eldee*); his wife, who is young (1526: *a ȝonke þynk*) and more beautiful than Guenevere; and an aged, hideous lady. At the high table the old lady is seated with the master, while Gawain and the fair lady (*þe gay burde*) sit together, enjoying each other's company thoroughly (1001 – 15). The pairing off corresponds to that in Type 313. The master of the castle there (in French called *le diable, le Vieux*, in the Welsh Gypsy tale "The Green Man of No Man's Land" called "the old lord"), I compare to Gawain's host (called in line 1124 *þe olde lorde*); the master's daughter (*la fille du diable*), who becomes the hero's sweetheart, I compare to the young lady in the romance, who in effect tries to become Gawain's; and the master's wife (*la femme du diable, la vieille*, in "The Green Man of No Man's Land" called "the old lady"), who in this demonic family with magical powers is said to be *plus fine et plus dangereuse* than her husband,[41] I compare to *þe olde auncian wyf* (1001), whom the Green Knight later makes out to be Morgan le Fay, the evil fairy with great powers of enchantment. The poet has laid the foundation of a moral test by making the young lady the host's wife instead of his daughter.

The stay at the castle shows how very significant the inspiration of Type 313 has been, since this section, which is unparalleled in Beheading Match accounts, in *Sir Gawain* occupies a commanding position, constituting half of its length and functionally containing its hub. The

---

41   The Devil is traditionally "old" (*antiquus hostis*). His wife is amply illustrated in Type 313 in France, as can be seen from Delarue (note 2 above). "Grey Norris from Warland", *Folk-Lore Journal*, I (1883), 316, habitually cited for the Irish form of Type 313, conveniently serves to show the evil being's wife in Ireland. "Grünus Kravalle" and Grimm, No. 113, do the same for Type 313 in Germany.

importance of the three successive days is reflected in the fullness of their scenic development. Now in the folk-tales we see the master of the castle setting out at sunrise and returning at sunset, with our entire attention fixed on the scene in between, a scene which concerns the hero and the young lady. But there is a significant balance in the romance: the course and the end of the hunt over the landscape are portrayed in fine detail, the activity and the pursuit to death outdoors forming an artistic frame, suggesting parallel and contrast, on either side of the central picture indoors at the castle. And in the romance the motif of decapitation threatened for failure in the tasks is transposed into the bond that binds the events at the castle to the Beheading Match: what happens at the return blow will turn out to depend on Gawain's performance on the three successive days. The daily obligation to the master is discharged, in the romance, as a result of what occurs in the bedroom, as the place where the young lady comes to hold privy discourse with the hero. In the folk-tales, his fate rests on the dealings with her because she saves him from the master, whereas in the romance the situation is reversed by her being secretly in league not with the hero but the host, and Gawain surviving by his own merit (and the support of Virgin Mary) in spite of her efforts to tempt him.

As we approach the climax of the three days, the host drops a hint that Gawain is engaged in a game there with life at stake. After the hero has fully discharged on the first two days the obligation placed on him, his host makes a remark which seems genial, but which hides a threat:

> "For I haf fraysted þe twys, and faythful I fynde þe.
> Now 'þrid tyme þrowe best' þenk on þe morne;[42]
> Make we mery quyl we may and mynne vpon joye,
> For þe lur may mon lach when-so mon lykez."
> (*Sir Gawain and the Green Knight* 1679 – 82)

The lord sees his daily tests of the hero as casts of dice, as if Gawain has so far won twice: "I have tested you twice, and I find you reliable. Now take heed on the morrow of the saying 'Third time, the lucky throw'; let us make merry while we can and be intent on joy, for a man may face misfortune any time he likes." That is, although Gawain should bear in mind the likelihood of his host winning on the metaphorical third cast of the dice, he is to postpone this thought to the next day. The ominous maxim[43] that follows does not suggest to Gawain the death penalty which losing this game might entail, for he is unaware that the game at the castle

---

[42] Semi-colon, as in the editions by A. C. Cawley (London, 1962) and R. A. Waldron (London, 1970).

[43] Cf. I Corinthians xv.32: "Let us eat and drink, for tomorrow we die."

is really where he puts his head at stake. He is distracted by the visible threat to his life, the imminent return blow of the Beheading Match, and so fails to hand over the love-gift of the lady's girdle, which she has persuaded him is a talisman with the power of saving him from death, but which (as suggested by its colour combination of green and gold) turns out to be the adversary's belt. In so far as the three days consist of a single sequence of events repeated three times and leading to similar results, they correspond to those which the hero survives with success in the folk-tales: Gawain resists the temptations of illicit love and duly delivers the kisses to the lord of the castle. But inasmuch as Gawain succeeds on the first two occasions and fails on the third, through his concealment of the lady's gift, the rhythm is that of the game-introduction to *The Tasks*, with its pattern of the hero winning twice but losing the third game.

When Gawain presents himself at the Green Chapel for the return blow, it turns out to be a hollow mound covered with vegetation, and Gawain observes that the place has a desolate appearance which makes it a suitable spot for the man dressed in green to hold his devilish rites; he thinks it is the Devil who, with the intention of destroying him, has imposed the obligation of meeting him there (2185 – 94). On the basis of this passage, D. B. J. Randall published an article in 1960 asking ''Was the Green Knight a Fiend?''[44] Indeed, the Green Knight's commanding presence, fine figure, and splendid array, as depicted when he arrived to make the challenge to the game, is paralleled in legends about the Devil. In Germany he often arrives on the scene as a fine, distinguished gentleman dressed in green, and his splendid green attire may also be described as adorned with the combination of gold with the green which is characteristic of the Green Knight.[45] Compare the Prince of this World (John xii.31, xiv.30, xvi.11), who appears in German medieval icono-graphy as an elegant figure behind which evil skulks.[46] Thus one can understand how Gawain could believe the knight in magnificent green

[44]   *SP*, LVII (1960 – 1), 479 – 91.
[45]   B. Baader, *Volkssagen aus dem Lande Baden* (Karlsruhe, 1851), p. 111: ''ein stattlicher Mann in grünen Kleidern.'' Kühnau (note 29 above), ii.665; ''ein Herr in einem schönen grünen Rocke mit goldenen Tressen.'' *Ibid.*, iii.43: ''ein schöner Herr in einem grünen Rocke.'' H. von Pfister, *Sagen und Aberglaube aus Hessen und Nassau* (Marburg, 1885), p. 25: ''in grünem Kleide ein stattlicher vornehmer Herr.'' F. Ranke, *Die deutsche Volkssagen* (*Deutsches Sagenbuch*, ed. F. von der Leyen, München, 1909 – 20, IV), p. 263: ''ein stattlicher Jäger.'' Schönwerth (note 29 above), iii,15: ''ein stattlicher Mann, ein grüner.'' Observe the description of what is specifically called *das stattliche Jägerhabit* of previous centuries, as worn by the phantom huntsman in R. Eisil, *Sagenbuch des Voigtlandes* (Leipzig, 1871), p. 62: ''grünes, reich mit goldenen Tressen besetztes Wamms'' (a green jacket richly trimmed with gold braid).
[46]   J. Réau, *Iconographie de l'art chrétien* (Paris, 1955 – 9), ii.2.355 – 7; *Lexikon der christlichen Ikonographie*, ed. E. Kirschbaum (Freiburg, 1968 – 76), iv.496 – 8.

clothes to be of the same nature as the challenger to the game whom we have seen in the folk-tales. This voicing of Gawain's thought invites us to have the same suspicion.

Gawain's head is apparently at stake when he lowers it to receive the blow, for it has not yet been revealed that what will happen depends on his performance on those three successive days. The Green Knight first makes two feints with the axe, and before the next and final blow (which nicks Gawain in the neck) he says:

> "Halde þe now þe hyȝe hode þat Arþur þe raȝt,
> And kepe þy kanel at þis kest, ȝif hit keuer may."
> (*Sir Gawain and the Green Knight* 2297 – 8)

Which means: "May the exalted order of knighthood that Arthur conferred on you preserve you now, and save your neck at this throw, if it can manage to." The noun *kest* has been taken to mean "stroke" here, but there does not seem to be any instance of such an application, the other examples of "a sudden movement; a blow" in the *MED*, s.v. *cast*, sense 1 (f), occurring in a phrase of different construction, *with (a) cast of* (the eye, the hand), which refers to sudden movement. What the phrase *at þis kest* resembles is *at last cast*, which is in the *MED* under sense 1 (b), "the throwing of dice". There is no dicing in the *Sir Gawain* context, but this does not present a difficulty. Compare the usage of Old Norse *kast* in *í fyrsta kasti* "the first time", *at seinustum köstum* "at the last moment". *At last cast* itself, for which the *MED* gives "at (one's) last throw, with (one's) back to the wall", was transferred from the game of dice, and used so idiomatically that among the *MED*'s citations there will be found an application to a bridge near the end of its life. Gawain's adversary has already used the language of dicing for his daily tests of the hero at the castle, and this time the metaphorical third throw of the dice in prospect is the final stroke of the axe. Once more we have the idea that Gawain has survived two gambles, and is being threatened with loss the next time. This conception in common strengthens the bond between the events at the castle and the return blow of the Beheading Match. Apt use has been found for a feature of the game-introduction to *The Tasks* — that the first two of the set go to the hero, and to his opponent the all-important third.

The poet has thus created three games. Gawain is enticed into the first game, which saddles him with what appears to be a death-contract, by a dominating green-clad figure who also deceives Gawain with the information that he will not fail to find him, because many people know him as the Knight of the Green Chapel (454 – 5); whereas Gawain cannot find people who know him. When at last Gawain finds someone who does know of the Green Chapel, he is a figure of burning intensity and striking energy who tricks him by concealing that he is the person Gawain seeks, and plays a second game with him, about whose nature Gawain is deceived. Now temptation — and consequently the Devil — has held an important place in Christian thought on spiritual development. The more ardent the desire for perfection, the more redoubtable the temptations of the Devil, who attacks by preference the most virtuous. And, indeed, the trials in *Sir Gawain* are aimed at an upright, blameless man, of whom we have been told that he is *Voyded of vche vylany* (634) and aptly bears on his shield the *endeles knot* of the pentangle, standing in sign of a righteousness seen as a complex of interrelated courtly and religious virtues. The Devil usually operates covertly and deceitfully, with ruse as his main weapon, and, in seeking to trick by artifices, here is how he often seeks to catch his victim: by a weak point; at a moment of negligence or distraction; by masking vice by the appearance of virtue; through good but indiscreet intentions; and in a minor matter, if he meets with resistance in major ones.[47] In the romance, the host sets temptation through the ruse of his wife offering her love to Gawain, with the illicit nature of the proposed relations cloaked under the seemliness of a chivalrous pastime, the courting of ladies, which he, to keep his reputation for courtesy, is urged to pursue in order to show some principles of the art. And Gawain, acting with the best of intentions, as he tries to pass between the Scylla of being discourteous by refusing the lady's love and the Charybdis of committing sin by accepting it and becoming a traitor to his host (1771 – 5), is drawn into the indiscretion of a covert relationship with his host's wife. A stratagem, relying on Gawain's fear of death, makes this relationship go so far as to cause him to be dishonest towards his host, even if not in a particularly serious matter. In the meantime, the attention paid to the host's activity while Gawain is being tempted suggests the significance of a metaphor which was associated with the Devil, the hunting of a soul, for his tempting of a Christian.[48] Finally, the Green Knight plays a third game, with Gawain's head, and it seems that Gawain cannot be put to death by him unless he first forfeits his soul, for by his lapse at the castle he does not pass any further into his adversary's power to destroy than to suffer a nick in the neck. The sinister resonances need not be dispelled by such a feature as the piety at the castle — the Devil could take on any appearance to further his deceptions. That the castle is the answer to Gawain's prayer for harbour does not stand in the way of the implications either. God put Job in Satan's power.[49]

---

47   *Dictionnaire de Spiritualité*, ed. M. Viller (Paris, 1932 –), iii.149, 189, 191, 237.
48   There are some instances in the *MED*, s.vv. *hunte*, (b); *hunten*, 2 (f); *hunter*, (b).
49   In his article Randall (note 44 above) noted the tradition of God allowing Satan to pursue Christians with temptations.

What different light is thrown upon the matter is due to the poet having it both ways. John Burrow has remarked that what goes a long way to explain why one carries away such a favourable view of the adversary at the end of the poem is the author's tendency to block, and sometimes even falsify, our view of his feelings and thoughts during the castle scenes; the poet seems, in fact, to cheat in a similar fashion with his wife.[50] So, too, the men at the castle whisper to each other their delight that the guest who has arrived is Gawain, the *fyne fader of nurture* (915 – 27). On such occasions the author has joined in the game and plays with his audience.

What are we to think, then, when the Green Knight gazes upon Gawain with heartfelt approval (2335: *in hert hit hym lykez*) after the Beheading Match has been consummated, reveals all and assumes the character of judge, with a verdict on Gawain's performance at the castle that justifies the sparing of his life as well as the punishment for his fault? He expresses open admiration of Gawain, praises his conduct under trial at the castle as showing him to be so faultless as to be unparalleled among knights, and minimises his lapse. Whether we take the Green Knight's behaviour at this point at face value or not, it should be observed that his very high praise of Gawain could lead to pride, and that the hero, in response, acts as if he resists temptation again. He is not deflected from judging himself by the highest standards. When the revelation of having been caught in a trap of unrighteousness has a devastating effect on Gawain, the Green Knight makes out he gives absolution, which, because of the hero's full acknowledgment of his fault and through the penance of the cut in his neck, wipes him as clean as if he had never sinned since he was born. And he enjoins Gawain to return with him to the castle in order to make merry. Yet *contricioun moste be continueel* (*Parson's Tale* 304). Slipping into priestly robes — the Devil could do this literally — the Green Knight has tried to extinguish in Gawain what in fact lends absolution lasting efficacy. He fails. Then, having previously indicated, by way of assurance as to what kind of people Gawain has been dealing with, that he himself is not supernatural or evil, his name being Bertilak de Hautdesert and the marvel at Arthur's court having been engineered by the old lady at the castle, who sent him in this fashion with malicious intent, but — being Morgan le Fay — is Gawain's aunt, the Green Knight leaves to go *Whiderwarde-so-euer he wolde* (2478) as if his castle does not exist after all, so reminding us of how it had suddenly appeared to Gawain in the forest.

[50] J. A. Burrow, *A Reading of Sir Gawain and the Green Knight* (London, 1965), pp. 59, 93 – 4, 112.

> "I look down towards his feet; but that's a fable.
> If thou beest a devil, I cannot kill thee."

Othello says this of Iago, in the final scene, and Iago pointedly replies, after Othello has stabbed him: "I bleed, sir; but not killed." To Shakespeare's contemporaries Iago may well have seemed to be Satan or his agent. As deliberately as Shakespeare with Iago, the medieval poet conveys such a suggestion about the Green Knight, but he does not leave it uncontradicted. The mystery is given a solution in which the Green Knight displays a complete change of attitude and lays off the responsibility for his fiendishness on a malicious fay. Yet the effect of the Satanic element is not fully eradicated, and it resounds in the deep structure of the story.

In combining the evil being of Type 313 who seeks the hero's destruction through punishment for failure with the supernatural adversary of a Beheading Match who ultimately pronounces an approving judgment on the hero, the poet gives the Green Knight an ambiguity exploited to create a figure, too large to be merely Morgan le Fay's agent, which fills the imagination and poses an enigma to the end. The opinion of Arthur's court that Gawain's lapse is not to be taken seriously agrees with that expressed by the Green Knight, but it stands for the worldly view, and so also begs the question. To the story of a Beheading Match the poet has added moral dimension by using Type 313 in such a manner that what was its fiendish setter of tasks is given the role of tempter, and the trials result in strengthening the perfect knight's humility by the knowledge of his own weakness, even as the Devil's temptations do with a religious man:[51]

> "therefore I find fault with myself,
> and repent in dust and ashes."
> (Job xliii.6)

---

[51] *Dictionnaire de Spiritualité*, iii.237: Dieu permet que ses serviteurs soient violemment tentés par le démon . . . pour affermir leur vertu, et notamment leur humilité par la connaissance d'eux-mêmes et de leur faiblesse.

Sir Gawain and the Green Knight:
The Underlying Myth

CHRISTOPHER WRIGLEY

The central mystery of the story told in *Sir Gawain and the Green Knight* is rarely confronted by critics. It is well formulated by Anne Astell in a valuable essay[1] which comments fruitfully on the *Gawain*-poet's techniques and values. She notes that after the apparent climax of the story, the feigned beheading, and Gawain's extravagant remorse over his peccadillo in retaining the lady's girdle, the Green Knight 'laughs goodnaturedly, forgives Gawain and pronounces him "polysed of that ply3t'''.[2] Neither Astell nor almost all other critics appear to see anything strange in this. Yet it is surely, by all normal criteria, quite extraordinary. One might have thought that if any forgiving is to be done it should be Gawain who does it. He has been grossly tricked and deceived. The Green Knight had behaved with the most refined cruelty, causing Gawain to spend a year in the belief that he is doomed to die in his first age, putting the lady up to assail the virtue and honour on which his life depends, and finally playing with him like a cat with mouse before allowing him to live.

The ready acceptance by critics of this amazing dénouement is indeed a tribute to the poet's skill. But unless, on further thought, we are to dismiss this apparent absurdity as the triviality of a weakly escapist romance plot — and no sensitive reader of the poem will agree to that — we must seek more fundamental explanations of a kind that do justice to the profoundly imaginative structure that leads us to accept with satisfaction this apparently illogical ending.

The present essay is an admittedly speculative and controversial attempt to restore to consciousness our response to the underlying archaic powers of the story of *Sir Gawain and the Green Knight*. It is on lines

---

[1]   Ann W. Astell, ''Sir Gawain and the Green Knight: a study in the rhetoric of romance'', *JEGP* 84 (1985), 188 – 202.

[2]   Lines 2389 – 94, ed. J. R. R. Tolkien and E. V. Gordon, 2nd edn. N. Davis, Oxford, 1967.

similar to those followed by Derek Brewer in *Symbolic Stories*, a work which was unknown to me when, as a by-product of studies of African traditions, I began to put together some thoughts about the story of *Gawain*. The concepts which I use are in a loose sense 'structuralist', and depend on recognising that a traditional story operates at several levels, some of them below the normal level of conscious awareness. These deeper levels often derive from traditional rituals and their associated stories, which continue as it were underground in the oral tradition, becoming imaginative rather than practical, after the ritual is abandoned, while retaining their power. By the same token, such stories derive also from universal, or almost universal, structures of the human mind in its relationship to the family, to society and to ever-present problems of life and death.

Western thought has also developed, separately from stories, more analytical approaches with which to raise problems and their solutions to consciousness. One of the applications of such analysis is to stories themselves. Of course all societies develop some form of analysis — cause and effect need to be linked in some way — but modern Western thought has developed some peculiarly powerful analytical tools, which both derive from, and may aid, literary analysis. Among these are the concepts of anthropological and psychoanalytical folkloric study, and the following essay borrows from these to attempt to elucidate and enrich our understanding of the deeper, imaginative logic of *Sir Gawain and the Green Knight*.

The poet of *Gawain* is himself conscious of a need to rationalise and motivate the action of his poem. He puts into the Green Knight's mouth a superficial reason which may content us for a moment, in the surge of eager reading, accepting the conventions of romance and in the grip of a powerful story, but can hardly survive reflection. The excuse offered by the Knight for his appalling behaviour is that he was merely the instrument of a malignant plot by 'the goddess Morgan', who had wanted to make Guinevere die of fright. Morgan is also credited, somewhat contradictorily, with another motive, to "assay the surquidré" of Arthur's court.[3] Astell, as others have done, seizes on this as a justification; it was right for Gawain to be chastened, even so brutally, because he and his fellow Arthurians were guilty of the sin of pride. That, however, is not what the poem itself suggests. Morgan did not seek to punish the pride of Camelot but to test it, find out whether it was well founded. And in the person of Gawain it passed the test with flying colours. For he is a truly heroic hero, not the prig that some over-solemn criticism makes him but a very brave and entirely likeable young man.

---

[3]   Lines 2456 – 62.

The Green Knight himself calls him the most faultless man alive. True, the praise contains the implication that no human being is wholly faultless. True, he accepted the girdle in the hope that it might save him, and he flinched once as the axe fell. But to criticise him for such lapses would be to judge him by an extraordinarily high standard.[4] In any case they explain why he received a small wound, not why he was subjected to the ordeal in the first place. Yet Gawain at the end is angry with himself, not with his tormentor, and they part on friendly terms. What is more, as Sir Bertilak in his castle and after the dénouement the Knight is shown as a rumbustious but genial character, well disposed towards Gawain, and it is perfectly clear that this is his real nature, the ogreishness of his other appearances being a kind of play-acting. But what the play is about is never properly explained; nor I believe, can it be explained within the accepted boundaries of naturalistic and literalistic analysis.

The basic premiss of nearly all contemporary criticism is that the individual composers of medieval romances were solely responsible for their design and content, and that the relevant context is limited to their own intellectual formation and the religious and political preoccupations of their own time. Anyone who pays attention to the traditional antecedents of a poem such as *Gawain* is likely to be dismissed as naive. It was not always so. There was a time when such works were almost buried in anthropology and when it was very necessary to remind readers that they were works of art. Nor would anyone in his senses dispute that the *Gawain*-poet was a superb storyteller, a master of language, a wise and sympathetic observer of human behaviour. But we should surely take heed of his own statement (lines 31 – 36) that he was going to tell the story "as I in toun herde, with tonge", and would use the appropriately traditional verse-form, "in londe so has ben longe".[5] Astell takes "in toun" to mean "in the court precincts", but that seems arbitrary; an equally natural rendering would be "in the village where I grew up". Without necessarily taking this too literalistically we should take into account the possibility that as well as written texts the story had its roots in what is often dismissively called folklore but was actually the venerable and still lively native culture of north-west Europe.

That culture, moreover, supplied the romancers not only with the narrative themes and decorative elements familiar to students of oral and traditional narrative but with the architecture, and thus the meaning, of

---

[4]   See also Derek Brewer, *English Gothic Literature* (London: Macmillan, 1983), p. 160: "Gawain, though not inhumanly imperfect, has triumphantly succeeded, not failed." See also Brewer's more extended treatment in *Symbolic Stories* (Cambridge, 1980, reprinted London, 1988), pp. 72 – 91.

[5]   The "Brutus book" cited in 1.2523 is the authority for the pseudo-historical frame, not for the story itself.

their poems. It is well known that the theme of the "beheading game" was the common property of storytellers over the whole region, and antecedents have been found for the other main component of the *Gawain* poem, "the bedroom temptation". I shall try to show, however, that these were not originally separate plots that were brought together by the genius of the English poet (nor by Kittredge's hypothetical "clever Frenchman" either)[6] but had always been integrally and naturally connected, being related episodes of the same immemorial myth. By "myth" I mean a fantastic story which accompanies or treats major problems and crises in a traditional, usually oral, culture.

This claim echoes the pronouncements of earlier critics, such as Francis Berry, who wrote in 1954 that "it is because of, and not despite the anthropological and theological background that the poem has such an ample power of realised and natural human observation",[7] or John Speirs, for whom the Gawain-poet, "a conscious and deliberate artist . . . has, as it were, cooperated with some inner organising, unifying and realising principle of life and growth."[8] It is a general rule, indeed, that the more closely a medieval writer was able to "cooperate" with his inherited material the more impressive and enduring would be his impact.

To understand the poem, then, one must understand the antecedent myth, and in this Speirs was only partly successful. The particular principle of life that he invoked, being derived from the cycle of the northern year, is not adequate to account for the emotional strength of the *Gawain* poem and its continuing vitality in an age that has lost intimacy with the natural seasons. "Mythological" criticism has in fact earned some of its present disrepute by using a concept of myth that was out of date a quarter of a century ago. In the larger perspective supplied by Lévi-Strauss, "nature myths" and fertility rituals take their place among the many codes in which the basic dilemmas of human existence can find expression. A fuller and essentially correct explanation of *Gawain*, and of romance in general, was given thirty years ago by Charles Moorman, who identified it as the product of a *rite de passage* myth.[9] And Morton Bloomfield's irritable question — "Just what has Gawain been

6 G. L. Kittredge, *A Study of Gawain and the Green Knight* (Harvard: University Press, 1916), p. 137.

7 "Sir Gawayne and the Grene Knight", in Boris Ford, ed., *The Age of Chaucer* (London: Cassell, 1954), p. 155.

8 "Sir Gawain and the Green Knight", *Scrutiny* 16 (1949), 274–90, reprinted in Denton Fox, ed., *Twentieth Century Interpretations of Sir Gawain and the Green Knight* (Englewood Cliffs, N.J.: Prentice-Hall, 1968). Cf. J. Speirs, *Medieval English Poetry* (London: Faber, 1957), pp. 215–51.

9 "Myth and medieval literature: *Sir Gawain and the Green Knight*", *Medieval Studies* 18 (1956), 158–72, reprinted in R. J. Blanch, ed., *Sir Gawain and Pearl* (Bloomington: Indiana University Press, 1967), pp. 209–35.

initiated into?''[10] — is easily answered: into manhood. To modern European ears ''initiation'' connotes entry into an esoteric cult or fraternity. In traditional societies, however, it is the destiny of all men (and sometimes of all women too) and it marks nothing more, or less, than the transition from childhood to the duties and privileges of adult life.[11] It has always been recognised in a general way that the romance heroes progress from innocence to experience. But whereas in modern societies this process is gradual and diffuse it used to be a dramatic change, compressed into a few months of intensive education and a moment of fierce pain; and it is from the emotional residues of that ritual that romance derives most of its energy. Romance is in fact about adolescence; and the reason why it was so popular in the Middle Ages is probably that most of the consumers of fictional entertainment *were* adolescents, the young apprentice knights and the maidens who were the resident population of the great castles. The making of knights, moreover, preserved many of the symbols and procedures of tribal initiation, so that the stories originating therein would have a still recognisable appeal.[12]

The initiatory character of the *Gawain* romance is not hard to see. Quite apart from the climactic ordeals, there is the lone journey through the wild country, where the youth must prove himself as a hunter and learn to cope with solitude and with the fell beasts and monsters that are the projections of his inner fears. The poet passes quickly over this phase of the story and fortunately refrains, unlike some others, from turning the ogres into highwaymen and the psychic conflicts into those interminable jousts that were so fascinating to medieval audiences and are so tedious to most of us. All the same, the winter journey has been recognised as a vital component of the poem, as it was of the initiation process. But the most interesting evidence comes from an earlier section. If Gawain becomes a man in the course of the story he must have begun it as a child; and it is very clear that children are what he and all the folk of Camelot are, at least metaphorically. The Green Knight says so, bluntly — ''there are none but beardless children sitting on this bench'' (1.280) — and no-one contradicts him. The poet says so too: ''all that fair folk were in their first age''. There is no warrant for taking the first age to be mature if young adulthood, especially as even the great king is described as ''somewhat

---

[10]   ''Sir Gawain'', *PMLA* 76 (1961), 7 – 19.

[11]   For a general discussion of such rituals see M. Eliade, *Initiations, rites, sociétés sécrètes: naissances mystiques* (Paris: Gallimard, 1956). Descriptions of African performances includer J. Vansina, ''Initiation rituals of the Bushong'', *Africa* 25 (1955), 138 – 53, and V. W. Turner, *The Forest of Symbols* (Ithaca, N.Y.: Cornell University Press, 1957), pp. 185 – 220.

[12]   Cf. J. H. Grisward, ''Ider et le tricéphale: d'une aventure arthurienne à un mythe indien'', *Annales* 33 (1978), 279 – 93.

childlike''. The atmosphere of Christmas at Camelot is exactly that of a children's party, with games, presents, lots of nice things to eat — and no sex. Even the kissing game alluded to in lines 67 – 70 evokes only the mild titillations of first adolescence.[13] As Dorothy Everett noted, ''while there is much talk of love at Bercilak's castle, which is a place of temptation, there is none at Arthur's, which is not.''[14]

Into these juvenile revels comes the Green Knight, who at first seems to be a part of them. It has been well observed that his demeanour was that of an amateur actor in a Christmas entertainment, ''a courteous gentleman masquerading as a monster''.[15] If we take this literally, he might well have been actually masked, with some accoutrement that could be cut off without damage to himself. There could have been some such Christmas game or 'interlude' (cf.1.472). But then, as Gawain duly ''beheads'' the visitor, it dawns on him and his friends that perhaps this is no joke at all. It was as though they had been playing Oranges and Lemons and suddenly see a real chopper that might really be going to chop off a head. The whole poem walks this knife-edge path between mirth and terror, and the true measure of Gawain's heroism is that mirth is finally restored. It is difficult for us modern readers with our built-in positivism to respond to this curiously ambiguous play-element that is also quite serious.

A very similar ambiguity informs puberty-initiation rites, wherever it has been possible to observe them. The boys (and their mothers) are supposed to believe that they are going to die.[16] After the first painful stage of the exercise they may even be given to understand that they *have* died and that the initiation camp is the land of the dead — a character which it retains in every version of the correlative myth. Their return to the village is represented by all possible symbolic devices as a resurrection or rebirth. By this time, of course, they know that the whole business has been a pretence; and even beforehand their real state of mind was probably just that uncertain half-belief that gives the *Gawain* poem its peculiar frisson.

There is evidence, too, that the ''death'' threatened to adolescent boys was sometimes a decapitation. In his exploration of world folklore

---

13 See the illuminating essay by John T. Leyerle. ''The game and play of hero'', in Norman T. Burns and Christopher J. Reagan, eds., *The Concept of the Hero in the Middle Ages and the Renaissance* (Albany: New York State University Press, 1975), p. 52.

14 ''The alliterature revival'', in Patricia Kean, ed., *Essays in Middle English Literature*, reprinted in Fox, *Twentieth Century Interpretations*, pp. 13 – 32.

15 Elizabeth Wright. ''Sir Gawain and the Green Knight'', *JEGP* 34 (1935), 157 – 79.

16 Even in the 1950s in what is now Zambia novices were said to be ''killed'' and the lodge where they were secluded was ''the place of dying'' (Turner, *Forest of Symbols*, pp. 192, 222, 231).

Kittredge found many stories about exchanges of blows and many others about replaceable heads, but no precise parallel to the "beheading" game outside the west European cultural province. There is one story, however, which seems to come very close. It belongs to the kingdom of Buganda in central Africa, and is one of the tales associated with the culture-hero Kintu, who is both the founder of the dynasty and the father of mankind.[17] Kintu, however, remains in the background on this occasion and the actual hero is Tortoise, to whom the role of Deceiver is often assigned in Africa. We are in the time before time, when the kingship was held by Bemba Omusota, that is Scaly the Snake. Bemba was a tyrannical ruler, and Tortoise, prompted by his friend or master Pangolin (the scaly anteater), undertook to get rid of him. Introducing himself at the court he tempted the king, saying: "As you know, tortoises live for ever, or nearly so. The reason is that every night we cut our heads off and in the morning they have grown again, so we are as good as new". To prove his point he showed himself in the evening with his head retracted and appeared next morning in his normal shape. So that night king Bemba and all his snake-retinue agreed to have their heads cut off, that they too might live for ever. Kintu, whose name means "Man" (in the sense of human being), then became king, and history began.

The formalists have taught us that the identity of the actors in a tale is unimportant, that what matters is the structural pattern. Both Bemba and Gawain are deceived by an ostensible decapitation into accepting a real one for themselves; and this is so odd a notion that the recurrence is unlikely to be due to chance. The European stories of the beheading game have to be seen as a subset of a larger and much older set to which the Ganda myth of Snake and Tortoise also belongs. There are of course some differences. In one case the deception relies on a natural ability to conceal one's head; in the other it is dependent on magic, a concept which in Europe wavers between supernatural power and technical trickery. Unlike Bemba, moreover, Gawain is not actually beheaded. But he narrowly escapes this fate, receiving a gash in the neck, the significance of which will appear shortly. The African version, however, completes the European one by explaining what the point of the deception was. The whole set of tales is concerned with the quest for everlasting life and the message, as of most myths, if that this quest is vain. It is conveyed by means of a splendid irony. It is very widely believed that by sloughing their skins from time to time snakes are able to live for ever — unless of course their heads are cut off. So Tortoise, purporting to confer immortality on Bemba, found the only way to deprive him of the immortality he already possessed.

[17]   J. F. Cunningham, *Uganda and its Peoples* (London: Hutchinson, 1905), pp. 170–78.

But why is it not possible to live for ever? The Ganda do not tell us directly, and for the answer we have to turn to a better-known member of the same or a related set: *Genesis* 3. Here there is no beheading, but there is deception leading to the loss of immortality. There is also Snake as a leading actor, and if he is here the deceiver instead of the deceived that is an inversion very characteristic of myth. It is likely that the biblical editor has developed the story, which originally had a much simpler point. Snake, working through the agency of Woman, tricked Man into eating from the fruit of (carnal) knowledge when he thought he was being offered the fruit of (everlasting) life — which the ever-juvescent serpent craftily reserved for his own use.[18] Here is the irony again: Man had really no need of the fruit of life, and had found the only possible way of removing himself from the garden of eternal youth. Likewise king Pelias would probably have been safe for ever if the Cunning Woman, here acting on her own account, had not tricked him into being cut up and stewed. Woman plays a similarly criminal role in a vast number of African myths which are explicitly about the origin of death.[19] Absent from the tale of Snake and Tortoise, she figures centrally in two other Kintu myths which convey the same message by other means.[20] The message is not that women are evil, but simply that the duality of gender makes us mortal; a reproductive being cannot also be a permanent one.

The necessary connection between sex and death was formerly taught to all boys at the time when they were becoming aware of the necessity of sex.[21] It was taught both by myths, that is by verbal demonstrations of the logic of existence, and by sharp ritual experience. And, given its main objective, it is not surprising that the most widespread and presumably ancient form of the ritual should have been an operation on the penis. The Ganda people, who preserved the tale of Scaly, did not practise the circumcision of adolescents in historical times, any more than Europeans did; but the ancient myth nevertheless alludes to it not too obscurely. It has been remarked that the four characters in the tale constitute a kind of evolutionary series: first the writhing Snake; then Tortoise, the reptile with inefficient legs; then Pangolin the slow-moving, anomalously scaly

18 Here I synthesise the interpretations of Sir James Fraser, *Folklore in the Old Testament* (London: Macmillan, 1923), vol. I, chap. 2 and of Sir Edmund Leach, *Genesis as Myth* (London: Cape, 1969).

19 H. Abrahamsson, *The Origin of Death: Studies in African Mythology* (Uppsala: Studia Ethnographica Upsaliensia, 1951), pp. 56–72, 90, 94.

20 J. Roscoe, *The Baganda* (2nd edition, London: Frank Cass, 1965), pp. 460–64; and "Further notes on the manners and customs of the Baganda", *Journal of the Anthropological Institute* 32 (1902), 25–26.

21 G. Róheim, "Dying gods and puberty ceremonies", *Journal of the Royal Anthropological Institute* 59 (1929), 181–97; James L. Brain, "Sex, incest and death: initiation rites reconsidered", *Current Anthropology* 18 (1977), 191–98.

mammal; and finally erect-walking, scale-free Man.[22] Since there is considerable overlap in Bantu languages between words for "foreskin" and the names of reptiles, the inference of the tale is unmistakeable: only by the removal of the last "scale" can the quasi-reptilian boy become fully human, licensed for sexual action and destined to a finite life.

The European version perserved in *Gawain*, however, is more nearly explicit. For the Beheading Game makes sense when it is seen to refer, not just to puberty initiation in general, but specifically to circumcision. That is represented by the gash in the "neck" that Gawain suffered in lieu of decapitation.[23] It may well be that in our ancestral cultures boys had to undergo a symbolic castration, as the Freudians have long maintained. "Come now", says the Deceiver, as Tortoise said to Snake, "let me cut off your 'head', and then you can live peacefully for ever." After this terrifying menace the actual operation would be a great relief, as it was to Gawain. So at one deep level the Green Knight represents Death, or Nature, or God, the demiurge who made the world as it is and in whose will is our peace;[24] but at another level he is simply the Circumciser, the man bound by inviolable custom to inflict pain on young kinsmen, neighbours' sons, for whom his real feelings may be entirely kindly.

Demonstrative proof of this interpretation is hardly possible, but unconscious memories of the operation may survive in the biographies of other romance heroes, at least three of whom lost a piece of skin, not far from the loins, in circumstances of mystery and terror. At the beginning of Chrétein's *Erec et Enide* there is a scene which might have been taken from the report of an African initiation. The boy is with the womenfolk when there appears a grotesquely masked figure (in the medieval convention a dwarf, in African tradition a spirit from the underworld), who drives the women away with his whip and causes the boy to follow him. Next day, Erec takes part in the ritual of the Sparrowhawk (in the convention, a joust). He confronts an older man and receives a wound: "the cold steel penetrated to the flesh on his thigh". Lancelot, likewise, lay down on the perilous bed and at midnight a flaming lance descended, "passing so close to the knight's side that it cut the skin a little without seriously wounding him." Yvain, too, had a strange experience on his first visit to the Fountain: the trap gate of the castle fell behind him,

---

[22] R. R. Atkinson, "The traditions of the early kings of Buganda: myth, history and structural analysis", *History in Africa* 2 (1975), 23.

[23] So Judith S. Neaman, who also notes that the ordeal takes place on the Feast of Christ's Circumcision. ("Sir Gawain's covenant: troth and *timor* mortis", *PQ* 55 (1976, 30 – 42).

[24] See for instance H. Zimmer, *The King and the Corpse* (Princeton, 1948); A. H. Krappe, "Who *was* the Green Knight?", *Speculum* 13 (1938), 206 – 15; and especially A. K. Coomaraswamy, "Sir Gawain and the Green Knight: Indra and Namuci", *Speculum* 19 (1944), 104 – 25; Brewer, *Symbolic Stories*, pp. 87 – 91.

cutting off his horse's haunches and grazing his back, after which he had to lie in the dark, like many novices, and hope to avoid being beaten. On a later visit he would actually be wounded in the neck.[25] Then again, what else could possibly be the meaning of the Bleeding Lance that was carried by a youth in the Castle of the Grail?

Evidence that traditions of puberty initiation remained in the subconscious or maybe conscious minds of storytellers close to the threshold of literary romance is supplied by the conclusion to the Welsh tale of *Peredur*.[26] The hero has gone through a great jumble of adventures, mostly taken from various versions of the French *Perceval* but with some Welsh material added. Then at last the yellow-haired youth who made two previous appearances in his own form kneels before him and confesses that he was also the black maiden who has been persecuting him through several episodes; that, before that, he was one of the boys who carried the Bleeding Spear and also one of the girls bearing the salver with the Bleeding Head; and, finally, that he is Peredur's cousin. This apparently crazy farrago is one main reason why critics have not been able to take the *Peredur* very seriously. Put it into the context of initiation ritual, however, and it makes sense at once. The youthful hero has been subjected to a series of frightening and bewildering experiences, and at the end it is disclosed to him that it has all been trickery and illusion; he has been the witness of an elaborate charade, in which many of the parts, including the female ones (no actual female would have been allowed anywhere near) were taken by the slightly older kinsman who went through it himself a few years earlier and now acts as guardian of the new initiand. How far the author of *Peredur* consciously understood this must remain a question, but he must surely have had some kind of grasp on its deeper significance.

In the perspective of initiation there is no longer anything surprising about the presence of the temptation theme in the *Gawain* version of the Beheading Game. Recent scholarship has tried to reserve for the Gawain-poet the sole credit for this conjuncture, and he certainly handled it with special sensitivity and skill. However, Gawain's sojourn in the bedroom at Hautdesert may be seen as one of a whole class of equivocal amorous encounters in which the natural dénouement is apparently evaded. Chrétien's Perceval, just before his visit to the Grail Castle, spends a night in the besieged city of Belrepaire in chaste embrace with its young chatelaine.[27] Chaste, certainly, even though they slept *boche à boche, bras à*

25 Chrétien de Troyes, *Arthurian Romances*, translated by W. W. Comfort (London: Dent, 1914), pp. 13, 277, 192, 225.
26 Gwyn Jones and Thomas Jones, *The Mabinogion* (London: Dent, 1949), p. 226.
27 Chrétien de Troyes, *Perceval, ou le Conte du Graal*, ed. W. Roach (Geneva and Paris: Droz, 1959), lines 1932–2074.

bras; for Chrétien was not unduly reticent and if there had been more to tell he would have told us; moreover in the morning the girl is still pointedly described as a *pucele*. Then there is the frustrating experience of the "Fair Unknown" in the Isle of Gold.[28] Here there is no lack of ardour on the hero's part. It is the Maiden with the White Hands who first offers herself to an almost naked embrace who abruptly withdraws, saying with belated primness that this would lead to lechery. The Fair Unknown's close counterpart, Malory's Gareth (the younger brother of Gawain), twice tries to enjoy the hard-earned favours of the lady Lyonesse and is twice interrupted by the onslaught of an armed knight. Each time he removes the intruder's head and each time it is replaced.[29] Lancelot's behaviour on the way to the land of the dead, on the other hand, resembles that of Perceval on his way to the Grail. A young woman insists that he spend the night with her and tries to stimulate him by staging an attempted rape. He does battle with the assailants but remains unstimulated.[30]

For a clue to the meaning of this recurrent theme we turn again to Africa, this time to the kingdom of Burundi, an isolated country where ancient tradition was preserved into the present century perhaps more faithfully than anywhere else, especially in the observances of sacred kingship. It is necessary to recall at this point that Sir Gawain is not just an ordinary knight. Like his Irish counterpart Cuchulainn and many other romance heroes he is a king's sister's son, which means — since both Irish and Arthurian myths contain ample hints of the royal incest once customary in Africa[31] — that he is also the king's son and heir in the original versions. The pristine sense of the Gawain-figure may well have been that he was the king in the younger phase of his life-cycle, the "Hawk of May" as the Welsh called him. For it should also be understood that a king was in the first instance not a governor but a boy chosen and set apart so that he might enact the great transitions with special solemnity on behalf of the people, and so assure the continued turning of the wheel of life. (This is the last function of monarchy, as it was the first; even sophisticated Englishmen acknowledge the emotion stirred in them by the recurrent dramas, the births, coronations, marriages, jubilees and deaths of their otherwise functionless and impuissant royalty.) Now in Burundi the chief national ceremony was the Feast of Sowing; and on that occasion the drum Karyenda, supreme symbol of the kingship, was

28   Renaut de Beaujeu, *Le bel inconnu*, ed. G. P. Williams (Paris: Champion, 1967), lines 2387 – 2456.

29   *Le Morte d'Arthur*, ed. J. Rhys (London: Dent, 1906, vol. I, pp. 214 – 16.

30   Comfort, *Arthurian Romances*, pp. 282 – 86.

31   L. de Heusch, *Essais sur le symbolisme de l'inceste royale en Afrique* (Brussels: Université Libre, 1958).

brought out and placed on a kind of altar, and the celibate priestess who was called its wife, having given the king porridge to eat, lay naked before it. If the king was a child, as he always was in the early years of his reign, he was made to simulate intercourse with her, but if he showed signs of going beyond pretence he was pulled away.[32] Our report does not say what happened then; but it is reasonable to suppose that, having given proof that he was no longer a child, he was put through the nine-day initiation rite called "the king's growing up", of which we have detailed accounts from Buganda, another kingdom of the same group.[33]

The simplicity of this African charade is of course far removed from the delicate wit of Gawain's encounter with the mistress of Bertilak's castle. On the other hand it has a very close parallel in another, less refined story of Gawain, *The Carl of Carlisle*.[34] Here Gawain is ordered by his monstrous host to get into bed with his wife. He complies, but when he begins to go further he is told that that game is forbidden. There follows a beheading, though not in the proper reciprocal form. Very similar too, in all probability, was the original form of the Irish myth of which several versions are clumsily collated in *Bricriu's Feast*.[35] The role of the Green Knight is here usually played by Curoi, who is described as a *bachlach*, that is to say a churl, or in northern English a carl. In one story he visits the king's court to play the beheading game with Cuchulainn, but in another it is Cuchulainn who goes to Curoi's castle and is entertained in his absence by his wife Blathnat. Set to watch the fort at night, he copes with the assaults of giants and monsters that are the usual prelude to initiation and then goes inside to be greeted by Blathnat — at which point Curoi suddenly returns. A series of earlier Arthurian scholars (Zimmer, Hulbert, Loomis, Buchanan)[36] argued, surely with justice, that the extant version draws a veil over an incident not unlike the one at Carlisle and

---

[32] J. Gorju, *Face au royaume hamite du Ruanda, le royaume frère de l'Urundi* (Brussels: Bibliothèque Congo, 1938), p. 48.

[33] Roscoe, *The Baganda*, pp. 210 – 13; A. Kagwa, *The Customs of the Baganda*, ed. M. Mandelbaum (New York: Columbia University Press, 1934), pp. 16 – 20.

[34] Donald B. Sands, *Middle English Romances* (New York: Holt, 1966), pp. 365f. L. E. Brewer, *From Cuchulainn to Gawain* (Cambridge: D. S. Brewer, 1973) translates the sources and analogues, including 'The Carl of Carlisle'.

[35] George Henderson, ed., *Fled Bricrend: the Feast of Bricriu* (London: Irish Texts Society, 1899). It is a sign of recent scholarly fashion that the analogy of *Twentieth Century Interpretations* published in 1968 contained no mention of Bricriu — or of Kittredge who in fact dominated Gawain studies for much of the century. But see L. E. Brewer n. 34 above.

[36] J. R. A. Hulbert, "Syr Gawayn and the Grene Knyght", *MP* 13 (1915 – 16), 49 – 78; R. S. Loomis, *Celtic Myth and Arthurian Romance* (New York: Columbia University Press, 1927), pp. 57ff.; Alice Buchanan, "The Irish background of *Gawain and the Green Knight*", *PMLA* 47 (1932), 315 – 38; H. Zimmer in an article of 1911 cited by Buchanan, p. 326.

that there has been an Irish precedent for the association of the temptation and beheading themes. It was pointed out in particular that in yet other tales (outside the *Bricriu* collection) Cuchulainn and Blathnat were avowed lovers, who conspired to kill Curoi. Blathnat's real function, however, like that of Blancheflor, of the lady Lyonesse and of the wife of Karyenda, was to test the hero, not for chastity or loyalty or courtesy or any moral quality, but simply for pubescence. By his reaction or lack of reaction to the woman's advances the boy king would show whether or not he was ready to be made into a man. All "Potiphar's wife" stories have the same origin; and the point is made very crudely at the end of the Irish beheading tale. When Cuchulainn bows his neck before the axe Curoi complains that it was too short to provide a target; so the hero makes an effort to stretch it, and at the second attempt, with good Irish hyperbole, makes it reach right across the hall. Only when the "neck" has shown itself to be extensible is it ready to be cut.

After all this, the role of Bertilak's wife presents little difficulty. Most critics have agreed that Gawain is *not* being tested for chastity. One finds "no suggestion that he is ever stirred dangerously by sexual desire",[37] and another states that "hardly for a moment does he feel drawn towards his temptress in a passionate way."[38] Reading the account of the first two bedroom scenes, one can hardly disagree. Yet surely there is a mystery here? The lady is very beautiful. She sits on the hero's bed, kisses him and announces her eagerness to be seduced with at least as much frankness as the manners of her class allow. How can he not be stirred by desire? The lady herself appears to be puzzled and says that he cannot really be Gawain. Here she has, so to speak, slipped out of the frame of the story, becoming a fourteenth-century lady who reads romances and knows that Gawain is a great lover. She is, however, supposed to be a character in his biography, and one whose part is played before the beginning of his amorous career. For the reason why he does not respond to her is simply that he is not yet old enough. He is an embarrassed youth, "a Gawain of ridiculous bewilderment, peeping furtively from under the blankets and coyly submitting to the kisses" of a woman who is outside his experience. But that is on the first two days only.

Between the *Gawain* "temptation" story and the Blancheflor episode of Chrétien's *Perceval*[39] there is a close similarity of pattern, one of the structural conformities which prove that medieval romancers were

---

[37] Fox, *Twentieth Century Interpretations*, p. 11; A. B. Friedman, "Morgan le Fay in *Sir Gawain and the Green Knight*", *Speculum* 35 (1960), 260–74.
[38] Larry D. Benson, *Art and Tradition in Sir Gawain and the Green Knight*, (New Brunswick, N.J., 1965), p. 38.
[39] Ed. Roach, lines 2138–2708.

indebted to the tradition, not just for bits and pieces of material, but for entire significant narrative designs. In both stories, three scenes of dalliance within the castle are counterpointed by three passages of manly action outside it. On each of the days when Gawain is snugly in bed being tempted by his hostess Sir Bertilak is out hunting in the wintry hills. In the Grail romance it is Perceval himself who sallies forth between flirtations, and his campaign is not against beasts but against human adversaries. There are, however, detailed correspondences that can hardly be ascribed to chance. On the first day Perceval engages in single combat with the enemy seneschal; on the second day there is a general mêlée; on the third day he jousts with the chieftain Clamadeus. Except that the order of the first two events is reversed, Bertilak's hunts follow the same pattern: a general slaughter of the deer; then the hunting of a boar; and finally the killing of a single fox. The amorous interludes are likewise parallel. Before the first battle in Chrétien's poem, as we have seen, there is nightlong innocent embrace. After it Perceval and Blancheflor kiss and talk and cuddle but with no more serious outcome than before. But at their third meeting, just before the final combat, Blancheflor's kisses take effect on Perceval; as Chrétien gently puts it, "they turn the key of love in the lock of his heart". So also at Hautdesert the third day is very different. The drift of lines 1762 – 4 is unmistakeable:

> Wiȝt wallande joye warmed his hert.
> With smoþ smylyng and smolt þey smeten into merþe
> That al watz blis and bonchef that breke hem bitwene.

And the poet intervenes to say that they are in great peril and will need Mary's help.

It is implied that, whether through celestial aid or a sense of obligation to his host, Gawain was able to restrain his passion, but it can no longer be said that he did not feel any. He has given proof that he *is* now old enough for the visit to the Green Chapel, which takes place on the following day. It is not certain, moreover, that we can believe in his continuing innocence. He did, after all, end up in possession of the lady's girdle, and he wryly admitted that she had successfully played the part of Eve, the Deceiver. Here again is the familiar irony. She had promised that the girdle would preserve his life, but instead it was in the end almost fatal to him. Because of it, he receives the wound that is the mark of his and our mortality. For there is a price to pay for the compromise that is circumcision. The cut that does not quite deprive him of his sexuality also just fails to free him from the human condition. Gawain is not going to die this time. A full life of adult achievement and adventure lies ahead of him.

But beyond it, beside the ancient tomb, the Green Knight will still await him, as he awaits us all.

When Gawain sets out from Camelot his baldric secures a shield bearing the sign of the pentangle, the endless knot that is the best possible symbol of eternity. On his return journey his baldric is the green lace, the token of both death and of human joy. And when he tells his friends the story of how he has acquired it he is greeted with what is surely bawdy laughter. Camelot too had lost its innocence, has grown up.

The poem has yet another dimension, which has been explored in the penetrating commentary of Derek Brewer. "At the deepest level of structure", he writes, "the story is a most original version of the family drama, in which the Green Knight is a father-figure and his lady the seductive aspect, and Morgan the malevolent aspect, of the mother figure".[40] A similar conclusion was reached by Maureen Duffy, who also saw that the two women in the castle, the old and the young were really one and the same, and suggested that the lady's bare bosom evoked for Gawain "the memory of another offered breast".[41] Though the poem describes Morgan as Gawain's aunt there is a strong tradition that he was in fact her son. The erotic fantasies of the young adolescent — for that is what the lady's visits at one level represent — are likely to focus on a youthfully disguised version of his mother.

Professor Brewer goes on to note that "the hero's quest, instead of being a departure from home, as is usual in fairy tales, is a return to home, where he must solve the problems of emotional bonds, and from which he emerges, not unscarred, as a mature though young adult". That is unquestionably what the *Gawain* poem is about; but its presentation, masterly though it is, does not have quite the originality that Brewer suggests. For the function of the initiation rite that we have seen as its ultimate source is precisely this: to help the boy to overcome his Oedipal emotions, to part from his mother and to come to terms with his father, and so with life.[42] And we can now see that Gawain's most serious testing comes after the axe has been laid aside. Sir Bertilak twice pressingly invites him to return to the castle, to enjoy further hospitality and renew his acquaintance with the lady. Gawain declines, the second time with a brusqueness[43] that is disconcerting until one recognises that this is the crux and climax of the whole adventure. If he had returned to Hautdesert he would never have got out alive.

---

[40] *English Gothic Literature*, p. 165.
[41] *The Erotic World of Faery* (London: Hodder and Stoughton, 1972), pp. 59 – 61.
[42] There is a poignant illustration of this theme in the autobiographical account by Camara Laye, *L'enfant noir* (Paris: Plon, 1955), pp. 130 – 35.
[43] Line 2471: "And he nikked hym naye, he nolde bi no wayes".

The structure of *Sir Gawain* is the structure of a very ancient myth. The poem is of course not itself in any simple sense a myth, but a rich synthesis which also includes popular humour, contemporary religious thoughts and feelings, the poet's personal sensibilities and skills and, very importantly, influences from the epic tradition, legacy of the successive warrior elites that had held dominion in these islands since the Bronze Age. Myth and epic are sharply contrasted modes. Boys in tribal societies have no choice about being circumcised or otherwise painfully inducted into adult life. Nor could the sacred king of the ancient sort choose when he should grow up, marry, beget an heir and die, for he was a mascot manipulated by custom and the priests along a predetermined path. Accordingly the hero of myth gives no impression of personal heroism. His adventures are ordained, his valour automatic, his victories magical. Gawain, on the other hand, surrenders himself to the Green Knight by his own unconstrained decision. The change owes much to the Christian example, the voluntary self-sacrifice of the Son of God, but probably even more to the aristocratic ethos which made life valueless when not enriched by courage and fidelity. It is the fusion of ritual and heroic themes that makes the story of Gawain so deeply moving. The youth leaves the fun and fellowship of Camelot behind him and goes alone into the winter wilderness to keep a bizarre compact which must, it seems, cost him his life. And then a second time he finds the strength to depart from the friendly refuge of Bertilak's castle, from his warm bed and from the flirtation that has just begun to be delightful, and goes out into the bleak January dawn to place his head upon the block. He is no pale martyr or twisted fanatic, but a robust young man who loves his life but does not value it as the highest of all goods. Certainly *Gawain* is a "festive poem",[44] and what it celebrates is victory over the knowledge of death.[45]

---

[44] Benson, *Art and Tradition*, p. 248.
[45] The article by P. L. Rudnytsky, 'Sir Gawain and the Green Knight: Oedipal temptation', *American Imago* 40 (1983) 371 – 83, is a psychological reading which makes some points similar to those of Brewer (n. 4 above) and also associates the cut in the neck with circumcision, but regrettably came to my notice too late to be used.

'Troilus' and the Disenchantment
of Romance

BARRY WINDEATT

'This sagacious person was Dan Chaucer; who in a reign, that almost
realized the wonders of romantic chivalry, not only discerned the absurdity
of the old romances, but has even ridiculed them with incomparable spirit.
His RIME OF SIR TOPAZ, in the Canterbury Tales, is a manifest banter on
these books, and may be considered as a sort of prelude to the adventures of
Don Quixot . . .'

Richard Hurd, *Letters on Romance and Chivalry* (1762), XI.

I

If medieval romance typically concerns itself with the idealized adventures of knights in chivalry and in love, within a world open to the
marvellous,[1] then it fits the modern understanding of 'ironic' Chaucer
that the poet's own unsuccessful tale in the *Canterbury Tales* should be a
parody of romance, with its ridiculous knight errant as passionate lover
and giant-slayer. An instinctive indifference to the marvellous as theme,
and an impatience with the episodic structure of repetitious exploits at
arms, has also been inferred in explaining why Chaucer abandons the

---

[1] 'Real romance is a pre-novelistic kind of narrative. It's full of adventure and
coincidence and surprises and marvels, and has lots of characters who are lost or
enchanted or wandering about looking for each other, or for the Grail, or something
like that. Of course, they're often in love too . . . In psychoanalytical terms, romance is
the quest of a libido or desiring self for a fulfilment that will deliver it from the anxieties
of reality but will still contain that reality . . .' David Lodge, *Small World: An Academic
Romance* (Harmondsworth, 1985), pp. 258 – 9.

129

romance of marvels and adventures which the Squire begins.[2] The Wife of Bath's tart assumption that the marvels and enchantments of England's Arthurian past survive no more (*WBT*, III, 857 – 81), and the Nun's Priest's arch assertion that his fable of cock and fox is 'also trewe, I undertake, / As is the book of Launcelot de Lake, / That wommen holde in ful greet reverence' (*NPT*, VII, 3211 – 4), have further seemed to reflect Chaucer's own detachment from Arthurian romance. That *Sir Thopas* is unendurable to the society of Canterbury pilgrims has suggested not only Chaucer's sophisticated distancing of himself from popular English romance,[3] but — by extension — his amused impatience with the characteristic concerns and forms of romance throughout his works.[4]

[2] On romance generally, cf. E. Auerbach, *Mimesis* (translated by W. R. Trask), (Princeton, 1953), ch. 6; G. Beer, *The Romance* (London, 1970); D. Brewer, "The Nature of Romance," (*Poetica*, 9 (1978), 9 – 48; N. Frye, *The Secular Scripture: A Study of the Structure of Romance* (Cambridge, Mass., 1976); K. Hume, "Romance: A Perdurable Pattern," *College English*, 36 (1974), 129 – 46; W. T. H. Jackson, "The Nature of Romance," in "Approaches to Medieval Romance," ed. P. Haidu, in *Yale French Studies* (hereafter *YFS*), 51 (1974), 12 – 25; D. Kelly, "*Matière* and *genera dicendi* in Medieval Romance," *YFS*, 51 (1974), 147 – 59; E. Vinaver, *The Rise of Romance* (Oxford, 1971); M. Bloomfield, "Episodic Motivation and Marvels in Epic and Romance," in his *Essays and Explorations* (Cambridge, Mass., 1970), pp. 97 – 128.

[3] On medieval English romance, cf. D. Everett, "A Characterization of the English Medieval Romances," in her *Essays on Middle English Literature* (Oxford, 1955), pp. 1 – 22; D. Pearsall, "The Development of Middle English Romance," *Mediaeval Studies*, 27 (1965), 91 – 116; D. Mehl, *The Middle English Romances of the Thirteenth and Fourteenth Centuries* (London, 1969); P. Gradon, *Form and Style in Early English Literature* (London, 1971), ch. 4 "The Romance Mode"; J. Stevens, *Medieval Romance* (London, 1973); K. Hume, "The Formal Nature of Middle English Romance," *PQ*, 53 (1974), 158 – 80; J. Finlayson, "Definitions of Middle English Romance," *Chaucer Review*, 15 (1981 – 2), 44 – 62, 168 – 81; P. Boitani, *English Medieval Narrative in the Thirteenth and Fourteenth Centuries* (Cambridge, 1982), ch. 3; Lee C. Ramsey, *Chivalric Romances* (Bloomington, 1983); P. R. Coss, "Aspects of Cultural Diffusion in Medieval England: The Early Romances, Local Society and Robin Hood," *Past and Present*, 108 (1985), 35 – 79.

[4] On Chaucer and romance, cf. Karl Young, "Chaucer's *Troilus and Criseyde* as Romance," *PMLA*, 53 (1938), 38 – 63; C. Muscatine, *Chaucer and the French Tradition* (Berkeley, 1957), ch. II; J. Burke Severs, "The Tales of Romance," in *Companion to Chaucer Studies*, ed. B. Rowland (Oxford, 1968, 1979), pp. 271 – 95; P. M. Kean, *Chaucer and the Making of English Poetry*, 2 vols. (London, 1971), ch. 2 "The *Canterbury Tales*: the problem of narrative structure"; R. T. Lenaghan, "The Clerk of Venus: Chaucer and Medieval Romance," in *The Learned and the Lewed: Studies in Chaucer and Medieval Literature*, ed. L. D. Benson, Harvard English Studies, 5 (Cambridge, Mass., 1974), pp. 31 – 43; R. M. Jordan, "Chaucerian Romance?" *YFS*, 51 (1974), 223 – 34; R. M. Jordan, "The Question of Genre: Five Chaucerian Romances," in *Chaucer at Albany*, ed. Rossell Hope Robbins (New York, 1975), pp. 77 – 103; D. S. Brewer, "Chaucer and Chrétien and Arthurian Romance," in *Chaucer and Middle English Studies in Honour of Rossell Hope Robbins*, ed. B. Rowland (London, 1974), pp. 255 – 9; A. C. Spearing, *Medieval to Renaissance in English Poetry* (Cambridge, 1985), ch. 2 "Chaucer's classical romances".

For Chaucer it is the unsustainable nature of human idealisms which both draws him towards some depiction of the characteristic experience of romance, and also necessarily leads him to show the qualifications and exhaustion of romance. For Chaucer the significance of romance is thus not so much an identifiably borrowed structural principle informing a whole work, an identifiable style, manner and tone within a poem.[5] It is not unreasonable to claim the *Knight's Tale* and the *Troilus* as Chaucer's two greatest single works, and not unreasonable to think of both poems as being in a real and important sense romances. For in both poems — in settings long past and exotically distant — the experience of the principal young characters is that of the typical protagonists of romance: an intense and transfiguring experience of love, as well as a kind of adventure. Dragons and enchantments are there none, apart from such mechanisms as the *furie infernal*. Yet the all-possessing nature of the experience of love of Troilus, as of Palamon and Arcite, makes that love to them a kind of inward equivalent of 'aventure', just as the strangeness of love to them, and that force of idealization which they each bring to their experience, gives to it the quality of a marvel and of an enchantment, the marvellous inward adventure of love.

In both the *Knight's Tale* and *Troilus* the heroes' identification with the life of romance heroes has been emphasized by Chaucer's adaptation of his immediate sources. But in both poems this involvement with the life of romance does not bring the conclusion that the romances of tradition generally have.[6] Both Chaucer romances end in an intensity of disappointment that invites comparison with some of the effects of tragedy, even though both poems have also contained and apparently endorsed the traditional experiences of romance.[7] The *Knight's Tale* and *Troilus* variously work through a process of disillusionment with the idealization of romance. It is in the wisdom of this disappointment that the two poems

---

[5] On medieval sense of genre, cf. P. Strohm, "Storie, Spelle, Geste, Romaunce, Tragedie: Generic Distinctions in the Middle English Troy Narratives," *Speculum*, 46 (1971), 348 – 59; P. Strohm, "The Origin and Meaning of Middle English *Romaunce*," *Genre*, 10 (1977), 1 – 28; H. R. Jauss, *Toward an Aesthetic of Reception* (translated by T. Bahti), (Brighton, 1982), ch. 3 "Theory of Genres and Medieval Literature"; P. Zumthor, "Le roman courtois: essai de définition," *Etudes littéraires*, 4 (1971), 75 – 90.

[6] Cf. 'The medieval English romances are stories in verse which deal with the adventures of noble men and women and which end happily,' A. V. C. Schmidt and N. Jacobs (eds.), *Medieval English Romances*, 2 vols. (London, 1980), Vol. 1, p. 1.

[7] Cf. K. Hume ("A Perdurable Pattern"): 'Comedy stays within the bounds of the probable; romance dips into a realm full of tragic possibilities. It is romance's nature to wrest success from this material, tragedy's to show failure . . .' (p. 143). Cf. also 'Romance . . . in my opinion is the real opposite of tragedy,' D. Brewer, *Chaucer: The Poet as Storyteller* (London, 1984), p. 81.

can incorporate and transcend the typical experience of romance in testing, refining and educating its characters. In these poems style reflects the aspiration of romance, which structure and context comment upon ironically. Indeed, the very notion of 'pure' romance was perhaps impossible for an artist as prone as Chaucer to create through and in terms of 'frames' and mediating or distancing devices. In a poem like the *Troilus*, where the outward enchantments of traditional romance have been internalized in the inward adventure of the hero's engrossing but eventually disillusioning experience in love, Chaucer's most distinctive development of the genre may be seen as the disenchantment of romance.

Although in creating his *Troilus* Chaucer is working primarily from Boccaccio's *Filostrato*, Boccaccio's own source was already famously a romance of the disillusionment of hope. In the twelfth-century *Roman de Troie* of Benoit de Sainte-Maure, which originated the story of Criseyde's betrayal and established her as a type, the relation of the history of Troilus and Briseida only begins at the enforced separation of the lovers at the exchange of prisoners. As a narrative the earliest version focusses entirely on the disintegration of the affair, and in his *Filostrato* Boccaccio had the inventiveness to provide a beginning for this story which first existed only as an ending, imagining his way back behind the conclusion to show how Troiolo first falls in love and wins Criseida. This newly-invented beginning is however a projection back from the established ending in the sense that its characterization of Troiolo and Criseida is designed to explain the given *dénouement* with its intrinsic antifeminist bias, and the *Filostrato* is in itself by no means a straightforward romance. Insofar as the *Troilus* resembles a romance, this is because Chaucer has worked to align *Filostrato* with romance tradition by addition and adaptation. At some important moments Chaucer ignores Boccaccio and goes back to the earlier romance tradition of Benoit in order to imitate or to borrow materials that give *Troilus* more of the setting and procedures of romance. Recurrently, Chaucer can be shown to use language and to represent behaviour in *Troilus* in ways which overlap with the English romances of his day and with romance tradition generally. *Il Filostrato*'s powerful drive away from romance still stirs beneath the English poem, however, and the *Troilus* like the *Knight's Tale* becomes an untypically uneasy romance, which eventually by its ending questions the presuppositions with which romances typically begin and proceed. Yet despite the example of *Filostrato*, and Chaucer's own apparent reservations about the characteristic forms and themes of romance, Chaucer will in the following pages be shown to make his Troilus and Criseyde story distinctly more of a romance than his immediate Italian source, so that his own poem can explore the disappointment of larger hopes and higher aspirations through the eventual disenchantment of the experience of romance.

II

In supplementing the narrative of *Filostrato* by drawing on the *Roman de Troie* Chaucer echoes something of the traditional romance narrative of both chivalry and love which marks Benoit's romance, where accounts of the chivalrous deeds at the siege of Troy are interwoven with psychologically subtle attention to the loves of Troilus, Briseida and Diomede, and of Achilles and Polyxena.

Looking first at Chaucer's added touches of chivalric texture: in *Filostrato* Boccaccio had kept little of the sense of battle in Benoit, whereas some of Chaucer's expansions of the Italian — as at the opening of Book IV — emphasize the background of the narrative in the battles outside Troy. While *Filostrato* simply says that Hector went forth against the Greeks (4.1), Chaucer elaborates on how his company was armed ('. . . brighte and shene/ . . . With spere in honde and bigge bowes bente,' IV, 38 – 40).[8] In *Troilus* Chaucer echoes the battles of the *Roman de Troie* through some of the phraseology used to describe fighting in the English romances. Chaucer's battle-description ('They fighte and bringen hors and man to grounde,/ And with hire axes out the braynes quelle . . .' 45 – 6) is made up of phrases echoing the ways of describing these actions in the metrical romances (e.g. Chetham MS *Bevis*: 'That hors and man to grounde he cast . . .'; *Ipomadon*: 'That hors & man boþe downe he bare . . .' 3735; 'Blode oute off the brenniys braste . . .' 3322).[9] The processions and ceremonial escortings that are part of the ritual action of many English romances were possibly also in Chaucer's mind when he turned Troiolo's simple passing by Criseida's house in *Filostrato* (2.82) into the triumphal procession when Troilus passes below Criseyde's window as a knight returning from battle (II, 610ff.), a ceremonious scene which is later repeated by Pandarus's plan (1247ff.). These scenes of Troilus's riding past in procession also echo the type-scenes of romance tournaments when the lady looks down on her knightly lover from some high place or vantage-point, or perhaps Chaucer is recalling the triumphal entries of Hector or Troilus in the *Roman de Troie*. The moment when Troilus recognizes his brooch on the 'cote armure' of Diomede, although derived from *Filostrato*, is stressed by Chaucer to be part of customary

---

8   All *Troilus* quotations are from my edition, *Geoffrey Chaucer, Troilus and Criseyde: A New Edition of 'The Book of Troilus'* (London, 1984). All other Chaucer references are to *The Works of Geoffrey Chaucer*, ed. F. N. Robinson, 2nd edn (London, 1957).

9   *The Romance of Sir Beues of Hamtoun*, ed. E. Kölbing, EETS, E.S. 46, 48, 65 (London, 1885 – 94); *Ipomadon*, ed. E. Kölbing (Breslau, 1889).

ritual ('As was the gise, i-born was vp and down,' V, 1650) and thus echoes the parading of trophies in some romances.

Chaucer's main debt to the *Roman de Troie*, however, lies in his use of it for two extended borrowings (V, 92 – 189, 995 – 1099) which present in much greater fullness than Boccaccio the process of Diomede's wooing of Briseida, and reflect in Chaucer's added soliloquy for Criseyde that sophisticated psychological interest found in the finest French romances. Where Boccaccio had compressed Benoit's account, in order to show a perfunctory and easy victory for Diomede, it suited Chaucer's approach to his heroine to go back to the ampler treatment of this episode in the *Roman de Troie*. With this reversion to the source-behind-his-source, Chaucer now includes the kind of exchanges between lovers in a knightly society which are no part of *Filostrato* but which do recall the world of some English romances. The developing relationship between Criseyde and Diomede is now expressed as in the *Roman de Troie* through the gift of the lady's sleeve or glove (V, 1043, 1013), while the lover sends his lady the gift of a captured horse (V, 1039), just as the heroes of *William of Palerne* and *Ipomadon*, and of other romances, send to their ladies presents of the horses captured in their battles.

Chaucer's absorption from Benoit of such social observance in the world of a chivalrous romance chiefly affects that last book of *Troilus* where Chaucer can make most use of the parallel narrative in the *Roman de Troie*. This has the remarkable consequence in *Troilus* that the betrayal and disenchantment of the hero's experience of romance is presented within some of the most quintessential conventions of romance tradition. Criseyde is most sustainedly referred to by the traditional epithets of English romance as the *lady bright* or *free*, or as the *may*, in that very fifth book where she can no longer be a heroine of romance. Both Diomede (V, 144, 162, 922) and Troilus (V, 465, 516, 669, 1362, 1390, 1405) refer to Criseyde as *bright* or *free*, and Troilus calls her his *lady bright* at some of his moments of keenest disenchantment (V, 1241, 1247, 1264, 1573, 1712), and only addresses her as his *may* at moments of farewell and relinquishing (V, 1412, 1720).

In the earlier books the developing relationship between Troilus and Criseyde — where Chaucer could derive little from the *Roman de Troie* — is not rewritten with such chivalrous romance texture: Troilus sends Criseyde no horses. But Chaucer does add moments to his Italian source narrative in which his lovers solemnly see their feelings as vested in significant and symbolic objects, in a way redolent of much romance. The brooch given to Criseyde by Troilus as a 'remembraunce' of himself at parting is indeed already in *Filostrato*, but after the consummation the lovers 'pleyinge entrechaungeden hire rynges' (III, 1369), and in addition 'a broche, gold and asure,/ In which a rubye set was lik an herte,/

Criseyde hym ʒaf, and stak it on his sherte. . .' (1370 – 2). Here Chaucer's Criseyde reifies her giving of her heart to Troilus in outward form, as in the lady's gifts in the *Roman de Troie*. Much later, Troilus's instructions to Pandarus about the arrangements for his funeral show Chaucer's classicizing of his source, with antique details drawn from *Teseida*. Yet the outcome of this pagan cremation is to be a gesture reminiscent of some of the 'love's reliquaries' of romance, like the reliquary for the nightingale in Marie de France's *lai* of *Laustic*. Troilus instructs Pandarus to present the ashes of his heart in a golden vessel to his lady 'for a remembraunce' (V, 309 – 15), just as in *The Knight of Curtesy* a dying lover orders that after death his heart be sent to his lady as a token.[10] At such moments, in the heart-shaped ruby and the golden reliquary of the lover's heart, the longings of Chaucer's lovers are concentrated in a precious object in a way reminiscent of the use of love-tokens by Benoit de Ste-Maure and in romance more widely.

But while Chaucer returns to some aspects of the *Roman de Troie* to supplement his *Troilus* with romance features, he entirely ignores that element of the enchanted and fabulous that he could find interwoven by Benoit with the story of his Troilus and Briseida. When Briseida leaves Troy she attires herself in a magnificent mantle of fabulous materials and decoration sent to Calcas by an Indian seer ('En Inde la Superior/ Firent un drap enchanteor / Par nigromance e par merveille . . .' 13341ff.), and when she reaches the Greek camp she is escorted to Calcas's rich tent, which had once belonged to that Pharoah who drowned in the Red Sea (13818 – 21).[11] Such exotic marvels of the French romance are pointedly not taken over by Chaucer into his own romance here, and such a disinclination to the outwardly marvellous in romance is characteristic of Chaucer's approach in the *Troilus*, where the central experience of love is intensified and internalized as the true inward 'aventure' and 'merveille', within a self-conscious sense of romance tradition and convention which anticipates the eventual disenchantment with the romance.

The focus of the *Troilus* narrative, at least before the hero's final ascent to the spheres, is accordingly this-worldly, and the marvellous or supernatural is either avoided or glanced at ironically, with the one significant exception of Troilus's moment of falling in love, where Chaucer revivifies the dead metaphor of Love's piercing in *Filostrato* (1.25) into a supernatural event, a confrontation with a god ('The god of loue gan loken rowe,' I,206). When Boccaccio's Diomede is wooing Criseida he mentions the possibility that he is of divine descent ('e, se

---

[10] *The Knight of Curtesy*, ed. E. McCausland, *Smith College Studies in Modern Languages*, 4 (1922), p. 14.

[11] Benoit de Sainte-Maure, *Le Roman de Troie*, ed. L. Constans, SATF (Paris, 1904 – 12).

creder si può, di dio disceso,' 6.24), but even so slight a hint of any supernatural dimension to one of the characters of his romance is dropped by Chaucer in translating (cf. V, 932 – 8), just as there is nothing otherworldly about the practical yet bookish character of Chaucer's Pandarus, that reader of romances and manipulator of the lovers' lives. When Criseyde has accepted the 'service' of Troilus, Chaucer has his Pandarus exclaim 'With-outen hond me semeth that in towne/ ffor this merueille ich here ech belle sowne . . .' (III, 188 – 9), which is an allusion to the tradition of the miraculous ringing of bells to signify a marvel in popular romances and ballads. Here the 'Trojan' Pandarus shows himself steeped in the motifs of the medieval English popular romances, but for Pandarus it is an artful literary allusion to associate the sequence of events in the lovers' lives which he has himself planned with the marvels of the old romances. In saving the appearances of the affair Pandarus in fact leaves nothing to enchantment. What may seem a destinal storm to the lovers in Book III — as in the story of Dido and Aeneas — cannot seem so destinal to the Pandarus who has chosen a rainy season to invite his niece to visit. And when Criseyde suggests sending the jealous Troilus the token of a ring, Pandarus shows his impatience with the enchantments of romance by ironically pointing out that it is not a ring with magical powers, as in the romances or in the *Squire's Tale* ('3e, Nece myn, that ryng moste han a stoon/ That myghte dede men alyue maken,/ And swich a ryng trowe I that 3e haue non . . .' III, 891 – 3).

The experience of Chaucer's Troilus and Criseyde is in this way recurrently associated or contrasted with some stock motifs of romance, even as it is eventually distanced from them. *Troilus* becomes so much more of a romance than *Filostrato* so that it can both contain and transcend the experience and the form of romance. In the portrait of Troilus in the 'Iliad' of Joseph of Exeter Chaucer could find that Troilus was a 'giant in spirit', and this Chaucer turns round to become 'Al myghte a geant passen hym of myght,/ His herte ay with the first and with the beste/ Stood peregal, to durre don that hym leste' (V, 838 – 40). Heroes of another kind of romance — like Arthur himself — may manage to overcome giants, but the emphasis in *Troilus and Criseyde* is on the hero's 'herte', and this does not make it less of a romance. The fact that there are indeed no giants or magic rings or bells that ring without hand in the romance of *Troilus* only emphasizes how much like a romance the perception of their inward experience by the characters has become. Troilus and Criseyde both see themselves in relation to the experiences of romance tradition. In Book I Chaucer's Troilus in his despair feels that if his hopeless love were known, 'I shal by-iaped ben a thousand tyme/ More than that fol of whos folie men ryme . . .' (I, 531 – 2). The reference is somewhat oblique, but Troilus is perhaps alluding to the madness of such great lovers in romance as Yvain, or Tristan in *La Folie Tristan*. Whoever the figure may be, Troilus is self-consciously comparing himself with a figure about whom men write rhymes.

A more evident self-comparison to the experience of romance characters is expressed by Criseyde when (like Lavinia gazing down at Aeneas in the *Roman d'Enéas*, 8031ff.) she has seen Troilus ride past below her window on his way back from battle, the very picture of a knight ('That to hire self she seyde, "who ʒaf me drynke?" ' II, 651). Here Criseyde associates her own first response to the sight of Troilus with the transforming effects of such magic love-potions of romance as those of the Tristan stories.

This vision of Troilus perceived by Criseyde as a knight of romance is partly stage-managed by Pandarus when he causes the vision to be repeated for effect (II, 1247ff.), and when he contrives that her knight submits himself to Criseyde's 'service' (III, 128ff.). Indeed, in the added 'feudal' language of love-service which distinguishes *Troilus* from *Filostrato* the Trojan prince Troilus expresses himself through the typical idiom of heroes of romance. The enhanced role of Pandarus in *Troilus* as the manipulator of the lovers' experience is important to the way Chaucer plays on the relation between his narrative of the Troilus story and the conventions of romance. When Pandarus thinks the lovers are brought together 'he drow hym to the feere,/ And took a light and fond his contenaunce,/ As forto looke vpon an old romaunce' (III, 978 – 80), and this reading of a romance suggests a return to the sources of Pandarus's inspiration in contriving the affair between Troilus and Criseyde.

III

For those medieval readers who took down *Troilus* to read by the fire ('I mend the fyre . . ./ I tuik ane quair — and left all uther sport —/ Writtin be worthie Chaucer glorious', Henryson, *Testament of Cresseid*), there were many echoes and resonances from their accumulated sense of 'old romaunce', and such echoes from medieval English romances recur through the *Troilus* in the nature of some archetypal episodes, formulas, gestures and ceremonies, in the handling of the narrative, the narratorial voice, and in attitudes to love.

Study of the patterns and formulas of both language and narrative-plot in romance has encouraged the discernment of 'type-scenes' and episodes within the structures of romance,[12] and although a scene in *Troilus* has actually been taken over from *Filostrato* it might well be referred by its original audiences to a wider context in romance. The scene of the hero's first sight of and love for the heroine while in church is such a type-scene. Troilus's first sight of Criseyde at the temple of 'Palladion' follows the parallel scene in *Filostrato*, but Chaucer's early audiences were more likely to see the scene in the context of thòse comparable moments of enamorment in pagan temples in the *Roman de Troie*. Benoit has Achilles first see and fall in love with Polyxena during a religious rite at Hector's tomb, and this may well lie behind Boccaccio's description of Troiolo in the temple, as may also (more distantly) Benoit's account of how Paris and Helen are first consumed with desire for each other during a ceremony in a temple. Dante's sighting of Beatrice, Petrarch's first sight of Laura, and Boccaccio's of the elusive 'Fiammetta' are all represented as occurring at church, the latter two at the feast of Easter, and reflect a sense of that type-scene of romance which Boccaccio develops in his *Filostrato* and which Chaucer takes over in *Troilus*.

While the temple scene is the dominant episode in the first half of Book I, Troilus's conversation with Pandarus dominates the latter half of the book and is itself no less surrounded with associations as a type-scene. Many romance plot-structures similarly contain a sequence involving the confession to a confidant of the hero or heroine's being in love, and the confidant's plan to gain the beloved. There are a number of parallels in the English romances for such confession scenes, handled with differing degrees of fullness and refinement. In its sparsest outline the type-scene is present in two stanzas of *Octavian* (1093 – 1116),[13] and is also suggested by some incidents in *Floris and Blancheflour* (385 – 424, 443 – 704)[14] and in *Sir Degrevant* (520 – 608, 803 – 939),[15] although it is developed more fully in romances like *Ipomadon* and *William of Palerne*, where there are a number of echoes of the exchanges between Troilus and Pandarus. In *William of Palerne* the heroine Melior confesses her love for William when her confidante Alexandrine begs her to reveal her feelings, and

---

12 Cf. S. Wittig, *Stylistic and Narrative Structures in the Middle English Romances* (Austin, 1978). Cf. D. Pearsall ("The Development of Middle English Romance"): 'Homogeneity is most evident in the observance of a wide range of formal and literary conventions, what we might call the "Grammar" of romance. The same plot-patterns, the same situations, the same phrases, recur insistently from romance to romance, providing much of their popular strength' (p. 11 above). For reference, cf. G. Bordman, *Motif-Index of the English Metrical Romances*, FF Communications (Helsinki, 1963).

13 *Octavian*, ed. Maldwyn Mills, *Six Middle English Romances* (London, 1973).

14 *Floris and Blancheflour*, ed. D. B. Sands, *Middle English Verse Romances* (New York, 1966).

15 *Sir Degrevant*, ed. L. F. Casson, EETS, O.S. 221 (London, 1949).

Alexandrine then offers to help Melior and plans to let William know (580 – 652).[16]

In the remarkable late fourteenth century tail-rhyme romance of *Ipomadon*[17] this type-scene is developed along similar lines, first for Ipomadon and his servant Thelamewe, and then for the heroine and her confidante. As with many other moments in *Ipomadon* which prompt comparison with *Troilus*, this scene is presented with a refinement of observation that provides some echo in contemporary English romance of the detail and delicacy of focus in Chaucer's poem ('In come his maystur Thelamewe/ And sawe, he was pale of hewe,/ So grette wo love hym wroughte./ His maystur than began to spere/ And sayd . . ./ The sothe to tell hym wold he nought,/ For no thyng, that he cowde owghte . . .' 1210ff.).[18] When the type-scene is again developed later, where the lady is found sighing and fainting in her bed by her maiden Imayne, there are a number of echoes in the friend's persuasions and the heroine's sense of secrecy of the parallel scene between Troilus and Pandarus. Just as Pandarus urges, 'And sith thow hast a felawe, tel thi mone . . .' (I, 696), so Imayne argues 'ofte sythe it dothe men good . . ./ To trewe felowe a tale to rehersse . . .' (1418 – 9), and just as Troilus is desperate to keep his secret ('3et Troilus for al this no worde seyde,/ But longe he ley as stylle as he ded were . . .' I, 722 – 3), so too is the lady in *Ipomadon* ('In faythe, I can not tell thee,/ Shuld I be dede þerfore . . .' 1431 – 2). The balance of warmth and wryness in the presentation of love in *Ipomadon* allows a

16 *The Romance of William of Palerne*, ed. W. W. Skeat, EETS, E.S. 1 (London, 1867).
17 The tail-rhyme *Ipomadon* was 'translated in the late fourteenth century' from Hue de Rotelande's Anglo-Norman original, and the unique fifteenth century manuscript (Chetham MS 8009) is in the "North Midland-Lancashire dialect" (J. Burke Severs, *A Manual of the Writings in Middle English 1050 – 1500*, Vol. 1 [New Haven, 1967], p. 153). For the Anglo-Norman poem, cf. A. J. Holden (ed.), *Ipoemedon: Poème de Hue de Rotelande. (fin du xii˚ siècle)*, Paris, 1979). As Robert W. Hanning points out ("*Engin* in Twelfth-Century Romance: An Examination of the *Roman d'Enéas* and Hue de Rotelande's *Ipomedon*," *YFS*, 51 (1974), 82 – 101): 'Hue's interest in *engin* focusses less on artifacts of rare accomplishment, more on wittily deceptive and manipulative behaviour" (p. 92). If the English *Ipomadon*-poet were influenced by Chaucer his lessons have been assimilated to the point where they are no longer directly apparent.
18 Cf. D. Pearsall ("The Development of Middle English Romance"): 'There is little concession to popular taste here, for *Ipomadon* is courtly, witty, smooth, enormously leisurely, technically highly gifted, and it opens up the tradition for a much more sophisticated audience' (p. 33 above). In discussing the 'pointing' of a scene in *Troilus* (II, 262 – 78), J. A. Burrow comments: 'Among the Middle English metrical romances it could be matched only in the remarkable tail-rhyme romance *Ipomedon A*, where some scenes . . . are pointed in enough detail for the reader to be reminded of Chaucer. But the author of *Ipomedon A* . . . was himself an exceptionally gifted writer, who might occupy a significant place in a comprehensive account of the Ricardian period,' *Ricardian Poetry* (London, 1971), p. 71. Cf. also A. V. C. Schmidt and N. Jacobs (eds.), *Medieval English Romances* (London, 1980), Vol. 2, pp. 40 – 9.

juxtaposition of the passionate intensity of the hero and the common-sense of the friend in a way reminiscent of the *Troilus*. The contrast within the scene in *Troilus* ('And wel neigh with the word for feere he deide./ And whann that Pandare herde hire name neuene,/ Lord, he was glad . . .' I, 875 – 7) finds some parallel in contemporary English romance in the contrast of tone in *Ipomadon* between hero and helper:

> 'And, mayster, or I my love shuld lese,
> In faythe, I wille be dede!'
> Whan Thalamewe herd þis tydynge,
> He sayd wyth hertte full well lauȝhyng . . . (2316 – 9).

As with such type-scenes of romance, so too with formulas and stock gestures which express the emotions: there is some common field of ideas, phrasing and stock situations between scenes in the *Troilus* and in the more refined romances, which suggest that — however extraordinary and special in its execution — Chaucer's poem could be related by its first readers and hearers to many of the traditions and conventions of what happens in the narratives of romance. Some of the expressions of sorrow used by Chaucer particularly echo the stock language of the romances. When *Filostrato* narrates how Troiolo could find no sign of life in the fainted body of Criseida the hero is described as *doloroso* (4.118), but in *Troilus* this becomes 'ffor which his song ful ofte is "weylaway" ' (IV, 1166), an added line which echoes a repeated refrain in some of the romances (e.g. *Amis and Amiloun*: 'Oft his song was "Waileway!" ' 1852; 'His song was "Waileway!" ' 2130).[19] When Chaucer goes on in the next lines to translate *dicea piangendo* [he said with tears] as 'with sorweful vois and herte of blisse al bare,/ He seyde . . .' (IV, 1168 – 9), he is again echoing some of the recurrent phraseology of romance (e.g. *Ipomadon*: 'His loue and I shuld forgoo,/ Off blis I were full bare!' 2203 – 4; 'To fight for that lady clere,/ That was of blis full bare . . .' 8214 – 5). The 'cares colde' of Troilus, mentioned recurrently through the poem ('And Troilus moot wepe in cares colde . . .' V, 1747), echo a phrase frequent and characteristic in some romances (e.g. 'As I be kepte frome carys colde,' *Ipomadon*, 7710). When Chaucer translated the account of Criseida's grief on the morning of her departure from Troy (*Fil* 5.1), but adds the line in *Troilus* 'ffor sorwe of which she felt hire herte blede' (V, 17), this echoes a formula recurrent in some romances (e.g. *Emaré*: 'For sorow hys herte gan blede,' [552, repeated at 609][20]; *Octavian*: 'For sorowe ther hertys can blede,' 288; 'For sorowe hur herte can blede,' 345). Pandarus's fierce oath 'Til I myn owen herte blood may see . . .' (II, 445) draws on the emphatic

---

19   *Amis and Amiloun*, ed. MacEdward Leach, EETS, O.S. 203 (London, 1937).
20   *Emaré*, ed. Maldwyn Mills, *Six Middle English Romances* (London, 1973).

language of romance characters (e.g. 'In feythe, or I frome the yode,/ I shuld se thy hertte blod . . .' *Ipomadon*, 1962 – 3). The regret that one was ever born, a note that Chaucer recurrently strikes in the *Troilus*, as when Criseyde in the Greek camp cries 'That I was born, so weilaway the tide!' (V, 700), is itself an outburst that recurs among the grieving characters of romance (e.g. *Emaré*: 'Sore he grette and sayde, "Alas,/ That Y evur man born was!"' 556 – 7; 'Alas,/That evur born Y was . . .' 772 – 3).

In Chaucer's use of gesture or body-language in *Troilus* there are also many parallels with stock gestures and formulas of the English romances. All the sore sighing that recurs in *Troilus* ('. . . she wepte and siked sore' IV, 716) echoes a recurrent token of distress in the narratives of the romances (e.g. *Floris and Blancheflour*: 'Sore he wept and sore he sight' 256, repeated at 270). Although some of the sighing in *Troilus* comes through from *Filostrato*, there is much addition reminiscent of the patterns of popular romance. Very much part of some more refined English romances are also the tremblings and swoonings through which Chaucer suggests a greater delicacy and timidity in the characters of his lovers. When Chaucer describes his Criseyde in the consummation scene ('Right as an aspes leef she gan to quake,' III, 1200) the comparison is one found in the gestures of other heroines of romance (e.g. *Ipomadon*: 'Then as an aspleff she quoke . . .' 6727; 'And as as aspenlleff she shoke,/ She was so sore aferde . . .' 6871 – 2). When Pandaro visits Troiolo in Book IV the latter runs weepingly to him (4.44), and when Chaucer elaborates so that his Troilus 'Gan as the snow aȝeyn the sonne melte' (IV, 367), he is adding the kind of stock figure which could recall the romances (e.g. *Sir Launfal*: 'All that he hadde before y-wonne,/ Hit malt as snow agens the sunne,/ In romance as we rede . . .' 739 – 41).[21] In *Ipomadon* the gestures and reactions of sensitive people stricken with suffering in love are observed with a detail and grace which parallels the *Troilus* in showing what some contemporary English audiences relished in romance. Just as Troilus — in a scene taken over from *Filostrato* — lies turning restlessly in bed ('To bedde he goth, and walwith ther and torneth,' V, 211, which in one MS reads 'and *waltryth* ther . . .'), so in *Ipomadon* a character goes to bed and 'Trobelyng too and fro she lyes,/ Waltryng on a woofull wyse' (7124 – 5). In the same scene Troilus pities himself that he has nothing left to embrace in bed but his pillow ('Saue a pilowe, I fynde naught tenbrace,' V, 224), and while this translates quite closely from *Filostrato* ('ora abbracciando/ vado il piumaccio . . .' 5.20), some contemporary English audiences could be familiar with a scene like that in *William of Palerne* ('þat puluere clept he curteisly & kust it ful ofte . . ./ He wende ful witerly sche were in is armes;/ Ac peter! it nas but is puluere to proue þe soþe . . .'

---

[21]   *Thomas Chestre: Sir Launfal*, ed. A. J. Bliss (London, 1960).

671ff.). The scene where Criseyde tears her hair, wrings her hands and prays for death (IV, 736ff.) is developed from *Filostrato*, but contemporary audiences of a romance like *Ipomadon* need not find the emotional tone and gestural detail of the *Troilus* unfamiliar, however superior in texture ('She tare hyr clothes & drewe hure hare/ Wyth many a carefull crye:/ "Thow dethe, thou come to me . . ./ And helpe, be lyve, that I were slaye,/ I praye the specyallye . . .' 4686 – 90). Just as Criseyde is described ('And on hire bed she gan for ded to falle/ . . . and ek hire fyngeres longe and smale/ She wrong ful ofte . . .' IV, 733 – 8), so too in *Ipomadon* comparable experience is narrated, however less intensely and acutely ('To hyr chambure gan she gonge/ Wepyng, and hure handes wrange/ And on here bedde hur layes,' 1814 – 6).

Such scenes of lamentation often include something of that sense of ritual and ceremoniousness which more generally marks the texture of romance, and which Chaucer draws on in *Troilus* at such moments as the hero's thanksgiving after the consummation, with its echoes of some stock emphases and gestures from scenes of thanksgiving in romance. When Pandaro comes to Troiolo next morning the hero emotionally throws himself on his friend's neck (3.56), whereas Chaucer has his Troilus solemnly kneel to his friend and 'gan hym thonken in his beste wise/ An hondred sythe, and gan the tyme blesse/ That he was born to brynge hym fro destresse' (III, 1594 – 6). Indeed, in some MSS Troilus thanks Pandarus 'A *thousand* sythe', and this thankfulness recalls some scenes of rejoicing in romance (e.g. *Amis and Amiloun*: 'þan was Sir Amis glad & bliþe/ & þanked him a þousand siþe/ þe time þat he was born' 1438 – 40: 'þan were þai al glad & bliþe/ & þonked god a þousand siþe,' 1402 – 3). The link between present happiness and a fortunate birth occurs here in *Troilus* as in the romances. The incidence of added kneeling and prayerful thankfulness in *Troilus* is a noticeable difference from *Filostrato*, just as some of the texture of social observance in Chaucer's poem seems to echo the emphases of the romances. When Chaucer alters *Filostrato*'s plain account of how Calcas received his daughter 'con gran festa' (5.14) so that 'And twenty tyme he kiste his doughter sweete' (V, 191), his inclination to elaborate this moment of greeting may recall some of the typical moments of greeting or reunion in the romances (e.g. *Sir Triamour*: 'Twenty tymys he dud hur kysse/ Then made they game and blysse,' 160 – 1).[22]

---

22   *Sir Triamour*, ed. J. O. Halliwell, Percy Society 16 (London, 1846). Some textual variation in *TC* MSS shows how some scribes registered and extended romance phraseology. In V, 669 ('. . . myn owene lady free') one MS, British Library Harley MS 1239, reads 'lady fair and free' (cf. *Ipomadon*: 'Tell me, lady fayre & fre,' 1415; 'Yon lady fayre & free . . .' 4881). In V, 64 ('This Troilus, in wise of *curteysie*') B.L. MS Additional 12044 reads 'wise of *gentell drewrie*'.

The English version of *Ipomadon*, moreover, provides at least some parallel in the English romance literature of the period for the sophisticated use of the narrating voice in Chaucer's romances. In effecting transitions in the narrative, indeed, Chaucer sometimes seems to echo the procedures of the English romances. When the narrative shifts back and forth between the separate lives of Troilus and Criseyde in Book II, it is Chaucer who has the poem's narrating voice articulate the transition in a way without equivalent in *Filostrato* but with many parallels in the English romances. The use in *Troilus* of such transition formulas as 'Now lat vs stynte of Troilus a throwe,/ That rideth forth, and lat vs torne faste/ Unto Criseyde' (II, 687 – 9), or 'Now lat hire slepe, and we oure tales holde/ Of Troilus . . .' (II, 932 – 3), closely recalls the familiar narrative transitions of English romance as developed at their more polished in the structure of *Ipomadon*, where we find such transitions as 'The damysell now leve we thore,/ And of hur louer speke we more,/ That leuythe in mekyll drede' (2285 – 7), or again: 'Ipomadon leve we thus/ And turne agayne to Cabanus,/ That was so good a knyght . . .' (8201 – 3).

But in *Ipomadon* the narrating voice in the romance is developed in a more sophisticated involvement with the story in a way that provides some English romance context for Chaucer's narrative method in *Troilus*. There is in *Ipomadon* some of that artful engagement of the narrator's tender feelings with the characters' lives which Chaucer deploys to his own effect in *Troilus*. When Criseyde is moved while looking at Troilus as he rides past her house for the second time, the narrating voice exclaims enthusiastically: 'To god hope I she hath now kaught a thorn,/ She shal nat pulle it out this nexte wyke —/ God sende mo swich thornes on to pike' (II, 1272 – 4). And when the narrator of *Ipomadon* describes a comparably important moment of perception about the hero by the lady in his romance he goes on to exclaim: 'In a stody full stylle she stode:/ I hope, here lokynge dyd here goode,/ Be god and my lewte!' (749 – 51). There is also more than a hint of the Chaucerian narrator's affectionately defensive loyalty to his heroine in the *Ipomadon* narrator's fond acceptance of the changeable nature of women ('There they haue byn most straunge,/ All att onys then will they chaunge/ . . . Godes dere blessyng and myne/ Muste they have therefore!' (7091ff.). Not unlike the device in *Troilus* where the narrator regrets what he has to relate ('I-wis, I wolde excuse hire ʒet for routhe,' V, 1099), the narrator in *Ipomadon* grieves over what he must narrate ('But a condycyon havys he,/ That I shall say, sore rewys me,/ All ladyes to love it lays . . .' 512 – 4). Some of that sympathetic and knowing observation in *Troilus* of the ways of lovers ('And this knowe I by hem that louers be,' III, 37) is also expressed in the narrative manner of *Ipomadon* ('They tremblyd bothe for gree,/ As lovers maners hathe bene,/ That long while no noþer hathe sene,/ Ye maye well witt there by . . .' 8744 – 7). That anticipation of a future at variance with the present which is expressed by the narrating voice of *Troilus* ('But Troilus, now far wel al thi ioie,/ ffor shaltow neuere sen hire eft in Troie,' V, 27 – 8) finds at least some parallel in the anticipatory narrative comments in a refined English romance like *Ipomadon* ('Joyefull was that maydon fre,/ But I trowe, by my lewte,/ That comnaunde will not holde,' 6008 – 10).

In romances where the narrative focusses on an experience of intense, carefully guarded secrecy and privacy from a wider world ('And they that nothyng knewe of his entente,' *TC*, II, 1665), one of the roles of the narrator is to share with the reader that secret inner knowledge of the lives of the hero or heroine ('But litill knewe þey his entente,' *Ipomadon*, 464). This sense of the inward intensity of love can often only be expressed through the paradoxes and contrarieties of love that Troilus voices in his *canticus* ('ffor hete of cold, for cold of hete, I dye,' I, 420) or in his letter ('My good in harm, myn ese ek woxen helle is,' V, 1376). But this intensity of feeling in love is not without almost equivalently courtly echoes in an English romance like *Ipomadon*, where the hero can declare in soliloquy: 'Of helle yt is the hottest payne,/ To love and be not lovyd agayne,/ There-on no wysdome lyese,' (1103 – 5). It is not only in the *Troilus* that love-stricken characters lament with gracefulness of language the near-madness and near-death that they suffer in love, for as Imayne exclaims to Ipomadon: 'Nere hand in poynt to rave,/ I love the so, wyth outen fayle,/ That, yff I lesse my travayle,/ I shall be layde in grave!' (7436 – 9). Just as in *Troilus* there is much sense of the constraints and binding power of love ('ffor loue hadde hym so bounden in a snare,' I, 663), so too in *Ipomadon*, e.g.: 'For love my herte hathe bovnde so faste,/ That euer more love will wyth me last/ To tyme, that I shall dee . . .' (1189 – 91).

In *Ipomadon* as in *Troilus* this kind of idiom is framed overall by a fond but quizzical narrative voice. In *Troilus* there is a six-stanza narratorial commentary after the hero has fallen in love, which begins with the example of 'proude Bayard' and develops the theme of love's power to overcome all resistance and to humble pride (I, 218 – 59). But some fourteenth-century English audiences could have heard in English a comparable discussion of the relation between love and pride in the tail-rhyme *Ipomadon*. Just as in *Troilus* there is commentary on the power of love to overcome princes ('So ferde it by this fierse and proude knyght:/ Though he a worthy kynges sone were . . .' I, 225 – 6), so too in *Ipomadon* the narrator comments on some events of the romance that 'Love is so mekyll off myghte,/ That it will davnte bothe kyng and knyght . . .' (7346 – 7), and earlier the narrator had commented on the mutual attraction of the hero and heroine: 'All othere thynges men davnte may,/ But, sertenly, be no waye/ Love wille no be davnte!' (800 – 2). In *Troilus* this narratorial passage comments: 'Men reden nat that folk han gretter wit/ Than they that han be most with loue ynome . . ./ ffor alderwisest han ther-with ben plesed . . .' (I, 241 – 2, 247), and in a comparable vein of commentary the *Ipomadon* narrator remarks: 'They, that wyseste is of witte,/ Fro tyme they be takyne wyth it,/ Hit takythe fro them there reasowne . . .' (7349 – 51). Indeed, just as in *Troilus* the audience is urged 'Refuseth nat to loue forto ben bonde' (I, 255) and persuaded 'The ȝerde is bet than bowen wole and wynde/ Than that that brest . . .' (257 – 8; or in some *Troilus* MSS 'Betir is the wand that bowen wole . . .'), so in *Ipomadon* the hero is advised by his confidant 'That lovers shold well leynand be,/ For mekyll I preyse that wande,/ That brekes not and will well bowe;/ Righte so it farythe be them, I trowe,/ That lovys and well can layne . . .' (2334 – 8). The witty archness of his Anglo-Norman model stimulates the poet of this English *Ipomadon* to a poised relationship with his romance narrative and with his audience which provides a rare parallel in the surviving English romances for the distinctive narratorial control and ironic detachment of the *Troilus*. For just as in *Troilus* the audience is addressed as 'ȝe wise, proude, and worthi folkes alle' (233) and urged 'Refuseth nat to loue forto ben bonde,/ Syn as hym seluen liste he may ȝow bynde' (255 – 6), so in *Ipomadon* the poet describes how his heroine's heart is not as yet 'dauntyd' with love and comments: 'But aftur sore it bande the fre,/ And so I wold, that all ye shuld be,/ That is of love so prowde!' (388 – 90).

IV

In Thomas Usk's *Testament of Love*, in response to Usk's request for instruction on the question of predestination, Love refers him to Chaucer's *Troilus*, remarking:

> 'Myne owne trewe servaunt, the noble philosophical poete in Englissh . . . in a tretis that he made of my servant Troilus, hath this mater touched, and at the ful this question assoyled . . . In goodnes of gentil manliche speche, without any maner of nycetè of storiers imaginacion, in witte and in good reson of sentence he passeth al other makers . . .'[23]

In distinguishing Chaucer from 'the foolishness of storytellers' imaginings' this contemporary reader of *Troilus* perhaps points to the gap — in

[23]   *Chaucerian and Other Pieces*, ed. W. W. Skeat (Oxford, 1897), p. 123.

subject matter, handling, and not least in structure — between Chaucer and the popular English romances of his day. Yet that Chaucer, unlike Boccaccio, shows characters of his romance reading a romance themselves within the poem is a token of the way that Chaucer plays on an awareness of romance conventions in his *Troilus*. When Chaucer's Pandarus visits Criseyde he finds her sitting with two other ladies 'and they thre/ Herden a mayden reden hem the geste/ Of the siege of Thebes while hem leste,' (II, 82 – 4). Criseyde tells him it is a romance ('This romaunce is of Thebes that we rede'), and that she calls the book a romance, which is being read to an audience of ladies, would probably suggest to Chaucer's audience a work in the vernacular, such as the *Roman de Thebes*, a *roman d'antiquité* like the *Roman de Troie*. But when Pandarus urges his niece to put aside her book and dance she dismisses this as unsuitable conduct for a widow, and in retort suggests a more fitting and alternative mode of life, which she characterizes as an alternative form of *reading* ('It satte me wel bet ay in a caue/ To bidde and rede on holy seyntes lyues . . .'). Here Criseyde briefly summons up the tradition of the desert saint, the female recluse living in prayer and holy reading in some desert fastness ('Who fedde the Egipcien Marie in the cave,/ Or in desert . . .?' *MLT*, II, 500 – 1). The moment is fleeting but remarkable, and the contrast could scarcely be sharper between Criseyde's refined and courtly ease, entertained by romance reading, and an ascetic life of prayer and pious reading of saints' lives. Such a contrast anticipates the eventual disenchantment with the this-worldly in *Troilus*, and that disenchantment is the more painful because the lovers' experience within the romance is so intensified and internalized. By removing the previous experience in love of the Italian Troiolo, Chaucer at once makes his hero's first experience of love much more of a personal 'aventure' and one in which, as Troilus's use of religious language shows, he finds something to him miraculous and marvellous. In its concern for secrecy, too, *Troilus* draws on traditions quintessential to much romance. Just as Troilus suffers secretly before Criseyde's empty house ('ffor which, with chaunged dedlich pale face,/ With-outen word he forthby gan to pace . . ./ That no wight of his contenance espide,' V, 536 – 9), so comparable moments characterize a refined romance like *Ipomadon* ('The lady satte and coloure keste/ And euer mornyd stille;/ She fadyd ofte, but she her feynde,/ And be resvn she her constreynede,/ That none parcevyd her wyll,' 5248 – 52).

A key difference, however, is that in *Troilus* Chaucer has so modified his source as to remove any strictly logical necessity for that secrecy which nonetheless the romance tradition insists upon. In a romance like *Ipomadon* the secrecy of the lady's feelings is necessitated, because in the disguised person of the hero she has fallen in love with somebody

146

apparently unthinkably beneath her in rank. Ipomadon's own repeated wish to disguise himself as an unknown knight or a comically cowardly servant, and recurrently to disappear after achieving victories, reflects the more mysterious need for secrecy in some heroes of romance, who seek disguise in order to put themselves successively to the test, to submit to 'aventure'. But while in Benoit or in Boccaccio the need for secrecy and the impossibility of marriage between Troilus and Criseyde was explained by the unbridgeable social disparity between the prince and the astrologer's daughter, Chaucer has so enhanced the social standing of his Criseyde as part of his presentation of her as the 'lady', the heroine of romance, that the immediate pressure for secrecy becomes much less real. Yet at the same time as making his Criseyde the valued friend of Troilus's family and endowing her with the palace and entourage of a noble lady, Chaucer also intensifies the lovers' concern for secrecy by comparison with *Filostrato*. That the conventions of romance form seem at such times to be pursued more urgently for their own sake in the *Troilus* is part of the way that Chaucer's poem works within and plays upon the expectations of romance, as it echoes some of the motifs of the English romances and their French forebears. The '*nycetè* of storiers imaginacion' Chaucer indeed avoids, yet the 'storiers imaginacion' of the romance tradition is still distinctively at work behind 'the noble philosophical poete in Englissh'.

Le Morte Darthur
and Romance

TERENCE McCARTHY

According to William of Malmesbury, King Arthur was "a man worthy to be celebrated not by ideal fictions, but by authentic history,"[1] and Malory, I believe, would have agreed. The "ideal fictions" of French romance provided the main bulk of his source material but certain features of his own redaction suggest a degree of disappointment with the genre. It could be argued that the *Morte Darthur* constitutes a movement away from romance, or that it presents that genre in a new light. Malory's *matière* is the *matière* of romance, but the *sen*, the 'feeling', is perhaps not.

There is no denying that individual adventures, whole tales even, abound in romance elements (magic, quests, adventure, inexplicable events, etc.), but the basic conception of the "hoole book" and its major narrative outline are presented in other terms. Romance takes us close to its heroes; we share their thoughts and see into their hearts. Malory takes us further away, replacing intimacy by respect. The romance features of his sources, the marvellous even, are not necessarily banished, for Malory the historian can encompass the casual mixture of magic and the everyday so typical of romance, but they are contained. They do not undermine the authenticity of the historical record; they become a testimony to a grandeur which has inevitably disappeared. Gawain's miraculous strength may be a remnant of folktale; in Malory's superlative world it is an agent of moral evaluation. But the central romance concern with private feeling is put aside and Malory allows himself no superior vantage

---

[1] I quote the translation of William of Malmesbury used by Gillian Beer (*The Romance* (London, 1970), p. 22) because the wording is appropriate for my argument. Other critics replace 'ideal fictions' by 'idle tales', 'fallacious fables' or 'foolish dreams of deceitful fables' for example. A shorter version of the present essay appeared under the title 'Private Worlds in *Le Morte Darthur*' in *Etudes Anglaises*, vol. XXXIX no. 1, janvier – mars 1986. I wish to thank the editor for his permission to re-use material first published in his periodical.

point. He handles the material of romance, as it were, from within, assuming the role of court historian and with it all the deference and distance that the public role requires. It is this outlook, I would suggest, which explains Malory's basic shift of emphasis. As he distinguishes between private and public worlds and, at the end, analyses their respective roles, Malory presents the material of romance in the historical mode. Leaving aside much of the incidental narrative, it is this central contrast I would like to discuss.

Le Morte Darthur is the history of a public world in which the central figure, the main hero, is the Round Table itself. The fellowship of knights is more important than any individual, and the honour achieved by an individual is, first of all, part of the collective honour of the community. The respect Lancelot merits from his fellow knights is not merely a reflexion of his own personally earned preeminence but a measure of the glory he has brought to them all. Members of the community have a proper role to play in a clear hierarchical structure and their personal identity is of little or no importance. For Malory, one's public identity and one's real identity are the same thing: a knight, if not a book, can be judged by his cover. Consequently, once a knight disguises his public image — his armour — he obliterates his identity. When Lancelot appears at a tournament in disguise, although his style of riding and skill in combat (both public, military traits) set people guessing, no one recognises him.[2] Lancelot's way of speaking was apparently distinctive (260.26), but no one even recognises his voice.[3] Modern readers of the Morte may well be tempted to look behind the public image, to peer inside the armour to find the real man, but when we do so we often find — to borrow Italo Calvino's amusing idea — il cavaliere inesistente. For Malory, private identity is of secondary inportance; one's role, one's official, public position is what counts. Significantly, Arthur in the depths of despair bemoans not the day he was born, but the day he became king (1183.7).[4]

In Malory's public world of action mere personal characteristics are a poor means of identification. Distinctive features such as Guinevere's recognisable cough, the scar on Lancelot's cheek or his accent are

[2]   The Works of Sir Thomas Malory, edited by Eugène Vinaver, 3 vols (Oxford, 1947). Second, revised, edition 1973. pp. 1070 – 77. Future references will be quoted by page and line number in the text.

[3]   The author of the Mort Artu does not turn his back on realistic details of this kind. Denying Lancelot's presence at a tournament Bohort says "se il i eüst esté, que il n'eüst parlé a moi et que ge ne l'eüsse conneü." See La Mort le Roi Artu, edited by Jean Frappier (Paris, 1936), 3rd edition, 1964, p. 33, section 34, lines 8 – 9. Future references will be quoted by page, section and line number in the text.

[4]   At the corresponding point of the Mort Artu Arthur "dit qu'il a trop vescu." (129, 99.7).

occasionally mentioned to serve the purposes of the plot,[5] but once they have done so they are forgotten. Despite his great gift for dialogue, Malory makes no attempt, as P. J. C. Field points out,[6] to distinguish between characters by the words they use. A knight's speech reveals the social group to which he belongs — "that is full knyghtly spokyn" — but not his identity. It is moral characteristics, how a knight distinguishes himself by his deeds, which, for Malory, are far more telling. As modern readers we might object that we do not even know what Lancelot and Guinevere, for example, looked like. Malory, I believe, would register surprise. Do we really mean to say that if the "most nobelest Crysten quene" walked into the room we would not know her? Lancelot may not be physically head and shoulders above all other knights; it is stature not size which makes him stand out in a crowd. Elaine and Lavayne, Urry and Fyleloly knew him for what he was at once. His moral excellence made him instantly recognisable.

In Malory's survey of the Arthurian world it is to public attributes that he regularly pays attention. Notice the importance of titles in *Le Morte Darthur*, especially in relation to Lancelot and Guinevere. Mark Lambert points out that in the early parts of the book "Malory follows period usage . . . and names characters either with or without their titles" but "in his later works Malory always names characters with their titles." Lambert's conclusions are to the point: "Sir Lancelot is essentially a knight rather than a man who happens to be a knight. We will be invited less often to share the private doubts and perplexities of Malory's character than of the *Vulgate* Lancelot," and the use of titles suggests "a particular view of reality." But it is not true that only the "mature Malory thinks of his hero as 'Sir Lancelot' rather than as 'Lancelot'"[7] for Malory throughout *Le Morte Darthur* is careful to use Lancelot's title. Apart from four references in Merlin's prophecies, where the name or the figure of Lancelot is more important than the man, and three references to Lancelot as a boy, I have traced only six examples where Malory himself (or his scribe) fails to use the title.[8] Concerning Guinevere the situation is even clearer. She is never referred to without a title (occasionally 'dame'

---

[5]   Oddly enough, the reference in Book III to Lancelot's speech does not really serve the plot even. The lady who says she recognises his way of speaking declares that she knows Lancelot anyway.

[6]   P. J. C. Field, *Romance and Chronicle* (London, 1971), pp. 120, 135.

[7]   Mark Lambert, *Malory: Style and Vision in* Le Morte Darthur (New Haven and London, 1975), pp. 66–7.

[8]   These are 804.29; 1017.19; 1255.21; and two references for which the Caxton text provides the title: 660.28; 1213.7. At 627.13 Lancelot's title is missing, but the name is supplied from the Caxton text to repair a corruption in the Winchester manuscript. On six occasions Lancelot is referred to without his title by characters in the story: 282.22; 867.13; 932.27; 933.9; 1014.13; 1259.9.

instead of 'queen'), except, appropriately, five times before her wedding when the title is not officially hers. And even before her marriage her future role is so important that she is called "Quene Gwenyver" twice.[9] Critics refer to the fictional character Guinevere; Malory, who writes with none of their objectivity or familiarity, never does.

What goes on in private at the court of Camelot is not Malory's concern and as historian — as opposed to omniscient narrator — is something to which he has limited access. The private details he can describe are those which have become public knowledge or those for which he has information from his sources because they influenced public events. Otherwise he can only be silent. Malory offers no scenes of private tenderness between Lancelot and Guinevere merely to give us an idea of the nature of their relationship. That the relationship existed is for him a historical fact we must accept, but the intimate details of it are not available to him. As a result we know precious little about Lancelot and Guinevere as individuals. Since the queen's personality — her unreasonableness, her jealousy, her possessiveness — have a direct bearing on events, we do learn something about her. But all those qualities which made her an exceptional woman, which made Arthur and Lancelot fall in love with her, and which kept Lancelot in her thrall for so many years remain unexpounded. If we at times wonder what Lancelot ever saw in this infuriating woman, Malory certainly gives us little help. She was exceedingly beautiful we know; the rest we must take for granted, for Malory shows us only the queen. Guinevere does not become Lancelot's (or Arthur's) "dearest chuck" once the court has withdrawn, for when the court withdraws so do we.

As Malory takes us on a guided tour round Camelot, the doors marked 'private' remain unopened. It is not his habit to peer into the hearts and minds of his characters and he regularly ignores the psychological insights provided by his sources. It could be argued, of course, that in any attempt to abridge a source, psychological description is obvious material to cut, and this is perfectly true. The essential narrative must come first. But Malory's lack of interest in the analysis of feeling has resulted in his producing a book which is not merely shorter but, quite simply, different, one which is less private than his originals, more a book of English history than a *roman français*. His attention is constantly on the public aspects of his material and Malory throughout respects the privacy of his characters.[10] It is not for the historian to enquire into the private motives of the court, nor indeed for the historian to repeat private information if it is

---

9   The unmarried Guinevere is referred to without her title at 97.16; 97.29; 97.34; 98.1; 98.14. At 39.16 and 98.19 she is given her future title.
10   Cf. Lambert, op. cit., p. 113.

available. Malory is aware that such details can even distort the facts and misrepresent a situation entirely. In general he remains silent, but on one (famous) occasion when he is forced to comment, he does so only to refuse, in the name of clarity, the information his readers are waiting for: "and whether they were abed other at other maner of disportis, me lyste nat thereof make no mencion, for love that tyme was nat as love ys nowadayes" (1165.11 – 13). What his characters think or do in private is less important than how things happened. When, in the *Mort Artu*, Bohort offers to fight for Guenièvre unless a better knight appears, the French queen is well aware that it is Lancelot who will come to the rescue after all and "si en devint moult liee" (102, 80.24). Malory preserves the suspense inherent in the public situation by keeping us totally ignorant of what the queen actually believes.

Malory's rejection of the private is more than a process of reduction, it enables him to focus his attention more fully on the public, an approach which can explain something of his attitude to one of his sources, the French prose *Lancelot*. It is by far the longest section of the Vulgate cycle and the central part of it, but although it is focused closely on Malory's favourite hero, he uses it sparingly. Fragments of it are adapted in Book III, one of its episodes is the basis of the Knight of the Cart episode in Book VII, but apart from occasional reminiscences there is little else. We cannot of course be sure how well Malory knew the *Lancelot*, and whether he had a complete copy of it at his disposal. "That Malory's source was simply a gathering of three sheets which had dropped out of a volume of the Prose *Lancelot*" is, Vinaver suggests, a "tempting but not very realistic" speculation,[11] and especially since the various reminiscences suggest a fairly full knowledge. But however well Malory knew this particular source, it is perfectly clear that much in the *Lancelot* is totally out of keeping with the spirit of *Le Morte Darthur* and as a result the tale he devotes to his favourite hero turns out to be, paradoxically, the shortest of all Malory's books.

As the French *Lancelot* progresses, as we move nearer to the Grail story, much emphasis is placed on the inferiority of earthly chivalry to heavenly chivalry, and Malory's own Grail book shows how ill at ease he was with that notion. But most important, a good number of the central incidents in the *Lancelot* are private scenes which form high points in the sentimental history of the hero. There is the first meeting between the timid, tongue-tied, adolescent Lancelot and the older, more worldly Guenièvre; the first rapturous kiss; the first night together and subsequent nights of sophisticated infidelity organised by a small circle of intimates. Lancelot is a lachrymose youth languishing with love for the

---

[11] *The Works of Sir Thomas Malory*, p. 1408.

queen when deprived of her company, inspired to paint masterpieces (icons almost) depicting the main stages of their affair when imprisoned by Morgain La Fée, and — but only after ''ii yvers et un esté''[12] — inspired by the beauty of a rose, a pale reflexion of his lady's beauty, to break the bars of his prison and seek her presence. A number of lengthy incidents are designed to emphasise the hero's infallible fidelity in his private devotion to the queen. On one occasion Lancelot is poisoned, and although bald and skinless as a result of disease his beauty is still so radiant that it arouses the passion of the maiden who nurses him. Having saved his life she feels a right to him, but Lancelot's love for the queen is such that he in no way feels morally bound and never gives in (vol.4, pp. 133 ff). In an earlier passage he is lengthily pursued by the attentions of a temptress sent by Morgain and beats a hasty retreat with all the terrified and injured innocence and none of the gallant but upright experience that reminds us of *Joseph Andrews* but not *Sir Gawain and the Green Knight* (vol.1, pp. 313 ff). Of course the tone of many of these incidents (and most obviously the last) is quite unMalorian in itself, but the essential point is that the French text gives Lancelot the kind of private importance Malory was unwilling to accord even his favourite knight.

Malory's lack of interest in moments of private experience and the refinements of courtly feeling shows a clear soldierly preference for the affairs of state. It may seem strange that in a book where the relationship between Lancelot and the queen plays such a vital role we should see almost nothing of the lovers together, but for Malory it is the public consequences of the love which is his subject; the liaison as such is one of the data of his story and requires little development in itself. Inevitably, the prose *Lancelot* could not help him much. He is writing the public history of Arthur's kingdom not the private history of Lancelot and Guinevere, and the book which, in Vinaver's edition, bears their name is no exception. In this context it is only natural that the lovers should in the end bemoan the destruction of the ''floure of kyngis and knyghtes'' rather than of their love, and that Lancelot, banished by Arthur, should lament not the ''most nobelest Crysten quene'' he was leaving behind, but the ''most nobelyst Crysten realme''(1201.9).

In *Le Morte Darthur* we are rarely privy to the characters' thoughts and feelings; Malory keeps us at a distance. Indeed, he keeps his characters at a distance from each other. Lancelot and Guinevere have none of the small circle of intimate friends who orchestrate their rendez-vous in the French, and even those who are presumably *au courant* speak with greater reticence. Lavayne's request to accompany Lancelot to the queen's room

---

12 *Lancelot*, edited by Alexandre Micha, 9 vols (Paris and Geneva, 1979 et seq.), vol. 5, p. 60. Future references will be quoted by volume and page number in the text.

in Meliagaunt's castle shows the understandable discretion and tact of a subordinate (1131.1 – 3), but even Bors' warnings are expressed with much formality (1164.20 – 1165.4). Not only does Malory himself choose to know less than his sources, he chooses also to let his characters know less and withholds from them a good deal of private information. In the *Mort Artu* after Lancelot escapes from the queen's chamber Bohort declares "Ha! . . . or vaut pis que devant, car ore est la chose descouverte que *nos avions* tant celee" (118,90.85 – 7, italics mine). There is little sense in Malory that Lancelot's party are all aware of what is going on and have been making a joint effort to keep the liaison secret. Indeed, Lancelot justifies himself to them with the same evasive, official version of the story that he uses throughout. "My lady the quene sente for me to speke with her" is all he confides to them (1170.30 – 1171.5). Similarly, Arthur in the *Mort Artu* is given clear proof of his wife's infidelity when he visits Morgain's castle and discovers the paintings Lancelot executed while in prison there. He knows what is going on and has no desire to cover things up, and Gauvain incurs his anger when he tries to dissuade Arthur from taking action: "Gauvain fet li rois, fuiez de ci, car vos estes li hom en qui ge ne me fierai jamés; car mauvesement vos estes contenuz envers moi, quant vos saviez ma honte et la soufriez ne ne le me fesiez asavoir" (112, 87.55 – 9). Malory's Arthur has no more than a "demyng" of the situation (1163.20 – 5), but if at this point Malory for once takes us into the mind of the king, it is only to show him choosing to put aside unconfirmed, private suspicions in the face of the evidence of much public service and for the sake of the public welfare. The French Arthur is acutely aware of how he has been betrayed: Malory's Arthur sees clearly how well he has been served. He is not naively blind; like his court historian he has other priorities.

For Malory, personal concerns remain of secondary importance because the community of knights represents a public ideal no private individual can rival. The greatest individual achievement a knight can obtain is, paradoxically, membership of the community, and striving for that achievement can inevitably provoke rivalry and resentment (131.1 – 2), while the harshest punishment a knight can suffer is the return to the status of an individual by exclusion from the group (120.19 – 20). The role one plays is more important than who or what one is, and it is a measure of the unimportance of individuals — and especially of individual women — in this military world of rank and role that although we know the names of several horses and several swords, the lady who was exceptional enough to capture the heart of both her king (Mark) and the finest knight in the land (Tristram) has no name. She is identified as Sir Segwarides's wife because for Malory her role as someone else's wife is all that matters. In this public world women naturally come off badly. The ones who are identified as belonging to the house of a certain knight are lucky; many have neither a habitation nor a name.

Modern readers, who generally come to Malory with literary habits based on the reading of novels, find this rejection of the individual for the collective, the private for the public something of a problem. Any community is made up of individuals and to establish the collective glory of the group Malory is well and truly forced to centre his readers' attention on individuals. Knights are singled out, that is, for their excellence within the group. But although the attention Malory devotes to certain outstanding knights is all the same regularly public, although his interest is primarily in social relationships rather than private relationships, he has a way of presenting his characters which makes them appear strikingly individual and intensely real. However formal and public his gaze may be, however much he reduces to a minimum the realistic description of both the characters themselves and the background in which they move, the knights and ladies who people his world are presented with great psychological insight. Much of this is due, of course, to Malory's fine ear for convincing dialogue and crisp idiom.[13] In a few words he can bring a scene to life and, beyond the formal, public situation we catch a glimpse of a real world of people we instantly recognise. There are scores of examples: the "full womanly" frankness of Torre's mother confessing that the stern King Pellinor took her virginity "half be force"(101.14); the brusque efficiency of the hermit who knows that weeping and wailing will not heal the injured Sir Lancelot: "lette us have hym in" (1086.22); the splendid comedy of the scene where Lancelot is wounded in the buttock by a lady: "the devyll made you a shoter"(1104.34); the finely controlled irony of Lancelot commenting on Guinevere's newly acquired prudence (1066.5 – 6); the heartfelt natural-ness of the Maid of Astolat's complaint (1093.3 – 1094.4); the cleverly modulated hesitancy and hypocrisy of Agravain breaking the news of the adultery to Arthur (1163.3 – 11). Malory rarely elaborates; he says little but has said, we feel, all there is to say. However, when the situation is more central to the narrative, Malory's terse dialogue can at times leave us unsatisfied. There are, we feel, (private) worlds which he leaves unexplained. We wish to translate the scenes into modern terms and give them the fullness of the novelistic technique. Inevitably we wish to make explicit what Malory has chosen to leave unspoken or merely implied. We wish to develop the individual, private aspect of a scene Malory is looking

---

[13] Malory's skill with dialogue has been widely admired. This should not make us overlook the fact that his characters do not always speak in such a lively manner. Frequently their speech is formal and stately. It is not that Malory's talent for convincing dialogue is occasional, merely that his interest in it is.

at with his more formal, public eye. We do not necessarily betray the spirit of his book but that is the risk we take. The danger is that we will produce interpretations which may well be appropriate for the sort of world we inhabit and are used to reading about, not necessarily apt for the court of King Arthur.

So, for example, Field argues that Bors is motivated by his "latent dislike of Guinevere" when "he first refuses to help her lest he should be suspected of complicity," when he "never mentions the possibility of her being innocent," and when "he makes no soothing exception for Guinevere herself" as he proclaims Lancelot's lack of interest in ladies.[14] It is worth pointing out, however, that no one else offers to fight for Guinevere — not even Gawain[15] — because "they all had grete suspeccion unto the quene" (1049.31 – 2); that Bors does protest the queen's innocence (1054.14 – 21) and, what is more, does so publicly; and that he is in no position to make a "soothing exception for Guinevere" because, however much he is aware of what is going on, it is hardly proper to speak so knowingly to a queen.

For a knight as honourable as Bors to dislike his queen seems unthinkable. Is he merely putting on a public face when he defends her so eloquently? (1053.32 – 1054.21). The words must have frozen on his lips. Bors is a man who has a genuine sense of the importance of keeping the peace and of public stability. When the queen banishes Lancelot, Bors does not seize the opportunity of putting in a bad word against a woman he dislikes, he advises Lancelot not to put a private quarrel before the "many grete maters ye have in honde" (1047.18). He should bide his time; the queen will get over it. And when trouble finally breaks the surface we still never know what Bors thinks. There is no time for private judgement: they must face and try to save the situation. "Whether ye ded ryght othir wronge" (1171.30-1) is as far as he ever commits himself.[16] Ultimately, I would suggest, the notion of a "latent dislike" is unnecessary and unhelpful. Knights show love, honour, devotion, loyalty (or their opposites), the public virtues and vices, but does anyone in Malory *like* anyone else? They are either closely knit by the bonds of family alliance and mutual regard or else fiercely at enmity, but public

---

[14]   Sir Thomas Malory, *Le Morte Darthur. The Seventh and Eighth Tales*, edited by P. J. C. Field (London, 1978), pp. 242, 251.

[15]   Gawain is the only one who, logically, is free to defend Guinevere. Since the poisoned apple was intended for him (he realises) he is hardly likely to be suspected of complicity.

[16]   Compare Lambert's remark concerning Lancelot: "we are not invited to share his private thoughts; indeed, we are not encouraged to suppose he has any." op. cit., p. 97.

allegiance does not allow the shades of meaning, the degrees of liking, that we are aware of at a personal level.

The public setting of the court is the world to which Malory's characters are wholeheartedly devoted and one which fully defines the contours of their identity. Those characters speak like men and women we all know, but the people we know are rarely in the same formal position. Behind the queen, for example, there is indeed a real woman, whose reactions are very much those of all her sex — and Malory at one point tells us this (1047.18 – 20) — but the behaviour of the average woman cannot justify our developing interpretations of scenes where Malory remains silent: other women are not necessarily queens. And if Malory is less interested than we in analysing secret, unofficial motives, it might be argued that it is this attitude which is responsible for much of the impact his characters have. In a few brief scenes he convinces us of their reality while at the same time keeping us at a sufficient distance from them for none of their mystery to be dispelled. We are aware of Guinevere's essential humanity — she is exasperatingly real — and at the same time she remains the queen. Malory's figures are at once larger than life and true to it, and his presentation of them is not unlike an assessment made of the British monarchy a generation ago: "a shrewd mixture of magnificence and ordinariness which in its central incompatibility bears all the signs of functional magic."[17] The publicity campaign of the present Royal Family seems bent on showing us the young man or woman behind the royal prince or princess, on revealing the ordinariness behind the royal exterior. We are regularly shown what they are like off duty, once the official engagements have been fulfilled. Although this in itself is merely another public image, the danger involved is that we will be convinced by how ordinary they all are. Malory will have none of this. His kings, queens, knights, and ladies are men and women we can all recognise, but they are never, for a moment, anything but extraordinary, they never shed their public image. There are times when it is fitting for a knight to divest himself of his armour, but if he divested himself of the public code that armour is worn to serve he would cease to exist. There are no moments when Malory's knights are off duty, no moments when, in private, they reveal what, unofficially, they really believe. Their engagement to the official, public world is total.

One thing which is vital to the public world, as the word itself suggests, is publicity. There is room for humility in the kingdom of Arthur but little room for modesty and none for false modesty. A knight in search of adventure does not relish the private satisfaction of having overcome an adversary, he sends him back to declare his defeat, to swear allegiance to

[17] Raymond Williams, *The Long Revolution* (London, 1961), Pelican edition, 1965, p. 345.

the court, and to say who sent him. At the end of the Grail quest Arthur has all the adventures put on record, even though the context of a spiritual quest might in theory be one where earthly glory — "vayne-glory" — is sacrificed for individual spiritual welfare. But the intensely private relationship between a man and his maker is of little interest to Malory; the pursuit of spiritual adventure has its *raison d'être* in the public eye and consequently "all thys was made in grete bookes" (1036.20 – 1). What people will say is of vital importance and no great deed can be concealed. When all the knights donate money at the death of Gawain we are told who gave and how much they gave. And it is fitting that Lancelot's generosity should outstrip them all. There can be no anonymous benefactors in Arthur's world. The hero of Jane Austen's *Emma* is knightly in name and nature, but the inconspicuous chivalry that makes him a gentleman in Highbury would have been his undoing in Camelot. In the same way, judged by the standards of Highbury Lancelot's offer of "a thousand pounde yerly" (1089.32) to Elaine of Astolat and her heirs smacks of showy vulgarity and is the "insult" Field takes it to be.[18] But in the kingdom of Arthur it is a sign of Lancelot's extraordinary generosity and concern. By refusing to become her lover Lancelot grieves the Maiden personally but he honours her family at the same time, and shows concern for Elaine by providing financial security for her future life in society. It would no doubt be a *faux pas* to everybody but Mrs Elton in Highbury, but for Malory it is perfectly fitting that the refusal and the offer should be made in public, in front of the father and brothers who are responsible for Elaine's welfare and to whom Lancelot is equally indebted. For in Malory the deed that is unrecorded, unspoken, unknown is a deed that does not exist, while on the other hand even the most ludicrously trumped-up accusation requires an answer once it has been publicly voiced. No one can afford to shrug it off with haughty indifference. No one rides through the streets of Camelot with his head held high certain of his own inner integrity and oblivious to ill-willed gossip. In a public world which thrives on publicity the "public word," as Lambert remarks, "has great power."[19]

A knight's chief aim is to achieve honour in the eyes of the world; when he is shamed his first impulse is to vengeance, to public restitution. Knights may well invoke the aid of Jesus, but their behaviour is more

---

[18]   ed. cit., p. 253. If the offer is an insult, Lancelot never realises. Indeed, he mentions it to the whole court to justify his behaviour and no one makes any criticism (1097.19 – 20). In the French source, Lancelot makes no such offer and his behaviour towards Elaine is criticised (90, 71.25 – 32).

[19]   op. cit., p. 194.

often in keeping with the Old Testament than the New. There is more of the Psalmist's demand for justice than the Christian's fear of judgement, more of an eye for an eye than turning of the other cheek — although Guinevere's clemency with Meliagaunt to avoid "every shamefull noyse" (1129.10) smacks somewhat of the injunction "judge not that ye be not judged."

At times — and inevitably — shame must be lived with; the damage done cannot be entirely repaired. In Book III when Lancelot saves a lady from the wrath of a husband out to behead her, he only manages to delay the husband's fury. The knight tricks him and the lady has her head lopped off while Lancelot is looking away. Lancelot is convinced that he is "shamed . . . for evir" (285.14). No amount of vengeance taking can alter the facts: he has failed to save the lady's life. Guinevere concedes that the "horryble dede" is a "grete rebuke unto Sir Launcelot," but adds that "natwythstondyng his worshyp is knowyn in many dyverse contreis" (286.4 – 7). That is, when a knight is rich in honour the impact of a single failure is minimised. The dishonour is not abolished but allowances can be made. Lancelot naturally feels his shame more acutely than we.

But there are occasions too in which shame must be lived with even when action is possible. Any dishonour suffered by an individual naturally reflects on the group, but any individual attempt to regain honour which undermines the unity of the group is worse than the initial shame itself. Arthur was well aware of this when he determined to prevent the sequence of private vendettas that could have followed the murder of his own sister (613.7 – 25). Honour may well have been at stake, but the disruption that would have been caused was intolerable. As he might have said: sisters I have enough but such a fellowship of good knights will never be together in no company. In a less ideal kingdom, Mark had to face a comparable reality when Tristram and Isolde were caught in compromising circumstances. Mark's initial reaction was to seek revenge but his barons advised him to swallow his private shame for the sake of peace. Tristram's reputation was such, they pointed out, that he would easily muster an army of supporters; Mark could not hope to win, and the stability of the realm would be in danger (427.5 – 16). Arthur, of course, found himself in a similar situation. Lancelot, even greater than Tristram, was able to rally much support and the unity of the realm was threatened. Egged on by others, Arthur at first failed to take the conciliatory course of action and then found himself a prisoner of the system. But he ought to have acted like Mark. And since Arthur, unlike Mark, was a man whose "worshyp is knowyn in many dyverse contreis" one slight to that worship would eventually have been seen in its proper perspective — and especially since "the quene shulde nat be seyde unto . . . for nothynge done of tyme paste" (1194.29 – 31). That silence would

159

not be a measure of the precariousness of the situation, but a proper refusal to give voice to secondary, private matters when the reunification of the realm was to be celebrated. Arthur could have followed the Pope's injunction with little loss of honour; although the disreputable King Mark's ready agreement with his barons' advice inevitably smacks to us of cowardly prudence, his decision was right.

In the public eye much honour cancels out a little shame. Sir Torre need not worry that anyone will call him a bastard or say that his mother was no better than she ought to have been: his father, King Pellinor, had honour enough for them all (101.22 – 5). And the honour of being Galahad's mother is such that no one could dream of pointing a finger at the unmarried Elaine — except Sir Lancelot, who points his sword (795.26) and realises bitterly how wrong he was to do so. When we consider the notion of shame as opposed to guilt in Malory's world, the presence there of natural children and unmarried mothers should remind us not to oversimplify. Illegitimacy may well be an obvious stain, even to our post-Victorian sensibilities, but it is not necessarily so for Malory. Camelot is not East Lynne.

Honour is greater, or more powerful, than shame and nothing is more honourable than wholehearted devotion to the group. No behaviour is more shameful than that which puts "private virtues and necessities"[20] before the interests of the fellowship as a whole. When Arthur, because of all the public evidence of loyalty, smothers his doubts about the possibility of his having been privately dishonoured by Lancelot (1163.22 – 5), he is acting honourably, not out of weakness. It is when he is urged to take action and lets his private anger lead him to hope for a shameful death for his finest knight that he loses something of our esteem, as he loses sight of a higher ideal. "Private virtues and necessities" must, in Malory's world, be controlled; the tragedy of that world is that, in the end, they are not.

From the very beginning of the final tales private affairs start to dominate the action and the results are inevitably disastrous. In this context Lancelot's three rescues of the queen are clearly intended to form a sequence. That sequence has been seen as a movement from innocence to guilt. In the first case Guinevere has been accused of a crime (murder) of which she is totally innocent; in the second she is technically innocent (she has slept with a wounded knight but not one of those accused with her); and in the third she is totally guilty (the deed and her accomplice are correctly identified). And yet is this quite how Malory presents it?

[20] This useful phrase is quoted from Sir Thomas Malory, *The Morte Darthur: Parts Seven and Eight*, edited by D. S. Brewer (London, 1968), p. 28.

Certainly her innocence in the poisoned apple incident is vindicated by Lancelot's might and the evidence (which Malory adds) of the "Damesell of the lake" — who would have saved a lot of fuss, of course, but would have spoilt the adventure by arriving earlier. The queen is no murderess, no "destroyer of good knyghtes" (1054.40); the accusations are preposterous. And yet, none the less, the evidence was against her. And that evidence existed because her private feelings had created a convenient situation which trouble-makers were able to use — or rather the private feelings of both Lancelot and the queen. The "prevy thoughtes" (1045.13) which had hampered Lancelot during the Grail quest are given such free rein that the lovers' "prevy draughtis" (1045.19) set the court talking. Lancelot is not unaware of the "sclawndir and noyse" (1045.28), but what he sees as their "boldenesse" and "wyllfull foly" (1046.22 – 5) is still not enough to lead him to reform. He merely puts on an outward show of proper knightly behaviour towards ladies, he merely cultivates the public image of a bachelor knight in order to quell the gossip. Private concerns are governing his public behaviour and when Guinevere sends Lancelot away she begins to do precisely the same thing. Her display of public indifference is merely to veil her private thoughts. The "pryvy dynere" (1048.12) she organises "in a prevy place by themselff" (1048.28) is a direct result of private feelings she seeks to misrepresent publicly.[21] Guinevere plans "to shew outwarde that she had as grete joy in all other knyghtes of the Rounde Table as she had in sir Launcelot" (1048.13 – 5). These, of course, are perfectly proper sentiments for a queen, but the motives are improper, and far from saving her good name she puts it in jeopardy. Her claim "I made thys dyner for a good entente" (1050.28 – 9) is not quite true and the situation created is eminently convenient for the private motives — envy and hate — of Sir Pynel; the queen has brought disaster on herself. Private sentiments are having distressing public repercussions. Their love is causing trouble; obliquely perhaps, as yet, but it is giving rise to disharmony. Significantly, Lancelot is privately glad that things have turned out as they have (1053.16 – 21), glad that he will be able to justify publicly, and earn public gratitude from, the lady who has wronged him in private.

As the adventures proceed, the conflicting claims of the public and the private worlds become increasingly clear, and private motives regularly lead to trouble. Lancelot's desire to fight in disguise, to shed his public

---

[21] That the effect of the private on the public is what matters in the final tales is underlined by the fact that it is Malory who makes the occasion of the poisoning a private dinner organised by the queen. Neither the stanzaic *Le Morte Arthur* or the *Mort Artu* have this detail.

identity for private reasons, leads to his being badly wounded, and by accepting a token from Elaine of Astolat to complete his disguise he contributes thoughtlessly to her sad fate. For him that token is no more than a detail in his private ploy; for her — and everyone else — it is a public display of a certain degree of attachment.

There are occasions when what I have called the obliteration of identity (when knights disguise or exchange their armour) can give rise to harmless confusion — as when Lancelot takes Kay's armour in Book III — but the situation is always potentially dangerous. When there is a difference between what a knight appears to be and what he is, things can get out of hand. And when the rift between appearance and reality begins to affect an issue more fundamental than that of identity, when questions of allegiance are at stake, the community as a whole is threatened. Lancelot and the queen no longer *appear* to be honest and the claim "she is a trew lady untyll her lorde" fails to convince as they fail to keep their private desires in check.

When Lancelot rescues Guinevere from Sir Meliagaunt their joint wish for further "prevy draughtis" leads him to prove his devotion with a somewhat ostentatious private show of strength — breaking the bars to gain access to your lady's bedroom, "Than shall I prove my myght . . . for youre love" (1131.19 – 20) is rather shoddy. This is a parody of knightly service. Lancelot is not putting his strength to the service of the lady's good name and, inevitably, the lady's good name suffers. She is accused of committing a "shamefull dede" (1132.20). Once again private feelings have created a convenient situation for trouble-makers to use, and the same thing happens in the third incident. Lancelot's urgent desire to go to the queen is such that caution is thrown to the winds, he refuses to hear the warnings of Sir Bors, and the lovers are caught together. Their "private virtues and necessities" have, a third time, paved the way for trouble-makers. The lovers have again played into the hands of cowards and, as Malory tells us, one is never in greater danger than when one is at the mercy of a coward (1126.5 – 6). Sir Pynel resorts to sly, underhand murder instead of knightly revenge, Meliagaunt's cowardice is even more evident, and Mordred is the worst of them all. In Guinevere's bedroom Lancelot fights "myghtyly and knyghtly" (1168.18); Mordred puts all his might into running away, he "fled with all hys myght" (1168.23 – 4).

If Lancelot's three rescues of the queen form a sequence, that sequence is not from innocence to guilt in terms of their relationship. Indeed, in the first incident their relationship is hardly relevant since the accusation concerns murder and not adultery. But there is a movement from innocence to guilt concerning that greatest of all sins in the Arthurian world — disruption and disorder. The accusation made against Guinevere at the poisoned apple incident was that she was a "destroyer of good knyghtes.''[22] In that affair she seemed entirely innocent. It is part of the irony of the final tales that it is precisely over this charge that she and Lancelot are seen, eventually, to be guilty. Their love — the private affair as such — was not in itself the crime, not even, in itself, the crime when it was made public, and Malory will not condemn it. Indeed, when accusations are finally brought he refuses to provide the evidence (1165.11 – 13). But those ''private virtues and necessities'' were allowed to get out of control and provoked disorder. Trouble-makers were able to use the relationship — which they totally misrepresented of course — for their own private disruptive ends. And it is their responsibility for the disharmony that the lovers come to realise. Lancelot and Guinevere, in the end, both accuse themselves not of the sin they were charged with during the third incident, but of the one they were charged with during the first — that of being destroyers of good knights. The day they were fully vindicated was the day they were most eloquently accused. Lancelot says ''I do nat as me ought to do'' (1193.23 – 4) not when he is smothering Guinevere with kisses, but when he is forced to take up arms against his lord in defiance of the unity of the land.

I have suggested a sequence of increasing danger in the three rescues — as the lovers' private world influences the public world it gives occasion for disruption and opens the door to subversive elements — because I am not sure that the queen (and Lancelot) are innocent, technically innocent, and guilty of the three different charges. It could be argued that they are innocent of the precise charges all along and that this triple innocence is a background to their real guilt, that of provoking instability, which is the only guilt they ever confess. For if we say that the lovers were technically innocent in Meliagaunt's castle we — of necessity — imply that the sin Guinevere was accused of committing with one of her knights was the sin she was committing with Lancelot, that Meliagaunt's accusation was carelessly worded.

It is true that Malory has made it plain that in Meliagaunt's castle Lancelot and Guinevere were in bed together. He was, after all, forced to give us this information for the sake of the plot. The incriminating blood-stains could hardly have been caused by Lancelot's sitting on the edge of the bed for a cosy after-supper chat. But Guinevere has not been accused

---

[22]   Although this accusation concerns only Guinevere, on another occasion Lancelot is accused in almost the same words. Gawain says ''thou haste . . . destroyed many of oure good knyghtes'' (1189.31 – 33). The force of Gawain's hatred is such that Lancelot appears to be unjustly accused, and yet his innocence of the charge is illusory. He later realises that Gawain was right. The charge is, of course, the most serious in the Arthurian world. The Orkney clan (except Gareth) are guilty of it, as is (notoriously) Morgan Le Fey. That Lancelot and Guinevere should find themselves in such company is a measure of how far the situation has deteriorated.

of sleeping with Lancelot and the precise charge that she has committed a "shameful dede" with one of her knights is outrageous on both counts. The queen would rather cut her throat than sleep with one of her knights (she tells Meliagaunt so quite bluntly and, later, Mordred too), and it is unthinkable to suggest that this "moste nobelest Crysten quene" would commit a sordid act of fornication. Guinevere is innocent for in Malory's world it is the precise crime one is being accused of which counts. In a society dominated by notions of honour and shame rather than guilt and innocence other, parallel but unspoken crimes do not exist. Modern readers with a greater awareness of — or obsession with — guilt will naturally ask: but what about the queen and Lancelot, what about the blood-stained sheets? To us those unexplained stains become the symbol of Guinevere's guilt: she was jolly lucky to get off. But surely not for Malory. When Guinevere slept with Lancelot she was not committing a parallel crime which, fortunately for her, remained unspoken. There is no parallel at all; her relationship with Lancelot was entirely different. Indeed, Malory has gone to great pains to make this point perfectly clear. It is surely no accident that at the very moment when the trouble caused by their relationship is about to dominate the action, Malory chooses to remind (even lecture) us about the "vertuouse" nature of their love. The famous May passage (1119.1 – 1120.13) is not introduced haphazardly; it forms a preface to the Knight of the Cart episode. As we call to "remembraunce the monethe of May, lyke as ded quene Gwenyver," as we realise that the queen's truth in love led her to a good end, can we believe that in Meliagaunt's castle she was guilty of "lycoures lustis" with anyone, least of all Lancelot?[23] And it is because of this that I am not sure how much irony there is (if any) — or where the irony lies — in Meliagaunt's warning to Lancelot that "God woll have a stroke in every batayle" (1133.28). Is the irony aimed at Meliagaunt, the complete rogue who thinks that *for once* he is in the right; at Lancelot, so accustomed to being in the right that he issues his challenge out of habit; or at the reader? Has Malory anticipated our modern reaction of seeing the lovers as only half innocent, as he later anticipates our modern reaction and refuses to provide the kind of clear-cut evidence our narrow minds require?

Of course those blood-stains remain unexplained; there can be no Lady of the Lake this time. Yet the absence of an explanation is not designed — I would suggest — to draw our attention to the reality of Guinevere's guilt on this occasion but to measure the precariousness of the situation. The

---

[23] By situating the final catastrophe in the same month and by echoing the words of the May passage then, Malory reminds us once more of the true nature of their relationship at the point where others will seek to misrepresent it.

lovers are not guilty; they are vulnerable. By giving free rein to their private desires they have provoked disharmony. Of course the accusations made this time were easy to handle — they were preposterous — but the lovers are none the less living dangerously. A more carefully plotted scheme — Meliagaunt, like Pynel, merely seized the occasion — is likely to come nearer the mark, near enough at least for the truth to be distorted into a convenient excuse for disruption.

And the third accusation is precisely that. Agravain and Mordred, motivated of course by a ''prevy hate'' (1161.12), have been on the look out for a long time. Their intentions are not unknown, but Lancelot's private affair is so important to him that he refuses to take the threat of possible public disorder seriously. The lovers are caught and this time the accusations made are more direct; the trouble caused by their love affair is no longer oblique or indirect, it goes straight to the point. Lancelot is ''takyn with the dede'' and this is the evidence to show that he ''holdeth [the] quene, and hath done longe'' (1163.7 – 8). And yet, of course, Lancelot is not ''takyn with the dede'': Malory refuses to provide the evidence required for a simple judgement because no simple judgement is possible. ''And whether they were abed other at other maner of disportis, me lyste nat thereof make no mencion, for love that tyme was nat as love ys nowadayes'' (1165.11 – 13). Malory's reticence here is, of course, important. We know the lovers were in bed together in Meliagaunt's castle; why then should he prevaricate here? Malory explains why: it is to prevent our misconstruing the situation, to prevent, I would suggest, our reading this scene in the light of the previous accusation. If Lancelot and Guinevere had been taken ''nakyd abed'' together (like Tristram and Isolde) we would have argued that in Meliagaunt's castle the queen managed to wriggle out of the charge because of a loosely worded accusation but that this time there can be no getting off scot free. But in Meliagaunt's castle the queen was not guilty of a ''shamefull dede'' (the queen of all people!) and nor is she now. Malory refuses to tell us what they were doing because he knows we will misunderstand. He refuses not because he has suddenly become squeamish, not because his commitment to the lovers will not allow him to confess the truth, but because what his (and modern) readers take to be the truth is a misconstruction.

We have all, surely, been placed in the awkward situation of having to give a simple answer to a question which is far from simple. Some people may well have been a defence witness and been required by the prosecuting counsel to answer yes or no. To say no would be perjury; to say yes will give an outrageously wrong impression. And it is this situation of moral ambiguity that Malory is forced to present. He is not on the side of Agravain and Mordred who think they have evidence of a ''shamefull dede''. There is no evidence and there was no ''shamefull dede.''

165

Imagine, after all Malory has told us, thinking of their "vertuouse" love as a "shamefull dede"! Malory's silence is not intended to blur the truth but to clarify it.

But the lovers have been trapped together — Malory cannot deny this — and are at the mercy of evidence their accusers will distort to serve their own ends. And that evidence exists because Lancelot and Guinevere are guilty of failing to control their private feelings for the sake of the public health; they have allowed those feelings to put them in a position where their relationship can become an excuse for others to undermine the unity of the realm. As Guinevere later realises, the disaster was caused "thorow", not *by* "thys same man and me" (1252.8). Their relationship itself was not the cause — not even when it was made public — because however much it may have challenged existing loyalties at a private level, it was not one to undermine the unity of the state. Lancelot's devotion in the service of the queen was a relationship everyone knew existed and one which brought public honour to all concerned. It was no cheap adulterous affair, a source of shame and disruption. That the queen should have sent for Lancelot is not surprising: he had frequently served her. For those who have the unity and well-being of the fellowship at heart all this is perfectly obvious.

The only people who give credence to the sordid interpretation are trouble-makers driven by private hatred and jealousy — Agravain and Mordred, and earlier, Morgan le Fey (617.14 – 16). They analyse the relationship in the lowest possible terms for their own ends. For the sake of fellowship and unity those who show fuller understanding and generosity — Gawain when he nobly puts aside his private sorrow, and Arthur himself when he smothers his doubts — are not blinding themselves to reality; they see things in their proper light. While the private nature of the relationship remained unspoken there were no public ill-effects, only honour. And when the relationship was voiced and made public, it appeared sordid and disruptive merely because there was disruption in the voice of Mordred and Agravain.

For Malory takes the love of Guinevere for both Arthur and Lancelot at face value. We tend to interpret any adultery in terms of a betrayal of one man for another. Malory sees Guinevere fulfilling a dual role. Her relationship to Arthur gives her the role of queen and wife with the duties and affections that role implies. To these she was true. For our modern understanding, which Malory anticipates, "she ys a trew lady untyll her lorde" (1171.18) may well appear to be a lie, but when Lancelot makes this assertion I am not convinced Malory means us to see it as a lie — even a gentlemanly one.[24] It is however, an avoidance of that yes/no opposition

---

[24]   Brewer, ed. cit., p. 29.

— were they in bed or weren't they? — which is insufficient to express the truth. And Lancelot realises that Arthur, for a time, fails to see that truth: "the kynge in hys hete, I drede, woll nat take me as I ought to be takyn" (1171.19 – 20). "He that hath a prevy hurte," Sir Segwarides remarks "is loth to have a shame outewarde" (395.15 – 6). The king, for a moment, is losing sight of the public cause in his anger over the exposure of his "prevy hurte."

For the reader too, if we lose sight of the public aspects of a situation and offer interpretations of private motives where the *Morte* has nothing to say, the danger is that we "woll nat take" Malory as he "ought to be takyn." This is particularly true of interpretations of behaviour concerning the relationships of Arthur, Guinevere, and Lancelot, which are central to the tragedy of the book. Discussing the causes of that tragedy, D. S. Brewer writes:

> Arthur himself may be thought to be at fault in that he is concerned so entirely with community, that is with public virtues and necessities, that he neglects private virtues and necessities: that is he fails to cherish his wife as an individual.[25]

My own impression is that if we see Guinevere as the neglected wife, if we rationalise her affair with Lancelot in such terms then we have trivialised the *Morte Darthur*. The love story becomes a rather commonplace *ménage-à-trois* and there is little point in pretending that "love that tyme was nat as love ys nowadayes." It is true that in the logic of an adulterous affair a neglectful husband is a cliché figure, but Malory says nothing. Since he says nothing, of course, we have perhaps the right to infer: Arthur may well have failed "to cherish his wife as an individual." After all, the king is so obsessed with community that the loss of his queen counts for little; Guinevere is eminently replaceable. And yet if Malory's silence gives us the right to infer, it does so only to the extent that our conclusions do not contradict what Malory does say. If Arthur's lament over the loss of his

---

[25] Brewer writes "Arthur *may be thought* to be . . ."; for the sake of my argument I wish to take this remark at face value. E. D. Kennedy has suggested that "Arthur's attitude to Guenevere changes from the devotion of a loving husband to the indifference of a king whose primary concerns are his realm and the knights of the Round Table." ('The Arthur-Guenevere Relationship in Malory's *Morte Darthur*, *Studies in the Literary Imagination*, 4, ii (1971), 29 – 40). Unfortunately, this point of view can only be justified by reading Malory in one hand and his sources in the other; by explaining the meaning of what Malory does not say and then interpreting what Malory does say along the same lines; and by refusing to admit (except when convenient) that the expressions of love between the king and queen are formal and public rather than evidence of their intimate feelings.

fellowship of knights rather than of his queen is evidence that Guinevere was neglected, it might be suggested that the queen herself would not have agreed, would not have urged her divorce lawyers to quote the king's words in court. For she too laments the tragedy in those terms. With all due respect to Guinevere, Arthur's words, in the public world of *Le Morte Darthur*, are perfectly true. This is not to underestimate the exceptional personal qualities which led her to being chosen by Arthur — her valiance and her beauty (97.20) — but as *queen*, if necessary, and with much ''sobbyng and wepyng for pure dole,'' she could be replaced.

If Arthur helps cause the tragedy by neglecting his private obligations, Malory portrays a man who remains unrepentent. Lancelot and Guinevere confess the private failings by which they jeopardise the public wellbeing; Arthur never regrets that if only he had found time for his wife none of this would have happened. The commonweal is such a vital concern for Malory that it is impossible to err by paying too much attention to it. A knight cannot have too great a love for the community. The only loves which are immoderate and ''oute of mesure'' are loves at the private, essentially secondary, level. A king who neglected his public role for the sake of his private occupations would be guilty indeed. But Arthur is quite the opposite. He is wholeheartedly devoted to his realm and that he regrets the loss of his wife less than the disruption of the realm is a measure of his greatness as a king not of his coldness as a husband. In our own times, the abdication of Edward VIII captured the romantic imagination of his people; Malory, one feels, would have sternly disapproved. His Arthur is perhaps not unlike the description E. M. W. Tillyard gives of Shakespeare's Malcolm:

> He is in fact the ideal ruler who has subordinated all personal pleasures, and with them all personal charm, to his political obligations. He is an entirely necessary and admirable type and he is what Shakespeare found that the truly virtuous king, on whom he had meditated so long, in the end turned into.[26]

If, by interpreting silences, we see Guinevere as a neglected wife and suspect Arthur's love for her, by interpreting silences we can also say that Malory does not. For when Lancelot returns the queen to Arthur there is one most pregnant silence. There is no scene where Guinevere complains; and one thing we do know about the queen is that she is not the sort of woman *not* to complain. Valiant and fair she may be; longsuffering she is not. There are no pleas to stay with Lancelot, no declaration that now it is

---

[26]   E. W. M. Tillyard, *Shakespeare's History Plays* (London, 1944), Peregrine Books 1962, p. 317.

all out in the open so much the better for she is far happier to be officially with Lancelot and away from a thoughtless husband who takes her for granted. There is no assertion to Lancelot that he does not know what she has been through: all those years of taking a back seat while Arthur was out playing soldiers. Malory gives Guinevere nothing to say. The private situation — whatever it is — is of no importance, is made totally subservient to the public. Her return is perfectly proper, a reunion of the throne, a first step to recovering the peace and stability of an ordered community, which is the fundamental good of the Arthurian world. And until that stability is completely retrieved there is nothing more the queen can do; for much of the rest of Book VIII Guinevere is, quite simply, absent.

On the nature of the private relationship between Arthur and Guinevere Malory is silent not because he hesitates to mention Arthur's failings as a husband, but rather, I believe, because there is nothing to mention. Their marriage was grounded on love we are told (even if that love is not scrutinised), and like any marriage it is a complex bond of duties and loyalties. In Book I we learn ''there had Arthure the firste syght of queene Gwenyvere . . . and ever afftir he loved hir'' (39.16 – 8), and as modern readers with our preference for psychological analysis and the dissection of motives we take that ''ever afftir'' with a pinch of salt, for fear of appearing naive.[27] Many a man has declared his undying love for a lady and by the following week been trying to cancel a rendez-vous. And yet with Malory perhaps we should have the courage to appear naive, not merely because ''love that tyme was nat as love ys nowadayes,'' but also, and most importantly, because it is not for us to ask indiscreet questions about the private life of a king and a queen. It is true that Malory gives us the occasional glimpse of Arthur and Guinevere together. We see them chatting at a window (1095.16); we know that Guinevere was planning to be back with Arthur by 10 o'clock on the fateful day she went maying (1121.1 – 3); and when Lancelot suggests that Arthur might have drawn the curtains of the queen's bed if he had wanted to lie with her (1133.12 – 15), the possibility of his doing so sounds perfectly natural. If the royal marriage was a loveless routine, the reaction of the king and queen after Guinevere is first saved from burning would not give that impression: ''aythir kyssed othir hartely'' (1058.9 – 10). Perhaps the relief of the occasion is such that an unburnt queen is willing to kiss even the most neglectful husband heartily, but perhaps too Malory is giving us a brief glimpse of their relationship, and the relief involved means that this time their private feelings of genuine wedded affection can justifiably be given public expression. But apart from these occasions Malory rarely

[27]   E. D. Kennedy (see note 25 above) takes ''ever afftir'' to mean to the end of Book I.

shows us the private life of the king and queen. In the French sources they live a life of cynical worldliness and sophisticated betrayal. When Arthur in the *Lancelot* tells Guenièvre he will be unable to join her one night — he has another lady to visit — the queen, who is not planning to be idle herself with Lancelot around, sees the happy irony of the situation and is careful to make no complaint: "ele n'en est mie dolante" (vol.8, p.442). But in Malory, the uneventful private life of the royal couple might be taken to argue a certain degree of domestic harmony, though Malory says nothing. Instead he constantly places the emphasis on their public roles, and there is every reason to believe that Guinevere was as fine a *queen* as Bors claims (1053.32 – 1054.21) and evidence throughout the *Morte* of the greatness of Arthur as *king*. What they were like as husband and wife is not, quite simply, Malory's concern.

As queen, Guinevere was a "trew lady untyll her lorde" and Lancelot's defence remains the same throughout. His assertions are a way of expressing the truth designed to prevent misconstruction. Guinevere is irreproachable: she has always fulfilled her duty to the king her husband. And if we with the cheapness of our modern minds keep asking "yes, but did you or did you not sleep with her?" Lancelot, like Malory, will avoid an answer, will assert the public honour of Guinevere, which is far stronger than any (supposed) private shame, and refuse to speak of his own part in the affair. And Lancelot will prove with his hands the right of what he has to say. As he is forced to point out to Gawain, his astounding physical success is clear evidence of the truth of his assertions. God was not on the side of his accusers (1197.29 – 31). Is this, however, merely a sign of Lancelot's retrenchment in lying? After all, Arthur suspects that might and right have perhaps parted company (1175.19 – 21). It is certainly true that the right Lancelot defends in the final books is not without ambiguity, and yet the idea that "God woll have a stroke in every batayle" has a certain non-ironic truth for Malory. For if it is a half-truth Lancelot is defending, that half-truth is far higher than the truth of his accusers. They are fighting for disruption; he is fighting to hold things together.

And it is because Lancelot (albeit a sinner) is fighting for a higher cause that he can invoke the help of Jesu (1167.5 – 6). Because he is fighting not only for his own honour and the queen's good name but also for the unity of the realm he can, without blasphemy or insolence, take the queen in his arms and call her "most nobelest Crysten quene" (1166.13) just at the moment when (our) suspicious minds find her behaviour the least noble and the least Christian. He can be sure that right is on his side not out of shameless arrogance but because of the urgency of his cause. And it is a measure of his glory and a mark that his sword is engaged in a rightful quarrel that he can even resist the "grace and gyffte" (1216.31) of

Gawain's miraculous strength. For ultimately Lancelot is not fighting for a wrong or half-right cause. Whatever may have permitted disruption to enter, however much he is privately to blame, the public cause he is now undertaking is the highest cause the Arthurian world knows. It is the survival of the Arthurian world itself.

Any allegiance to a code is, of necessity, an abnegation of individuality; knights taking the Pentecostal oath divest themselves of personal opinions to take on a shared ethic. Private convictions or conscience can only weaken a political group and as the "private virtues and necessities" of the Arthurian world get out of hand, the unity and public welfare of the realm are inevitably lost. Chaos comes again and society returns to a more primitive level of clan rivalry and unrest, of fickle allegiances and political dissent, of scavengers and private profit.

As Lancelot repeatedly defends the queen, verbally and with the challenge of his sword, he is defending the fellowship the others are seeking to destroy. Till now, it is true, he has been "so concerned with his private obligations . . . that he denies public values,"[28] that he has put the public realm in jeopardy. This is his (and Guinevere's) sin and this is the sin they lament. But from now on it is Lancelot who wholeheartedly devotes himself to the realm as others become entangled in private obligations and deny public values. With a clever piece of legal irony he points out "for and the quene had be so dere unto me as ye noyse her, I durste have kepte her frome the felyshyp of the beste knyghtes undir hevyn" (1202.6 – 8). By putting public duties first, by putting his private feelings aside, Lancelot is suggesting his indifference to Guinevere and her consequent innocence. One has the feeling that the earlier, more headstrong Guinevere would have been the first to misunderstand — she would surely have gone into a sulk — but Lancelot's return of Guinevere is accompanied by a public and perfectly fitting restatement of his total allegiance to her. Their love, in no way diminished, is restored to a proper footing. For now it is they who are able to control their private desires — Guinevere does not return to Arthur muttering "Oh well, if I must!" — while all the other characters begin to lose sight of the public well-being. Agravain and Mordred have a "prevy hate," Arthur is (at first) driven by his private feelings of anger, and Gawain, who stoically overcame his personal grief at the death of his sons, gives way to private vengeance at the death of Gareth, and vows that vengeance to God and knighthood (1186.1 – 12), thus keeping his personal feud alive with public justification. Once Gawain realises his error we return to Mordred, the ultimate trouble-maker, the personification of (Arthur's) private sin disrupting the public life, the man who fights not only against his own king, but his own

---

[28]   Brewer, ed. cit., p. 28.

father. Even Lancelot's supporters are eager for battle; only he remains true. And the failings of the others are not put forward to palliate the lovers' sin, but rather to show that sin in its proper light. It is not that guilt has no importance for Malory, but the real sins of the Arthurian world are public not private. The lovers take to a life of penitence not because they finally see the evil of their adulterous ways but when they are faced with the evidence that the wages of sin is the death of the "floure of kyngis and knyghtes". Theirs is not a sexual error (Malory refuses the necessary evidence for that to be made good), but they are guilty of provoking disharmony when the private roles implicit in their relationship take on such importance that the public roles can be misinterpreted.

It is the intrusion of the private into the public which forms the basis of the tragedy of the *Morte Darthur*. The one knight who has devoted himself entirely to the shared code, the one who (in theory) has denied himself even the private pleasures of marriage to follow the life of knightly service, the one who has brought greatest honour to the community, the one who was the chief cornerstone of the chivalric structure turns out to be the one whose self-abnegation fails as his private world of allegiance to his lady disrupts the order of the public world of allegiance to his lord.

In *Le Morte Darthur* private worlds when not fully restrained and subjected to public order are totally disruptive. Arthur was not to blame when he sent Guinevere into the arms of another man by being "concerned so entirely with community" and failing "to cherish his wife as an individual" for we do not know whether this is true. It is a rationalisation of adultery based on modern notions of love; and we know what Malory has to say about them. But Arthur is clearly less than admirable when he fails to assert his public authority to curb the private rancour of his nephews. He allows them to convince him that his right hand has offended him, and is trapped into granting their demand for amputation. He is aware that the law they are invoking will provide a cure more crippling than the disease, but he fails to take the only course of action open to him — and the course the Pope orders him to take — that of coming to terms with the law rather than following it through to the letter, coming to terms with his private dishonour for the sake of the public welfare. As his nephews make a public issue of their private hate, the bonds of allegiance that once held the realm together become a source of blackmail and division (1186.5 – 9). The tragedy of the *Morte Darthur* is the conflict between private worlds and public worlds, the ruin brought to the community when private grievances rig themselves out in the trappings of a public cause. When the letter of the law is invoked for private ends even a king's earnest wishes are powerless to restore the public health. In such cases the letter killeth.

172

And as the letter begins to kill we can justifiably wonder if *Le Morte Darthur* is a romance at all. It has neither the happy ending characteristic of the genre (although we could say, as Geoffrey Shepherd said of *Troilus and Criseyde*, "it is a romance in a tragic mode"[29]), nor does it place the emphasis firmly upon the value of private feelings. The importance of private feeling in romance, of course, does not constitute a denial of the public values of society. Heroes and heroines belong to the social group and even if the testing of a knight involves his temporary exile or isolation, he inevitably returns, better equipped to take his place again — a romance pattern present in the incidental narratives throughout Malory's book. But the overall or final 'lesson' of *Le Morte Darthur* is that when the ideals of behaviour that motivate a knight are no longer the desire to increase the collective worship of the group and to occupy his public position more deservingly, things inevitably go wrong. Lancelot's private itinerary leads to his exile not his integration, and to the destruction of society.

Malory's shift of emphasis from private to public values inevitably calls to mind other associations — older, oral traditions, from which, perhaps, the romance was born and of which the romance is a development, as the remote heroes of legend were brought closer to us, refined, civilised and given inner lives. As Malory rejects the analyses of private feeling that point forward to later literary developments, so he turns back to the spirit of those older traditions where action not abstraction is important and where a hero fights for a public cause not for private ideals of conduct. And it is in this, of course, that Lancelot is Malory's finest knight. He is — because the source imposes it — the hero of romance fighting for a private motive in his defence of the queen, but he is also the heroic warrior taking up arms, above all, to save the realm. The duality of Lancelot's position makes him akin not only to the Lancelot of French romance, but also to Beowulf and the warriors at Maldon.[30]

Critics have frequently commmented on Malory's lukewarm interest in love and his heroic concern for the better part of valour: martial achievement and the bonds of masculine loyalty. Lancelot's rejection of the attentions of other women is not (as in French romance) the gallant equivocation — naming no names — that his heart is otherwise engaged, but the soldierly affirmation that he has better things to do (270.28 – 271.4). And however uneasily Lancelot's words fit the inherited material — they are totally alien to the spirit of the French *Lancelot* — they

---

29 G. T. Shepherd, '*Troilus and Criseyde*' in *Chaucer and Chaucerians* ed. D. S. Brewer (London, 1966), p. 86.

30 Compare the remark in the editor's preface, *Essays on Malory*, ed. J. A. W. Bennett (Oxford, 1963), p. vi.

are a statement of an ethic the author seems entirely in sympathy with. Malory sees his knights as warriors, men of action, silent (not inarticulate) and almost entirely untroubled by thought. They may have amorous attachments, but Malory prefers to spend as little time as possible analysing these, no more time than his sources impose. For him they are merely one of a soldier's privileges. The importance of women and the emphasis on love account for the basically feminine temper of French Arthurian romance, a characteristic which as it developed seems to have been one of the factors in the decline of the genre. Joachim du Bellay, in a remark to which the Nun's Priest might have nodded assent, dismissed the Arthurian romances as ''beaucoup plus propres à bien entretenir les demoiselles.''[31] It is Malory's return to the more sober, masculine virtues of public allegiance rather than private devotion, the *sen* of heroism and ''authentic history'' which colours his romance *matière*, which both characterises *Le Morte Darthur* and, perhaps, accounts for its impact and survival.

Heroic, tragical, historical — I do not wish to be accused of piling up the genres like Polonius, but it is important to see how Malory has changed the temper of his romance material. But a change of temper does not imply a change of genre, and although he may have sought to invigorate his material by stripping away the excessive concern with sentiment and by turning back to older, more sturdy modes of perception, there is a sense in which the meaning inherent in Malory's romance material resists a total rejection of the genre. Lancelot and the queen represent — and do so in their private devotion to each other — all that is fine in the Arthurian world. Lancelot, we feel, could not have been a better knight. We do not share Bors' desire that Lancelot should love and settle down with Elaine of Astolat; his love for Guinevere — the inherited part of romance — is no tragic flaw, it is essential to his greatness. The private virtues that give life to Lancelot's knighthood are indeed the forces that destroy, and this is the tragedy; but that tragedy is, none the less, in its own way an affirmation of those virtues, for no comfort can be offered. There is no public, political comfort because the continuation of the realm under Constantine is without imaginative power, and no spiritual comfort either. In turning to a life of devotion the characters come to a good end, but not one which alleviates the reader's sense of loss. Even Lancelot finds no comfort in religion: '' 'Truly' sayd syr Launcelot, 'I trust I do not dysplese God, for He knoweth myn entente: for my sorow was not, nor is not, for ony rejoysyng of synne, but my sorow may never have ende' '' (1256.26 – 29). The unorthodoxy of the position (original to Malory) fixes

---

[31] *Deffence et Illustration de la langue françoise* (1549), livre II, ch. v. Compare also lines 446 – 7 of the Nun's Priest's Tale.

the response clearly. The lack of comfort is firmly centred on feelings which Malory as historian chooses never to elaborate but which he none the less endorses.

Folktale, Romance and Shakespeare·

JULIE BURTON

In this paper I am going to consider *The Winter's Tale* as part of the long line of stories in folktale and Middle English romance dealing with the separation of family members and their eventual reunion. I shall argue that *The Winter's Tale* is closer to the romance tradition than is *Pandosto*, Robert Greene's prose romance which is generally held to be the play's immediate source. Comparison of the two works by Greene and Shakespeare certainly shows how similar they are in their plots as well as in language;[1] but comparison also reveals striking differences between them. Pandosto has marked incestuous feelings towards his daughter: Leontes has not. Pandosto dies at the end of the story: Leontes lives on. Pandosto's wife dies: Hermione lives and Leontes enjoys a complete family reunion. These deviations from *Pandosto* place *The Winter's Tale* firmly in line with the medieval romance tradition.

The separation of family members and their eventual reunion forms the basic pattern of events which, being shared by a distinct body of Middle English romances and *The Winter's Tale*, links them together. In each work the pattern unfolds in four distinct phases, each phase being characterised by certain criteria. The sequence of phases and their characteristic manifestation, I shall refer to from now on as the Pattern. It runs as follows:

A woman is separated from the father of her child or children,

---

·   I would like to thank Mrs Felicity Riddy of the University of York for the help and encouragement she gave me in developing these ideas.

[1]   For evidence of the close relationship of *The Winter's Tale* to *Pandosto* see K. Muir, *Shakespeare's Sources*, 2 vols (London, 1957), I, pp. 240–247.

She is usually driven away from home by a hostile situation of some sort. Often there is a body of people sympathetic to those leaving home, but they cannot prevent it. The separation is inevitable in the circumstances.

The child or children are reared away from home.

The children may leave home when young, or they may be born in difficult circumstances while the mother is in exile. Sometimes the mothers rear the children at a foreign court, but in other cases the mother and child are separated and the child reared by animals or strangers. Often the children are stolen by animals.

A long time lapse ensues, during which the child or children grow up.

The hostile force which separated the couple may no longer be active, but reunion does not occur until the children have grown up and can take part in adult activities, these being predominantly fighting and marriage.

The family is reunited.

This is often brought about the activity of the children.

The Pattern is given expression by different means in each individual work: on the surface no one story is exactly the same as another. Each story is formed from one of only three types of folktale. The first is that of the 'Calumniated Wife'.[2] In this, a woman is banished from her home because some slander is spoken against her. If she does not already have a child, one or two are born shortly after she leaves home. After a long period of time she is reconciled to her husband and the family is reunited.[3] Several folktales include this type within their structure,[4] and several romances too, for example *Sir Triamour*, *Sir Eglamour of Artois*, *Torrent of Portyngale*, *Octavian* and *Valentine and Orson*. *The Winter's Tale*, also, is based on the 'Calumniated Wife' tale type. Hermione is slandered

---

[2] The 'Calumniated Wife' is a folktale type according to the definition given by Stith Thompson in his book *The Folktale* (London, 1946), p. 415, where he says that a tale type is a combination of motifs, usually in a specific order, which can stand up independently as a complete tale; and a motif is "the smallest element in a tale having the power to persist in tradition".

[3] This outline is taken from G. Gerould, 'The Eustace Legend', *PMLA*, XIX (1904), pp. 335 – 448 (p. 342).

[4] Numbers 451, 706, 707, 712, 883a and 892 in A. Aarne and S. Thompson, *The Types of the Folktale*, second revision (Helsinki, 1973).

and leaves home to live in hiding at Paulina's house. She has a child from whom she is parted and who is reared away from home. After a long period of time during which the child grows up, the family is reconciled and reunited. In each of these works the sequence of events remains true both to the criteria of the 'Calumniated Wife' tale type and to the underlying Pattern.

The second folktale type is 'Man Tried by Fate',[5] in which a man leaves home, often for religious reasons. He is separated from his wife and children and undergoes great suffering, but he is eventually reunited with his family.[6] The romance *Sir Isumbras* is of this type.

The third type is not listed in formal lists of types of the folktale but comprises narratives which are built on the sequence of a hero's exile and return.[7] A hero must leave home for some reason and becomes separated from his family, but he returns home after many adventures and is reunited with his wife and children. In *Apollonius of Tyre* Apollonius plays the role of the father in the Pattern. In *King Ponthus and the Fair Sidone* Ponthus is the child. In *Bevis of Hampton* Bevis at first fulfils the role of the child being reared away from home, but later takes on the part of the father. *Sir Degarré*, too, belongs to this group, with Degarré as the child.

The three tale types which I have outlined are the vehicles by which the Pattern is conveyed. The Pattern is the basic level, but there is another level in each work by which the tale types themselves gain expression. This level is largely composed of what are called motifs which, like the tale types are traditional, limited in number and character, and occur with remarkable regularity throughout the body of stories.

The principal motifs as they appear in *The Winter's Tale* are as follows.[8] Hermione, a wife and mother, is persecuted (S410) by being slandered as an adultress (K2112). Her child, Perdita, is driven out by a hostile relative (S322) and abandoned (S301). She is reared by a herdsman (S351.2). The eventual reunion of father and daughter is accidental (N732).

---

5   *The Types of the Folktale*, number 938.

6   Gerould, 'The Eustace Legend', p. 338.

7   Exile and Return is not a folktale 'type' but from the early days of folktale study it has been recognised as a common pattern of events in folktales. The earliest use of the term is, as far as I know, by J. G. von Hahn in *Sagwissenschaftliche Studien* (Jena, 1876), p. 340, who refers to a 16 point sequence of events as 'Arische Aussetzungs-und-Rückkehr-Formel'. For convenience I will imply its inclusion whenever I use the words folktale 'type'.

8   Stith Thompson, *Motif-Index of Folk Literature*, 6 vols (Bloomington, 1966). For the definition of a motif see above, note 2.

The play is faithful to the folk and romance tradition in the use of other common motifs. Difference of social rank between lovers (T91.6) is a frequent theme, and Perdita's seemingly lowly station in life precludes her from marrying a prince. Cruel fathers and husbands are not unusual (S11; S62). Episodes of trickery are numerous and in *The Winter's Tale* Hermione feigns death (K1860), Florizel disguises himself as a shepherd, and Polixenes poses as a swain (K1816.6; K1816.9). Leaving tokens of royalty with an abandoned child (S334) is not uncommon, and in *The Winter's Tale* a letter and mantle, left with the abandoned Perdita by Antigonus, allow her to be recognised later by Leontes. Prophecies (M300) are another shared feature: *The Winter's Tale* contains both the oracle's prediction and Antigonus's dream (D1812.3.3). The latter is of the same limited effect that prophecies tend to be in the romances.

So, as the play itself acknowledges, *The Winter's Tale* is indeed like "an old tale" (5.ii.28).[9] This is true of the level of motifs, at the level of the tale type and of the underlying Pattern. At the actual verbal level such stories of course differ considerably in detail, and the verbal realisation in many cases may seem illogical in terms of everyday cause and effect: some events may seem superfluous or implausible. But the surface level has primarily to obey the underlying logic of the Pattern, and many of the difficulties in the stories disappear if we see the stories in terms of the underlying sequence.[10]

Before we move on to consider the way specific romances and *The Winter's Tale* reflect the Pattern which shapes them, it is essential to investigate the Pattern itself. It is concerned with a family group during a period of transition: it spans the time from when the children are young (or their birth imminent) to when they are adult and ready to be married. The movement through time which this suggests is like a spiral: we begin with parents who have young children, and by the end the children are in a position to become parents themselves, so the sequence can start again. We have returned to the beginning only to find that we are one step further on. Each main character is to a large degree a representative type, for the problems he or she faces as a parent or child during the period of transition are representative of what every parent or child faces. Its

---

9   W. Shakespeare, *The Winter's Tale*, edited by J. H. Pafford, The Arden Shakespeare (London, 1982).

10   The many layered nature of stories and the symbolic function of the surface level are discussed by D. S. Brewer in the introduction to his book *Symbolic Stories* (Cambridge, 1980). He, in *Symbolic Stories*, and Anne Wilson in her book *Traditional Romance and Tale* (Cambridge, 1976), make the point that a story does not have to be logical on the surface in terms of everyday cause and effect for us to be able to enjoy and appreciate it: we can allow its inner logic to speak to us, although we are not always conscious of this happening.

representative nature allows the Pattern to serve as a medium to convey the idea that life proceeds from generation to generation by a sequence of cyclical renewal.

The transitional period begins when children are born to, or are about to be born to, a loving couple. Their arrival alters the relationship between the parents, for the woman becomes primarily a mother rather than a wife. At the literal level this is realised by physical distance being put between the parents: in this way their emotional disunity is highlighted. Resumption of harmonious relations between the parents cannot occur until the children reach adulthood, since only then can the mother drop her maternal role and become primarily a wife to her husband again. The maturity of the children is marked by family reunion and reconciliation, which signifies that all are happy with their relationships as adults.

The child's maturity is reached in stages. Firstly he must achieve self recognition; that is to say he (or she) must recognise his own nature (which is that by which others will identify him). This may be dramatised as the child's realisation that his foster parents are not his real parents. Secondly he must show that he is able to fulfil an adult role, and male and female children go about this in different ways. Men are generally considered to be the more aggressive of the sexes, and fighting is the sign of this aggression, so the male child must become adept at fighting. Correspondingly, since the ability to bear children is the ultimate feminine quality, the female must prove her fitness to marry and become a mother and she does this by preserving her chastity. Once mature, the children are able to meet their parents as adult to adult. With males, this is often represented by the meeting of father and son in combat. This should result in each admitting the adult male status of the other but without the son trying to usurp the father's role in the family.

The key concept here is that of recognition: the child must learn to recognise himself, and himself in relation to others. As an adult, the child will need to be able to distinguish between his parents and other adults in their relationships to him. (For example, the mother's sexual role must be acknowledged by the male child as being forbidden to him, but until he recognises her this taboo cannot come into play.) On the surface level this is dramatised by the child leaving home so that he has literally to recognise at least one parent, and it is often through this very process of recognition that the parents are brought back together.

The reunited family marks the maturity of the child and is a stable base from which he or she can proceed to the adult world of marriage. In this world he may take on the role of parent himself, so continuing the cycle of reproduction. He leaves behind him the stable, loving relationship of his own parents. This is the natural pattern of development.

Anything which disturbs it (for example, incest) is 'unnatural' because it prevents the continuation of the cycle as 'nature' intended it.

We turn now to the romances themselves. It is the role of the father on which we focus in *Sir Isumbras*.[11] The opening of the poem sees Isumbras swiftly stripped of all the trappings of his life: horse, dogs and hawks; buildings, beasts and men (70 – 96). All that remains to him is his role as father and husband, family protector and provider.

> He toke his mantell of ryche pall
> And ovur his wyfe he lette hit fall
> With a drewrye mode.
> His ryche sirkote then toke he
> To his pore chyldren thre
> That naked byfore hym stode.
>
> (127 – 132)

In this one image we see Isumbras in the role of provider to, and protector of his family, but at the same time the stark contrast between his rich clothing and the nakedness of the other members of his family singles him out. Soon, the focus will narrow still further and concentrate on Isumbras alone in order to show the nature of his isolation during this period of family life.

As the children grow older they must leave their father's protection and face the dangers of life alone. This is inevitable: if they are to become mature adults, Isumbras must expose his children to life's traumas. The logic of the underlying Pattern accounts for his leaving his second child unattended in the forest even though he knows that when he exposed his first child in such a way it was stolen by a lion. Subsequently he neglects the third child so that it is taken by a unicorn, even after the second child has been stolen by a leopard (169 – 186; 365 – 372). There is a great emotional trauma involved in this disruption of family harmony, but it is unavoidable (being the will of God).

> The knyghte seyde his lady tyll,
> 'Take we gladly Goddes wyll,
> Hertyly I yow praye.'
> The lady wepte and hadde grette care;
> She hadde almoste herselfe forfare,

---

[11] *Six Middle English Romances*, edited by Maldwyn Mills (London, 1982), pp. 125 – 147.

On londe ther she ley.

(187 – 192)

The loss of his wife to the heathens, soon afterwards, completes the father's isolation. The separation of the parents during the transitional period is required not only because it represents their emotional disunity, but because each parent must undergo the period of change as an individual. The roles of the male and female are different; so too is their development.

There is an inevitability about Isumbras's isolated suffering just as there was in the loss of his children. The trouble begins because "Into his herte a pryde was browghte" (37), the use of the passive suggesting that Isumbras was not responsible for his pride. The pride is a rationalisation to explain the cause of the trouble, but it is not wholly convincing, for Isumbras's repentance on hearing the bird's admonishment is immediate and the poet has previously emphasised that the hero is an exemplary knight. That the sequence of events which manifest the Pattern is set in motion inevitably, and arises from within the father figure himself, are features which *Sir Isumbras* shares with many of the other romances and are particularly interesting in *The Winter's Tale* where Shakespeare highlights them in Leontes's sudden and unreasonable jealousy.

When the children reach maturity, the father must relate to each of them as one adult to another. He must shed the role of protector and provider. This is dramatised by the re-emergence of Isumbras as a fighting knight. For many years he has not existed as a knight but has lived humbly as a wanderer and labourer. Armour is the outward sign of knighthood; of manhood as distinct from fatherhood. The making of his own armour symbolises the process of reforging his identity that the father must undergo as his children become adults.

At the end of the romance occurs the scene, incredible by naturalistic standards, where the three sons, mounted on wild beasts, join their parents as their equals and assist them in the defeat of some thirty thousand Saracens in battle (751 – 762). This bizarre image symbolises the concept that the united adult family is strong enough to resist even the greatest power which threatens to destroy it. That the children control the "wylde and wode" (757) beasts which stole them from their parents is an indication that they have turned the dangers which threatened them to their own advantage. It is only by knowledge of evil that one may confront and defeat it, gaining thereby a moral awareness which is a mark of maturity. In *Sir Isumbras* this is given a specifically Christian context: the victory of the family in battle is, the poet emphasises, one of Christians over heathens. (Hence in this case the mother too wears armour and fights in battle, indicating her inner strength.) The idea of strength through knowledge of sin is found in other romances, and is taken up by Shakespeare in *The Winter's Tale*.

It is to the roles of mother and male child in the Pattern that we turn in *Octavian*.[12] Firstly, the necessity of the cycle of regeneration is established. The long term stability of society depends on continuity of leadership, and one human lifespan alone cannot supply this.

> . . . we no chylde have us betwen,
> And here we schall not leve but a stownde;
> Y wott not how thys londe schall fare,
> But leve in warre, in sorowe and care,
> When we are broght to grownde.
>
> (65 – 69)

Seemingly ironically, trouble strikes the couple at the time of their greatest happiness, the birth of their children. The seeds of the trouble lie in the very cause of the joy which the parents so eagerly sought: the children give the Emperor's mother a tool to use against her daughter-in-law. The credulity of the husband does not depend upon outside factors. His reaction is well rationalised at the literal level by the plot of the mother-in-law which offers 'proof' against the wife, but even before this the husband never seriously doubts the accusation. As in *Sir Isumbras*, the cause of the trouble comes from within the family itself and springs from the very nature of the situation: the cycle is self-perpetuating.

The aggressive role of the mother-in-law represents the familiar aspect of the mother who wishes to dominate her son — a reversal of that other Oedipal aspect of the hero who wishes to marry his mother. This aspect of the mother, who does not want to lose her son to another woman (his wife), asserts itself when she slanders her daughter-in-law with accusations of adultery with a "cokys knave" (116).

The mother herself cannot be cast convincingly in any destructive role during the period of motherhood because the fertility of women means that they are naturally associated with procreation. Mothering children is essential to the life-cycle and therefore good. The aggressive male reaction may well be rooted in the jealousy familiar to fathers whose wives are suddenly preoccupied by children.

Children make a woman vulnerable. This is realised at the literal level in the pitiful image of the lady lying exhausted after childbirth while her husband indulges in the frenzied slaughter of an innocent beside her (154 – 180). Description of death and horror is punctuated by images of the lady resting after childbirth, suggesting that life and death are closely

12 *Six Middle English Romances*, pp. 75 – 124.

bound, for the knave's death depends on the birth of the children for its causation. The lady's obliviousness to the frenzied horror beside her emphasises the bizarre, nightmarish quality of the scene. Curiously, no suggestion is ever made that she knew about the killing. In this way she is totally disconnected from the evil.

The wife is pious and protected by God. "Thorow Goddys grace" (460) the lioness allows her to take the child, and then follows her to the ship.

> There men myght game see!
> Fowrty men lepe ynto the see,
> So ferde of the lyenas they were.
> By the lady the lyenas downe lay
> And wyth the chylde can sche play,
> And no man wolde sche dere.
>
> (475 – 480)

The juxtaposition of the images of the weak but courageous woman and the strong but cowardly men highlights both the lady's goodness (for she is divinely protected), and the courage she derives from motherhood which enables her to rescue her child. So this is a goodness closely associated with procreation. The incident shows how goodness, rather than physical strength, can conquer evil. Knowledge of evil becomes a strength when held in check by goodness, as the help which the lioness later gives to Octavian in battle suggests.

After her initial suffering, the mother retires into obscurity to await events. Attention now turns to the child. With Florent we see the preliminary but necessary procedure of self-identification when he, whilst being reared by a commoner, unwittingly displays signs of his noble rank by his impulsive purchase of a hawk and a horse, creatures of the aristocracy. Florent shows no regard for the value of money in what he does: he is more concerned with beauty than with the necessities of life. Clement, his merchant foster father, beats him for having wasted money, but

> As sore beton as the chylde stode,
> Yyt he to the ffawcon yode,
> Hys fedurs forto ryght.
>
> (682 – 684)

In continuing to attend to the appearance of the hawk, Florent acts according to the aristocratic nature which is his birthright. His behaviour is an indication of his "blode", the social status of his family.

> 'Owre feyre chylde bete ye noght!
> Ye may see, and ye undurstode,

184

> That he had never kynde of thy blode,
> That he these werkys hath wroght.'
>
> (753 – 756)

This process of recognition is crucial at the literal, as well as the underlying level, for if Florent had tried to be a bourgeois he would not have fought the giant and so never have been recognised by his true father.

This self knowledge is here achieved against a loving, stable family background.

> Bothe Clement and hys wyfe
> Lovyd the chylde as ther lyfe;
> For hym they wept full sore.
> To Jesu Cryste faste can they bede,
> To sende hym grace well to spede —
> They myght do no more.
>
> (907 – 912)

Here, Florent is leaving to fight the giant. This passage expresses the parents' grief at the child's exposure to danger, but also their trust in God and a sense of the inevitability of Florent's acceptance of the challenge. Clement represents that aspect of fatherhood which, although it regrets the 'loss' of his child to adulthood, nevertheless accepts it as inevitable. Just as there are two facets of womanhood represented in this romance, so there are two aspects of fatherhood: that of Clement and that of the Emperor. *Octavian* also presents us with two sides of family life: that in which Clement plays a paternal role is one in which parents delight in their children, and in which father and son derive mutual benefit from their relationship; that over which the Emperor presides is one full of hostility and tension. In the universal family, these two aspects exist side by side.[13]

Soon Florent has completed as much of the process of maturation as he can from within the family, so he must move into the outside world, a world peopled by kings, giants and princesses. Now love, combat and recognition are closely bound. Skill at fighting marks mature masculinity, and combat is the means by which males recognize each other. Maturity is necessary for marriage, and the hero usually wins his lady by means of combat. In *Octavian* this interdependence is suggested structurally by the interweaving of combat, love and recognition scenes. Florent kills the

---

[13]   D. S. Brewer discusses the idea of a character being 'split' to represent different aspects of itself in *Symbolic Stories*, contending that there are in fact only a few basic characters, and that many of the personages whom we meet in the stories are 'splits'. See also p. 7 above.

giant and so is brought to the attention of the Emperor which leads eventually to their recognition of their relationship. Florent then takes the giant's head to the princess to win her love.

> 'Damysell,' he seyde, 'feyre and free
> Well gretyth thy lemman the
> Of that he the behete;
> Here an hedd Y have the broght,
> The kyngys of Fraunce ys hyt noght:
> Hyt ys evyll to gete.'
>
> (1003 – 1008)

How Florent knows about the giant's promise to Marsabelle is never explained at the literal level: the underlying logic of the Pattern predominates over the simulation of everyday cause and effect.

Yet winning love, and marriage, are not the same thing. Although love may be felt at any time, marriage demands a relationship between two mature people who are fully aware of their own identity in relation to others, particularly their parents. Love felt by someone mature and stable is less subject to sudden change than if it is felt by one still developing, and the role of the parent, which follows marriage in the cycle, demands maturity so that there will be the natural discrepancy between parent and child. Maturity is necessary for marriage although not for love. It follows that Florent is premature in carrying off the princess, and this is shown by his somewhat abrupt desertion of her when he meets the chance of battle. Curiously suddenly, the love scene is over.

> Florent let the maydyn adowne
> And made him bowne to fyght.
>
> (1025 – 1026)

The maturity of the children is symbolised by the family reunion, which shows parent and child relating as adult to adult. Only after the reunion can the parents resume their relationship as husband and wife, abandoning their maternal and paternal roles; and only then is the child ready for marriage. The recognition of parents and children takes place differently according to the gender of the participants. Recognition between males is normally made by means of combat in some way. Mutual recognition between father and son results from killing a giant, in Florent's case, and rescuing his father and brother from captivity, in the case of young Octavian. Combat is also the means of the mutual recognition of the two brothers, and of their establishment of their equal status within the family unit. The brother of whom we have seen no proof of maturity rescues the one whose ability has been shown. In this way he takes upon himself an equal degree of competence, and therefore, maturity. A similar situation occurs in *Sir Isumbras* where the equal fighting ability of father and sons suggests their equality as adults.

A child is often the instrument of his parent's reconciliation. Octavian intends this, and offers to fight to prove that the accusations made against his mother are false. In the event this is unnecessary: mother and son are both immediately welcomed by the Emperor. This is because time has run its course. Here, the Emperor's realisation of his wife's innocence is never explained, although in other romances it is rationalised by proof. Acceptance of the mother's guiltlessness always happens before reconciliation can occur, but it is not the factor which determines the reconciliation. The essential factor is the maturity of the children, which takes time.

Recognition of the mother figure by a son requires a different process and is best illustrated by *Sir Degarré*.[14] Here, the need to recognise the parent as a mature adult, but in a separate category to other adults, is very marked. This is particularly important when a child is different in sex from the parent, because confusion could lead to incest, preventing the continuation of the natural cycle of family life.[15]

At first, Degarré's mother shows an unwillingness to consider her son in relation to any other woman but herself. She writes to whoever will find her infant son:

> 'Taketh him this ilke gloven two,
> And biddeth him, whar-evere he go,
> That he ne lovie no womman in londe
> But this gloves willen on hire honde —
> For siker on honde nelle thai nere
> But on his moder that him bere.'
> (213 – 218)

The word 'lovie' here is ambiguous. It could mean maternal love, or sexual love. The last lines imply that she means only maternal love, but they do not remove the ambiguity. The lines suggest the danger of future incest between mother and son as well as her reluctance to 'lose' her son's love to another woman.

---

14   *Medieval English Romances*, edited by A. Schmidt and N. Jacobs, London Medieval and Renaissance Series, 2 vols (London, 1980), II, 57 – 88. In quotations from this text 'th' has been substituted for a thorn.
15   This view of incest prompts the reminder that this set of tales and the scheme which underlies them is probably valid only in those areas where the family structure is informed and shaped by a specifically Christian moral system.

The first woman whom the male child knows is his mother in her maternal role. As he grows older, he comes to realise his own sexuality, simultaneously recognising that of women. Now he can appreciate the dual role of his mother (maternal and sexual) and for a while he confuses both roles in all women. Learning to separate them is part of the process of maturation. Degarré's confusion about his mother is clear, for after he has married her, he reflects on what the holy man told him.

> . . . he scholde no womman take
> For faired ne for riches sake
> But ȝhe miȝte this gloves two
> Liȝtliche on hire hondes do.
>
> (641 – 644)

Here, by using the word 'take' to suggest marriage, it is implied that Degarré should marry a woman who could wear the gloves. Yet previously he had been quite clear as to the purpose of the gloves.

> That bi the gloven he sscholde i-wite
> Wich were his moder . . .
>
> (312 – 313)

They are to be the means of identifying his mother. When he expresses his difficulty to the bride's father his words bring together the two views of the purpose of the gloves:

> 'I schal never, for no spousing,
> Therwhiles I live, with wimman dele,
> Widue ne wif ne dammeisele,
> But ȝhe this gloves mai take and fonde
> And liȝtlich drawen upon hire honde.'
>
> (658 – 662)

The addition of ''mai take and fonde'', and the use of ''dele'' rather than ''take'' (641) make all the difference. Here Degarré is not saying that he will not marry a woman whom the gloves will not easily fit, but that he will not consider marrying a woman who will not try on the gloves. The fact that these words come so soon after his previous thoughts (641 – 644) might appear to add weight to the suggestion that his words imply that he will marry only the one whom the gloves fit. However, he may be implying, on the contrary, that he will not marry the woman who can wear them. The ambiguity reflects his confusion over whether his mother should play a maternal or sexual role towards him, and what role he should play in his relations with her.

188

At the climax of his confusion, when, in his mother's words, she is "his moder and ek his wive" (700), comes the moment at which Degarré realises that his bride is his mother. This recognition immediately removes the sexual tension from the situation (hence the great importance of the gloves as a means of recognition).

> Sir Degarré tok his moder tho
> And helde here in his armes two,
> Keste and clepte here mani a sithe —
> That hit was sche he was ful blithe.
> (677 – 680)

Now, Degarré recognises his mother as a purely maternal figure, and loves her as such.

The resolution of the tensions regarding his feeling for his mother frees Degarré to love another woman, but he has yet to resolve his confusion over a woman's maternal and sexual roles with respect to his lover, as he did with his mother. When he falls in love with the lady of the castle, and visits her bedroom, he is overcome by the soothing comforts of the wine and the harp, and falls asleep.

> The levedi wreiȝ him warm apliȝt
> And a pilewer under his heved dede,
> And ȝede to bedde in that stede.
> (854 – 856)

This, the climax of the scene, emphasises Degarré's susceptibility to the woman's maternal role. He might have interpreted the wine and music as being sexual, rather than as comforting, as the lady's jest about him displaying no interest in her ladies suggests (862 – 864). Just as Degarré failed initially to see his mother in a maternal role, he now fails to see his future wife in a sexual light. In the end, the promise of her hand in marriage if he defeats her suitor makes him "glad al for to fizte" (925). As in Octavian, fighting and love are closely related.

In Sir Degarré, Degarré's incestuous inclination towards his mother is consistent with the confusion he later experiences regarding his lover. It arises as part of the normal process of growing up. The child must first love his mother, and only as he grows older can be recognise that her role towards him is completely different from that of other women. For the mother too, there is a natural development from demanding her son's whole love, to requiring an asexual, filial affection. Things are different when the potential incest derives from the misdirected affection of a parent, as in Pandosto. Excess parental affection is a menace to the natural cycle because it threatens the natural development of the protagonist's feelings away from the parent and towards the lover. It is essential to the natural law that whatever seriously threatens the continuation of the cycle of generations should be eliminated. So *Pandosto* must end as a tragedy with the death of the parent from whom the threat has sprung.[16]

The Winter's Tale, however, is not a tragedy. There is no need for Leontes to die, since he has no incestuous feelings for his daughter. It is true that he recognises her attractiveness, but this serves as a reminder of his wife, as the exchange between Paulina and Leontes makes clear (V.i.222 – 227). In this respect, Shakespeare radically changes his source, remaining rather in accordance with the tradition which dramatises the healthy and natural cycle of renewal in the family. In thus deviating from his immediate source he also broadens the meaning of the shared Pattern.

The Winter's Tale is of the 'Calumniated Wife' tale type but it is unusual in concentrating firstly on the father figure, before shifting its attention to a female child. This change of focus is given greater meaning than any such shift in the romances. It divides the play into two distinct parts. The first (Acts One-Three) is a tale of destruction, death and apparent tragedy: the second is, by contrast, a story of healthy growth, life and hope. Nonetheless the two parts are linked to form a whole, not only by the plot, but by, amongst other things, the vein of nature imagery which runs throughout, closely associated with the characters. Such imagery constructs a direct link between the human subject and nature itself, and is one of the main devices by which we see the seasonal parallels that Shakespeare makes with the human drama. Shakespeare puts the human action into the context of a wider pattern of existence; the natural cycle of the seasons. In so doing he clarifies and highlights a theme implicit in the romances. The ideal of the human cycle as the only way to ensure continuity over a long time span is present in *Octavian*, but putting the human drama so explicitly into the context of the greater natural cycle of the seasons (which itself reminds us of the passing of time) is Shakespeare's own innovation.

In *The Winter's Tale* man is not shown as a mere animal in the great cycle of existence. Shakespeare shows the possibility of man rising above this base state, ironically by means of his sexuality (so necessary a part of the cycle, but at the same time that by which man is most usually equated with lower forms of life). Shakespeare establishes this concept near the beginning of the play.

Polixenes   We were as twinn'd lambs that did frisk i' th' sun,

16   *Apollonius of Tyre* illustrates the destructive nature of father-daughter incest.

190

> And bleat the one at th' other: what we chang'd
> Was innocence for innocence: we knew not
> The doctrine of ill-doing, nor dream'd
> That any did. Had we pursu'd that life,
> And our weak spirits ne'er been higher rear'd
> With stronger blood, we should have answer'd heaven
> Boldly 'not guilty', the imposition clear'd
> Hereditary ours.

Hermione   By this we gather
> You have tripp'd since.

Polixenes   O my most sacred lady,
> Temptations have since then been born to's: for
> In those unfledg'd days was my wife a girl;
> Your precious self had then not cross'd the eyes
> Of my young play-fellow.

Hermione   Grace to boot!
> Of this make no conclusion, lest you say
> Your queen and I are devils.   (I.ii.67 – 82)

Polixenes describes his youth with Leontes in an image of weak innocence: the lamb, creature of the spring, small and defenceless. It is "stronger blood" which causes them to leave this state and become "higher rear'd". The reference here (lines 74 – 5) to Original Sin suggests that "stronger blood" refers to sexual passion, and from this we might suppose that the departure from innocence is regrettable. But "higher reared" has an elevated ring to it, suggesting that the stronger state is more desirable than weak innocence. So strength, which is by implication the higher state, is only to be obtained by knowledge of sexual passion, or "ill-doing". There is no strength in innocence. (This concept, of strength through knowledge of sin, is present in *Octavian*.) Ironically, Polixenes's relationship with a woman is the means by which he has sinned, but at the same time his knowledge of sin is the source of his strength and enoblement, and the index of his adult maturity.

The defeat of the sinful aspect of sexuality is possible through grace. That sexuality is a feature of the non-innocent state lines 75 – 80 acknowledge. Here the duality of how women are regarded becomes clear. Hermione, as a woman, is a "temptation" and the cause of man's fall from innocence, but at the same time she is "sacred" and "precious", terms which elevate her almost to the divine. With her expostulation "Grace to boot!" Hermione reminds Polixenes that only without the grace she brings as a woman does sexuality become base and a woman's inherent ability to tempt a man wicked. Female grace, which elevates sexuality, corresponds to the female goodness which tames evil in the romances, but in *The Winter's Tale* the power of goodness over evil is explicitly related to human relationships.

The first part of the play focuses on the destructive jealousy of the husband and the misery which it causes. By the end of the section, Leontes has destroyed his loving relationship with family and friends, and must prepare himself for a lifetime of "nothing but despair" (III.ii.210). This is a low point in the play: evil appears to have triumphed and the future looks bleak.

As in the romances, the cause of the trouble arises from within the family itself. Shakespeare emphasises this: we see Polixenes and Hermione innocently alone together, and so know that Leontes's jealousy, which appears unexpectedly and surprisingly during a happy scene, is irrational. Once in the grip of this passion, Leontes sordidly degrades human sexuality to a bestial level, calling his formerly beloved wife a "hobby-horse" (I.ii.276) and his son's "dam" (I.ii.137).

The grip of passion has put Leontes into an abnormal, unhealthy state. He should be ruled by 'Right Reason', but he is allowing his jealous passion to rule him, and so is reasoning wrongly. He is "in rebellion with himself" (I.ii.355). This is like a sickness: his suffering is described as "the infection of my brains" (I.ii.145) and a "diseas'd opinion" (I.ii.297). The imagery of disease, suggesting the blight and death of life in winter is aptly centred on Leontes, whose vengeful behaviour and its outome represent the destructive character of that season.

This aggressive energy is followed by a long barren period in which the consequences of destruction must be endured. The association with winter of the years of Leontes' repentance, in which he regrets the loss of his family, is directly shown in the imagery Paulina uses.

> . . . A thousand knees
> Ten thousand years together, naked, fasting,
> Upon a barren mountain, and still winter
> In storm perpetual . . .
>
> (III.ii.210 – 213)

Leontes' jealousy, like winter, began spontaneously, also, they are both inevitable. Camillo says of Leontes

> . . . you may as well
> Forbid the sea for to obey the moon,
> As or by oath remove or counsel shake
> The fabric of his folly . . .
>
> (I.ii.426 – 429)

192

Once again, nature imagery is used to equate human behaviour with nature and time.

The two parts of the play are interdependent, whether they are seen as focusing on winter and spring, parent and child, or death and life. Spring depends on winter to be able to arrive, just as children depend on parents. Conversely, spring leads to winter, as childhood leads to parenthood. This cyclical motion is reflected in the structure of the play, and gives it unity. Perdita, who largely represents the spring and dominates the second part of the play, is a child delivered "before . . . time" (II.ii.25) in the winter of her father's rage. Similarly, Antigonus's death in part one, is essential if Perdita is to live:

> I'll pawn the little blood which I have left
> To save the innocent.
>
> (II.iii.165 – 166)

The old must die in order that the new may live. (Antigonus may perhaps be regarded as that aspect of man which 'sacrifices' itself in fatherhood in order that his child may thrive.)

The two parts of the play are necessary to develop the theme of the passage of time, essential to the play's meaning. We look forwards and backwards in each part, both overtly as in Polixenes' nostalgic reminiscences, and less obviously through nature imagery, as when the young prince Mamillius is referred to as "this kernel, this squash" (I.ii.159 – 160), an image of a seed, an unripe fruit which suggests promise of future fruition. Time, personified, stands at the division of the parts to give visual reinforcement to his centrality. Immutable, he presides over the change:

> I turn my glass, and give my scene such growing
> As you had slept between . . .
>
> (IV.i.16 – 17)

The turning of the glass suggests that just as we have witnessed the progression of life to death, we are about to see the reverse, passing to the "growing" of spring from the dormancy of winter. Time will work through Perdita:

> . . . what to her adheres, which follows after,
> Is th'argument of Time.
>
> (IV.i.28 – 29)

What "adheres" to Perdita is the family reunion and before this can occur, she must mature, which takes time. Correspondingly, in the seasonal cycle (where Perdita is a representative of the spring, by her youth), time is necessary for life to re-emerge in the spring.

The importance of Time's function in the play is suggested by his very appearance as an allegorical figure, a dramatic convention from a past age. His arrival amongst the other relatively 'realistic' characters surprises us, immediately distancing us from the drama in which we have been absorbed, thus drawing our attention to the representational function of the characters, and to the fact that the story is one of a small cycle of time set in the larger framework of the continuity of nature.

The second part of the play focuses mainly on Perdita. In contrast to the first part, the mood is much lighter, for here we are concerned with an optimistic story of young love. Events and mood correspond to the achievement and optimism of spring. By the end, the family is happily together again, through the maturing and reconciliation of the young who are now ready to become parents themselves: seasonally, spring's arrival means the return of life as before winter, only a year further on. Romance, like the seasons, deals with the recurring cycle of life.

Perdita is closely associated with the spring. She is called "Blossom" (III.iii.46) and "Flora" (IV.iv.2). She is beautiful, young, and the hope for the future, but this is only one aspect of spring as we meet it in the play. There is another aspect — amoral — represented by Autolycus, who embodies the pure *joie-de-vivre* of the season. In his song (IV.iii.1 – 22) he tells us that he is out of work but does not care, he is a wanderer by nature and thinks of no-one but himself. He is unashamedly a petty thief and revels in the thought of "tumbling in the hay" (12). There is hint here neither of love nor of sordidness. His is an uninhibited enjoyment of the physical pleasures of being alive.

Autolycus is dishonest and selfish, so we cannot condone him, but he has an enviable freedom from anxiety and makes an amusing contrast with the cares with which the play has so far been concerned. He represents the amoral side of spring as it rejoices in breaking forth from the constraints, physical and emotional, of winter. This is appealing but antisocial, and spiritually unrewarding when translated into terms of human relationships. In contrast is the family unit, which demands loyalty and restrains behaviour, but gives ample spiritual reward. The importance of these demands and restraints is suggested when Florizel tries to ignore them. When he insists on retaining his disguise and keeping their love a secret from his father, Perdita is uneasy.

> How would he look, to see his work, so noble,
> Vilely bound up?   (IV.iv.21 – 22)

She knows that Florizel is degrading himself in socially lowering himself by his disguise, and by deceiving his father, guardian of the family tradition.

> The father (all whose joy is nothing else
> But fair posterity) should hold some counsel
> In such a business.
>
> (IV.iv.409 – 411)

If the father's authority is ignored, family relations will break down. The cycle of renewal within the family unit is at risk, and this unit is essential for human beings to achieve their natural high potential. Polixenes' anger when his son challenges this reminds us of Leontes's wintry rage, but in this case the anger is rational and protects the future.

It is natural that Perdita, and not Florizel, realises this since she has a woman's inherent grace (IV.i.24). It is grace which elevates human sexuality and makes family relationships possible. As Hermione says, grace has for her "earn'd a royal husband" (I.ii.107).

The reason that Shakespeare chose to make the child of his 'universal' family a female rather than a male is now clear. With her innate quality of goodness and her association with procreation, a female represents the spring, season of new life, growth and hope, as a male child, with his aggressive characteristics could never do. The female qualities are also necessary for the new dimension of the human family which was not present in the romances: its explicit elevation above the rest of nature.

The family reunion at the end of the play is unmarred by incest since incest is a destructive force for which there is no possible parallel in the seasonal cycle. Since the family and seasonal cycles only correspond when the family cycle is in its healthy natural form, the incest motif in Shakespeare's source *Pandosto* had to be omitted in *The Winter's Tale*. Family reunion is the appropriate end in terms of the family drama, and for this it is necessary that both Leontes and his wife live on.

Why, then, does Hermione pretend to die? The curious scene where her statue 'comes to life' at the end of the play is a rationalised marvel, and it represents, in terms of the family and the seasons, both the impossible and the inevitable. This tension emerges early in the play when Paulina tells Leontes that it is unnecessary for him to marry again in order to get an heir, since his lost child will return. His continued fidelity to Hermione is necessary in order to ensure the family reunion. In terms of the seasonal drama the barren winter must be endured in the faith that spring will come.

> . . . the gods
> Will have fulfill'd their secret purposes;

195

For has not the divine Apollo said,
Is't not the tenor of his Oracle,
That King Leontes shall not have an heir,
Till his lost child be found? which, that it shall,
Is all as monstrous to our human reason
As my Antigonus to break his grave
And come again to me; who, on my life,
Did perish with the infant.

(V.i.35 – 44)

Paulina's belief that the oracle meant that the baby will return is an act of faith, for it seems impossible. That the return is to the "purposes" of the "gods" means that it is inevitable, since the gods are all powerful. However, since it is a "secret" purpose, she and Leontes as human beings can only have faith that it will happen, living accordingly, although it seems unreasonable to them. Similarly, that the spring will come seems impossible during the long 'death' of winter, but in fact, it happens inevitably. The impossibility and unreasonableness of what will happen is contained in the image of Antigonus, who is certainly dead, returning to life. That Perdita (presumed dead) should return, or the life of spring return from the dead of winter, are equally "monstrous to our human reason".

Hermione's return is just such an offence to reason. A statue is lifeless, like the dead, but here, as if by a miracle, the impossible happens and it comes to life. The family reunion of which it is a part is the "argument of Time" (IV.i.29) and therefore inevitable. So, the 'rebirth' of Hermione expresses the miracle of the inevitable spring.

In romance, as in fairytale, where the protagonist is a girl, it is often the case that the mother or mother-figure must die or at least appear to undergo the experience of death (consider for example 'Cinderella' and *Apollonius of Tyre*). Shakespeare chooses to follow the gentler of these traditional patterns so that Hermione's 'resurrection' may parallel the resurrection of nature each spring in the cycle of the seasons.

To summarize, one may say that Shakespeare is imbued with traditional folktale types and motifs as they were told in mediaeval romances, but unlike almost all folktales and romances, *The Winter's Tale* uses a special combination of tale types. Ultimately the dominant tale type is that of the 'Calumniated Wife' with which the play begins and ends, for it is through this type that the paralleled human and seasonal cycles complete their circle. The 'Exile and Return' type, which involves the maturation of a new generation, is inserted into that part of the 'Calumniated Wife' sequence which is usually devoid of detail, thereby clarifying the relationship of both types within the Pattern. Finally, Leontes' experiences are similar to those of the protagonist in 'Man Tried by Fate'.

Although the series of events is improbable by the criteria of the everyday explanation, the traditional elements used to create the series bear witness to the kind of deep psychological need (and some would say truth) which they satisfy. But Shakespeare puts the human cycle into the context of the wider pattern of life and death in nature, and against the background of the natural cycle man emerges as being inherently capable of rising above the animal. By such treatment, Shakespeare both extends and makes more explicit the universality of the Pattern.